Ever tried. Ever failed.
No matter.
Try again. Fail again.
Fail better.

Samuel Beckett, 1983

Marc Angélil
Manuel Scholl
Sarah Graham
Matěj Draslar

FLUX REDUX

9 Sites of Experimentation in Stocks and Flows

PARK BOOKS

	State of Errors	7
1	Pioneering Environments Esslingen Triangle	21
	An Engineer Reflects (Ernst Hofmann)	45
2	Stripped Down Zurich Airport Terminal	63
3	Minor Architecture Zurich International School	91
4	Balancing Performances International Union for Conservation of Nature	115
	Housing Technology (Margarete von Lupin)	143
5	B35 Prototype Apartment Building	157
6	Ceçi n'est pas un musée Guggenheim Helsinki	185
7	Experiments in Timber Prefab A Genealogy of Projects	213
8	Experiments in Harvesting Solar Energy A Genealogy of Projects	239
	99¢ Space (Rainer Hehl)	259
9	Almost Off-Grid Refugio Road Ranch	271
	Living a House (Álvaro Siza)	301
	Acknowledgments	307

State of Errors

Successive Trials in Designing Sustainability

State of Errors
Successive Trials in Designing Sustainability

Much can be read from laundry lists, especially one itemizing all the technical utilities needed to create a well-tempered living environment that is properly heated, cooled, ventilated, humidified, and constantly monitored. This is to say that to temper any habitat requires a significant amount of technology. In design, the recurring question remains as to how to deal with all this technical stuff architecturally. Is it hidden, exposed, integrated, celebrated, or does it subsume architecture in its entirety? Add concerns about climate change to the matter and such disciplinary preoccupations are compounded by the broader issue of architecture's impact on the environment at large.

    A Home is Not a House

It might be worth recalling a notable laundry list addressing such issues from none other than architectural historian Reyner Banham, who, by the way, had also studied mechanical engineering. His provocative essay entitled "A Home is Not a House" from 1965 critically assesses the relationship between architecture and technology, being inspired as he was by Buckminster Fuller's statement that "the environment will be completely controlled and that the very concept of the house will be eliminated." Banham's essay

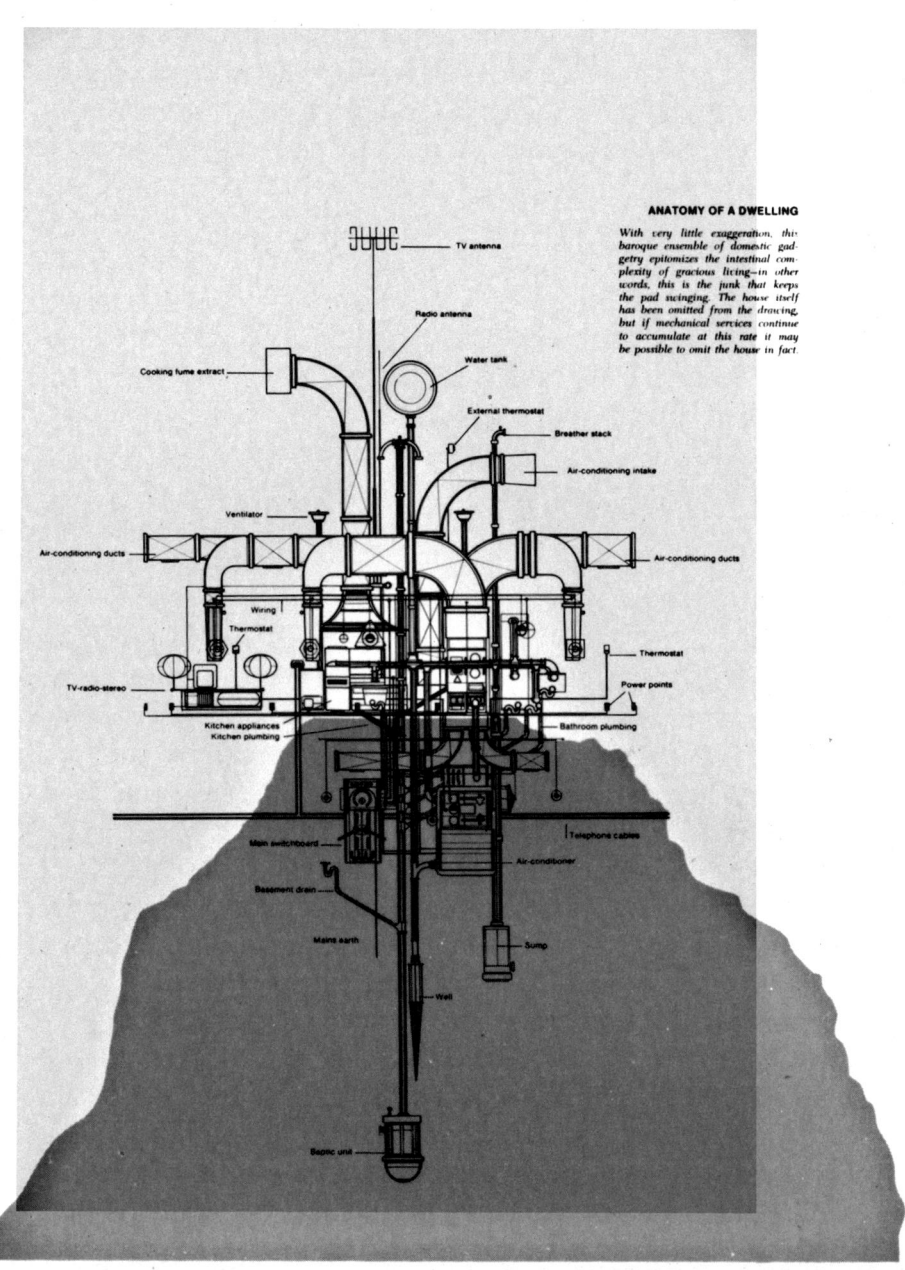

François Dallegret, *Anatomy of a Dwelling*, drawing for "A Home is Not a House" by Reyner Banham, *Art in America*, 1965

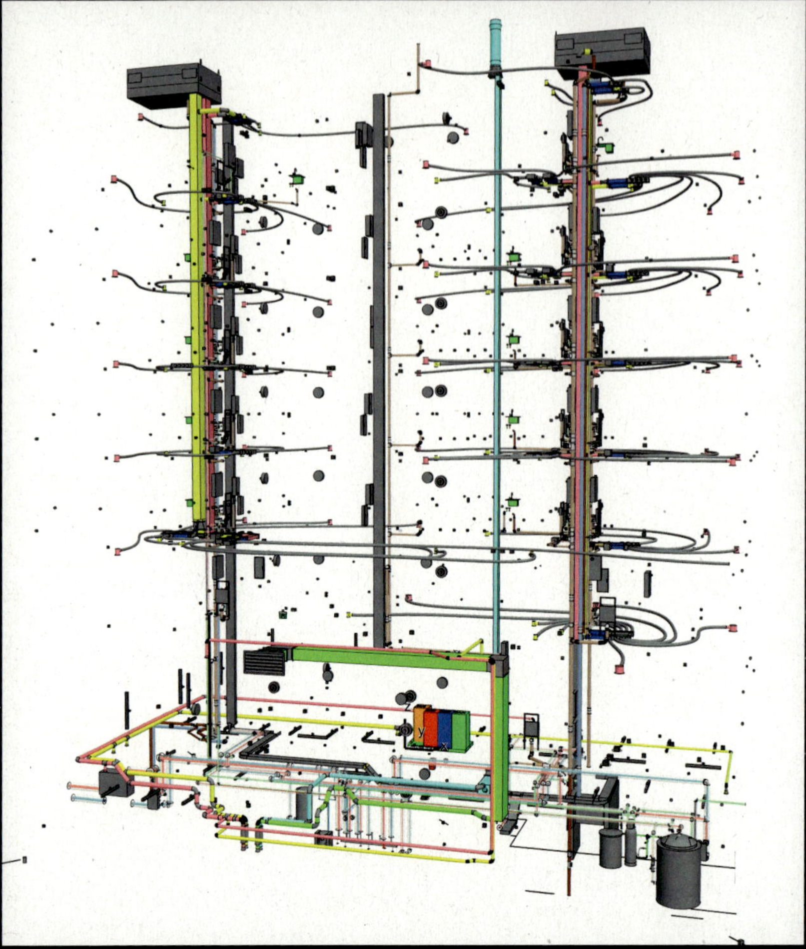

Digital model of the mechanical systems for the Argovia mixed-use building, Aarau, Switzerland, 2018–2022

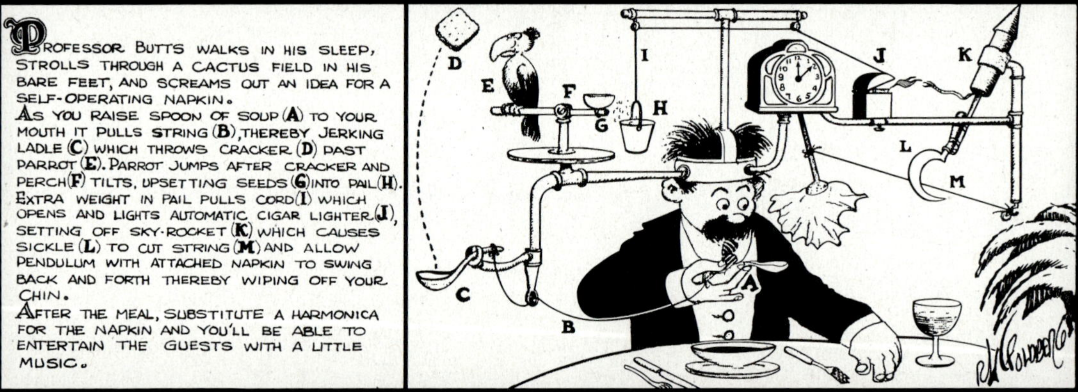

Rube Goldberg, *Self-Operating Napkin*, 1931; soup spoon (A) is raised to mouth, pulling a string (B), thereby jerking another spoon (C), which catapults a cracker (D) past a parrot (E) sitting on a swivel (F); a napkin at the end swings back and forth wiping off Professor Butt's chin (© The Rube Goldberg Institute)

opens by depicting a house as a machine, a *machine à habiter* in the Corbusian sense, albeit minus the house. The quote from Banham reads:

> When your house contains such a complex of piping, flues, ducts, wires, lights, inlets, outlets, ovens, sinks, refuse disposers, hi-fi reverberators, antennae, conduits, freezers, heaters – when it contains so many services that the hardware could stand up by itself without any assistance from the house, why have a house to hold it up?

Banham's heretical text is accompanied by a drawing from the French-Canadian illustrator and artist François Dallegret entitled *Anatomy of a Dwelling*, showing the sum of mechanical systems that comprise the 'home' that is not a 'house,' while nonetheless creating a fit environment for human activities. The caption reads:

> With very little exaggeration, this baroque ensemble of domestic gadgetry epitomizes the intestinal complexity of gracious living – in other words, this is the junk that keeps the pad swinging. The house itself has been omitted from the drawing, but if mechanical services continue to accumulate at this rate it may be possible to omit the house in fact.

The essay and the image seem to settle the issue of architecture's relationship to technology once and for all; namely, by eliminating the prop of architecture altogether because it is no longer necessary. From Banham's perspective, technology *is* the architecture. This provocation need not come as a surprise from someone who revered – or even fetishized – anything technological as an emblem of progress in what he called our machine age, be it the first, second, or third.

The relation of architecture to technology would later be picked up by Banham in his seminal book *The Architecture of the Well-tempered Environment* published in 1969, though, surprisingly, without reference to either his earlier essay or Dallegret's image, as if to retract his earlier, more radical position in favor of a less polemical, more palatable treatment of architecture as being served by its environmental control systems.

In the interim since Banham's writings, ecological concerns, which he mentions only in passing, have increasingly played a determinant role in architectural design by bringing the environmental ramifications of buildings to the fore. Not a day goes by without a reminder that the construction sector accounts for roughly 40% of the world's energy needs and CO_2 emissions, with 30% of that share being linked to the production of materials and the remaining 70% coming from operations. Given these alarming statistics, it comes as no surprise that sustainability now sets the agenda at all scales of the discipline and that an even greater range of technologies are being rolled out to make buildings more ecologically sound, so much so that they have become veritable environmental machines sanctioned by the mantra of 'net-zero' emissions.

Any drawing of this or that technical system tells the story. Every piece of equipment – every cable, conduit, coil, dial, duct, panel, pipe, probe, pump, switch, and whatnot – is calibrated to a specific function and interconnected within a larger system that winds its way through and beyond a building to channel flows of required – hopefully renewable – resources *ad absurdum*.

One is reminded of the contraptions of American cartoonist, inventor, and engineer Rube Goldberg, whose popular caricatures depicted the interaction of complicated gadgets performing simple tasks in indirect and absurdly convoluted ways. And one is left to wonder what kind of architecture would house such contrivances and still be sustainable at that. But this is just the challenge in practice when trying to design a building, for example, that connects hybrid photovoltaic and hot water collectors to heat exchangers to geothermal probes to a heat pump to floor coils to airboxes to digital sensors, and so forth.

So it goes in architectural practice as it does in the short video *Der Lauf der Dinge* (*The Way Things Go*) by Peter Fischli and David Weiss from 1987. The chain reaction of cause and effect among an odd assortment of common objects is "punctuated by eruptions, spills, collisions and other 'mini catastrophes'" that, while being highly controlled in their choreography, take on a life of their own. This is not so dissimilar to the challenge in design practice when having to account for the interworkings of a building's mechanical systems. While being highly controlled and engineered to the last detail, these systems have their own dynamic beyond their specific function due to their interaction within a building and with an environment undergoing constant change. And with the evolution of environmental awareness, building systems are becoming ever more complex with ever more demands for building performance.

Living a House

Still another laundry list of sorts comes from a short essay by architect Álvaro Siza entitled "Living a House," written in 1994, in which he depicts the house as a machine – not unlike Banham – yet this time, as a machine made of parts that break down and need to be repaired. Siza writes:

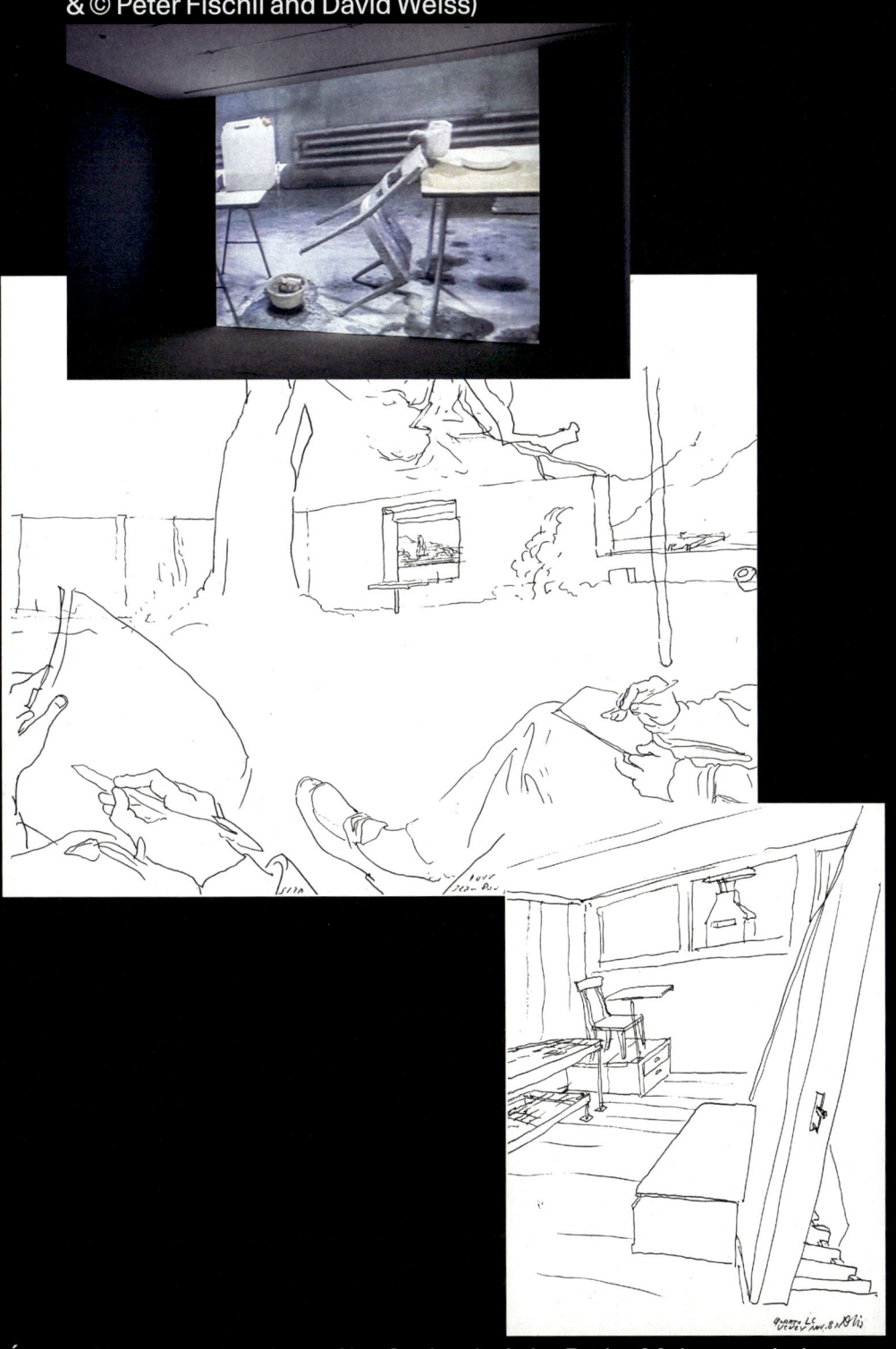

Projection of *Der Lauf der Dinge* by Peter Fischli and David Weiss (1987), Musée d'art contemporain de Montréal, 2021 (Richard-Max Tremblay & © Peter Fischli and David Weiss)

Álvaro Siza, 1981 sketches of Le Corbusier's La Petite Maison on Lake Geneva illustrating Siza's essay "Viver uma casa" from 1994

> The idea I have of a house is that of a complicated machine, in which something breaks down every day: a lamp, a faucet, a drain, a lock, a hinge, a socket; and then the heater, the stove, the refrigerator, the television, or the video player; and after that, the washing machine, the fuses, the curtain springs, or the security bolts of the doors.

The text proceeds by pointing out that living in a house brings with it the added measures of cleaning up and fixing some part of the constructed realm we inhabit to truly "live the house." In view of the fragility of all the stuff that facilitates everyday activities in human-made environments, the essay essentially asks: Are we not now in constant repair mode with every issue that we face?

Siza's reflection could be read as a parable about stewardship, one that is timely, inasmuch as it bears particularly on our relationship to the built and natural environment today. Moreover, his text highlights the inevitable breakdown of technologies and their relatively short life spans compared to that of, say, a house. And the critical question now in the age of climate change is how sustainable a building's technical hardware really is in the long term, considering that it will have to be replaced again and again.

The text is illustrated with sketches that Siza made while visiting Le Corbusier's La Petite Maison on Lake Geneva, a house built in the 1920s, which has since been repeatedly transformed, upgraded, restored, and even outfitted with a new facade and an addition on the roof. Here again, a modest dwelling lives through numerous iterations of maintenance, mending, and modification. Curious enough, one wonders if the chimney for the oil-burning furnace from the original design would be maintained as an architectural feature from a bygone era or removed when a more sustainable system is installed.

Looking more closely at Siza's sketches, what appears to be a bucolic setting – with the Alps in the background and Lake Geneva in the foreground – is actually nothing other than a *machine à habiter* in its own right, simply at another scale. For the Swiss landscape could be interpreted as the proverbial 'wolf in sheep's clothing.' The Alps are replete with military installations, transportation networks, tourist resorts, and infrastructure for generating and distributing power (hydroelectric dams, transmission lines, pumping stations, and the like), all encased in picture-perfect scenery. Multiple water treatment plants ensure that the lake water is clean, and this in turn is increasingly used as thermal storage via countless heat pumps serving houses and buildings in surrounding communities. Somewhere out of view in Siza's sketches are the expansive logistics arteries of one of Switzerland's largest metropolitan regions, which make it a well-tuned machine operating with clockwork precision, though far from sustainable.

Extrapolating from Siza's essay, one could even say that buildings – such as La Petite Maison – are indeed embedded within machinic urban landscapes or what could be called 'man-machine-environments' that are literally plugged into broader apparatuses, much like David Greene's *Logplug* from 1969 representing an elementary component of a machine-environment for living in. Siza's call for "Living a House" or, by extension, for "Living an Environment" underscores the profound care required to sustain any habitat, while stressing the custodial obligation that comes with any architecture of habitation. We would seem to have come a long way, from the house as a machine, to the house as a machine in the garden, to the garden as a machine for living in, which is now scaled to the territory of the planet itself. And given the condition of the world environment, who could argue that we are not constantly in repair mode at all scales?

An image by illustrator Jon Berkeley for the May 2011 cover of *The Economist* entitled "Welcome to the Anthropocene" shows Earth as a technical contraption somewhere in the process of being put together and taken apart again, with its substructure partially exposed and jets of steam escaping from its interior – a product of geo-engineering or geo-architecture run amok. It is no news that we have fundamentally altered the face of our terrestrial habitat. Needless to say, the contraption that we call 'home' is unsustainable. Any effort undertaken to fix the situation, some argue, will require more technology – a grand techno-fix, so to speak, to mitigate the negative effects of our way of inhabiting the world.

Such is the context in which architectural design must operate, bound as it is to the ongoing give-and-take between technologies deployed and their effects on the environment. Yet, as reliant as we are on technical systems – their production, their performance, their prevalence – to make buildings ecologically viable, the systems inevitably fail and must be repaired, as Siza's parable reminds us. What is more, technologies harbor many externalities often unaccounted for, most notable among them being their short life span, their embodied energy, and the operational resources required to make them work, not to mention their socio-ecological and underlying political ramifications as conduits of human conduct.

This is to say that there is more to technology than meets the eye with regard to making the future of architecture viable. Accepting, that architecture is bound to technology, design practice will

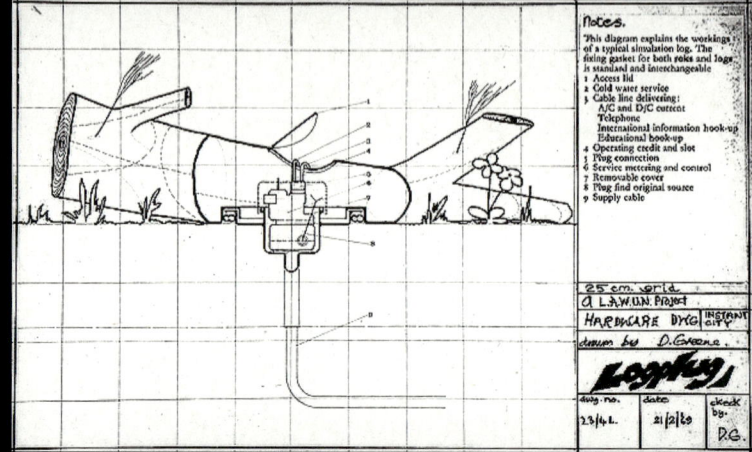

Logplug by David Greene, co-founder of Archigram, 1969

Cover image of *The Economist*, "Welcome to the Anthropocene: Geology's New Age," May 28, 2011 (Jon Berkeley for have to become more strategic in its purview by treating the architecture-technology-environment triad as an integrated nexus of relations that cannot be parsed into separate concerns. Perhaps then we might learn to 'live the house' or, for that matter, the environment as a whole by way of more calibrated means that make sustainability genuinely sustainable.

Trials of Design

The genealogy of projects comprising *Flux Redux* reflects on the relation between technology and sustainability in architectural practice. The book surveys a succession of nine design experiments undertaken by a group of architects over a span of some 30 years, addressing the evolution of a body of work relative to the evolution of environmental discourse. In so doing, the projects themselves register shifts in how architecture is thought about and how it is made. Though most of the buildings were realized, all of them had their share of setbacks, and each project stands as an attempt to overcome them by way of more trial and error. Every possible mistake was made. But in line with Samuel Beckett's appeal, each succeeding experiment involved trying again, failing again, and failing better by taking previous lessons learned as the basis for further experimentation.

Each case study project is accompanied by a diagram that plots out the work in a larger narrative concerning shifts in use requirements, energy measures, material properties, economic considerations, and policy specifications, with a focus on how they all bear on architecture and technology vis-à-vis environmental exigencies. Across the diagrams one can read broader paradoxes inherent to the ongoing debate about sustainable architecture. A case in point is the tendency for more and more technology to be used to increase building performance, which requires more material and therefore results in more embodied energy as well as more emissions, 'green' intentions notwithstanding. Consequently, long-standing design concerns about operational energy requirements were eventually attuned to the embodied energy of a building's requisite materials and technologies. Such shifts would show up in various iterations in different projects. If there is a red thread that runs through this genealogy of experiments it would have to be the continued effort to minimize the amount of technology for a project altogether, without compromising its functionality, its spatial quality, or environmental responsiveness. In sum, the diagrams chart the trials of a design practice as it developed different methodologies over time when trying to navigate the barrage of changing parameters, which unavoidably brought with it a slew of contradictions, some resolved, others not. It is these trials of design that make up the story of *Flux Redux*.

The *flux* of the title has several connotations. In its most direct sense as used herein, the term *flux* refers to the rate of transfer of any resource into and through a building – water, energy, materials, money, labor, data, waste, and so forth – as so many stocks and flows within which architecture is situated and, in turn, which it channels to specific ends. Yet architecture is also subject to the flux of discourses and policies that frame the discipline and orient its practices, among the most prominent being the discourse and policy debates surrounding sustainability, which are in a state of flux due to that of the environment itself.

As for *redux*, one of the rare adjectives used postpositively after a noun to qualify it, the term literally means 'brought back' or 'bringing back.' For architecture and the case studies of the book, *redux* refers to getting beneficial returns from the stocks and flows channeled throughout a building and its host environment. The word is also meant to highlight design attempts made to recirculate those stocks and flows in continuous, closed loops so as to enhance a building's environmental performance. In so many words, *redux* means getting as much back from a building as is possible. In a more metaphorical sense, the term *redux* recalls the Roman epithet for the goddess Fortuna, who figured as "the one who brings others safely home." In our time and with a considerable amount of good fortune, this would require a concerted rethinking of the stakes involved in how we inhabit our terrestrial home, ultimately in terms of how it is built, operated, and maintained.

State of Errors

Pioneering Environments

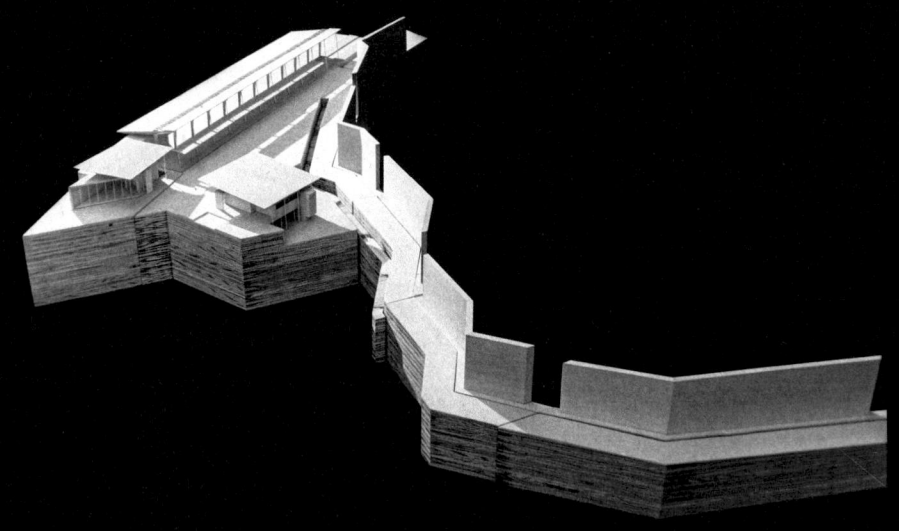

Esslingen Triangle

Drawing from the Site | Experimenting with Sustainability

Discourses

Use

Energy

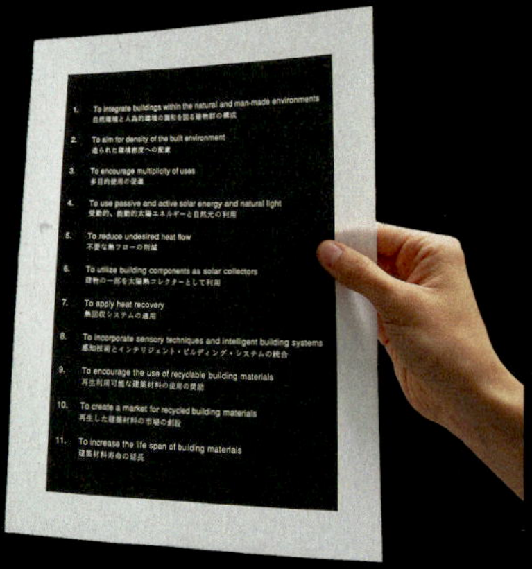

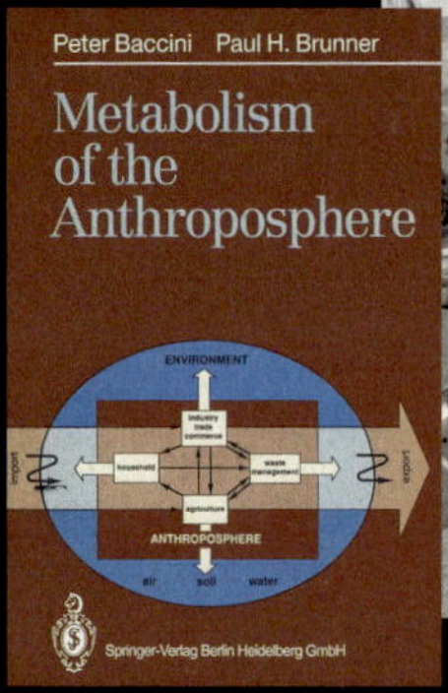

Peter Baccini and Paul Brunner, *Metabolism of the Anthroposphere*, 1991

11-point program for sustainable construction

suburbia

trial and error

Materials

material stocks and flows of human settlements

Economy

Rolls Royce vs. Deux Chevaux

Technology

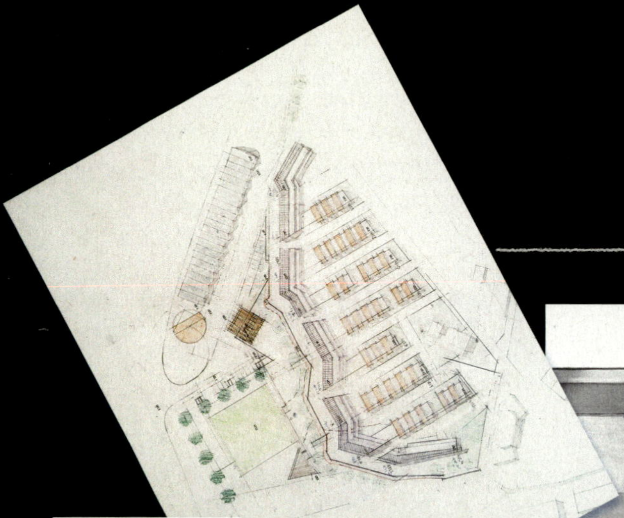

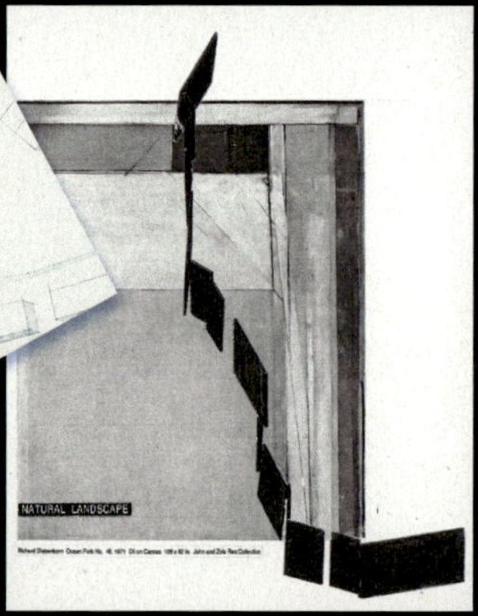

Methodology

drawing from the site

Policy

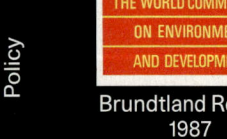
Brundtland Report, 1987

Intergovernmental Panel on Climate Change (established

(1) environment-conscious land use
(2) environment-conscious energy use
(3) environment-conscious material use

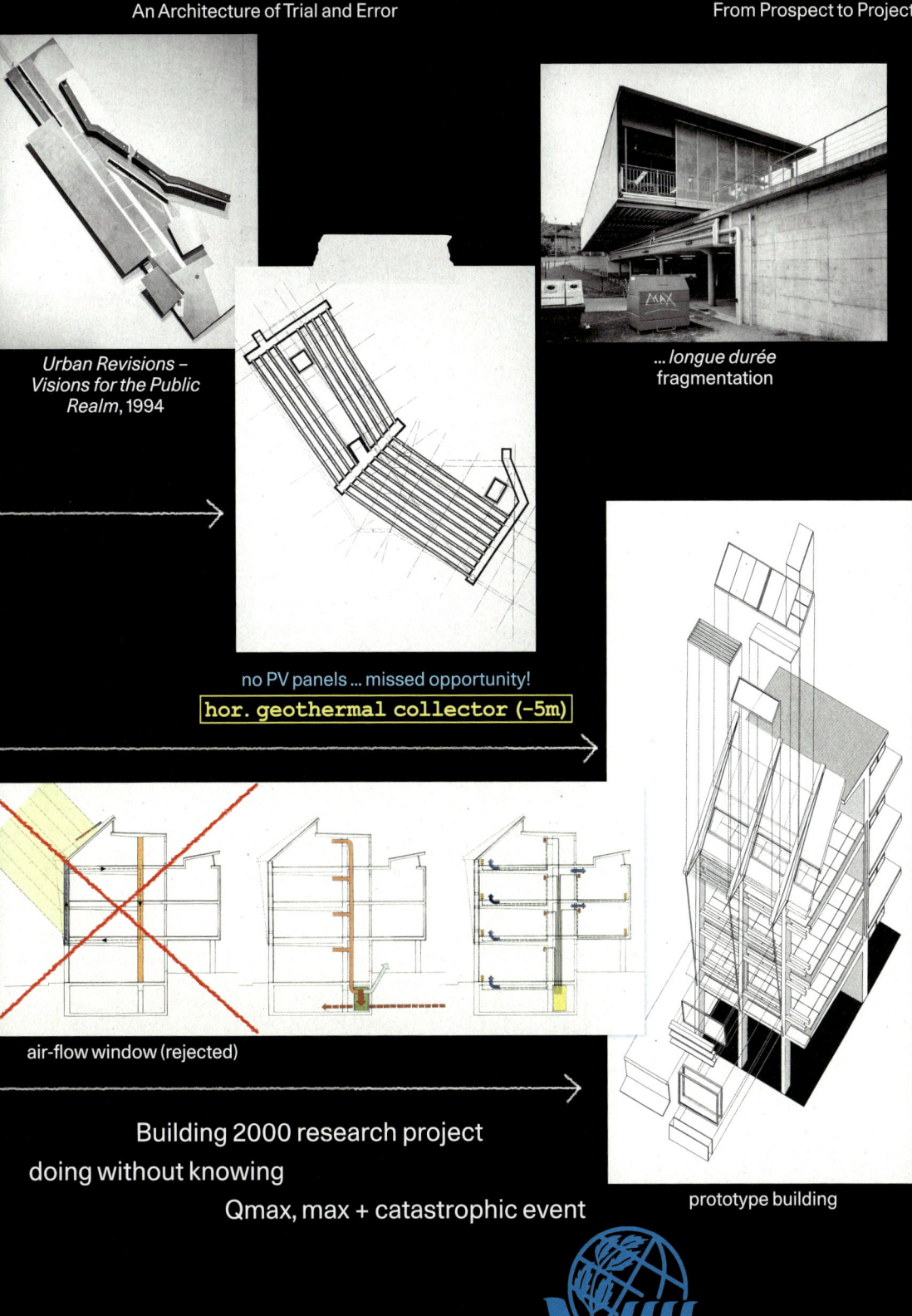

Pioneering Environments
Esslingen Triangle, Community of Egg, Zurich
1989–1995

The small town of Esslingen is a long way from Los Angeles and the distance between them proved decisive for a group of young architects in the United States working on a design competition for a new ensemble of public and private buildings in Switzerland. At least for the design team, a transatlantic flight to visit the site was out of the question for economic and ecological reasons. Hence, a postcard image of the triangular lot to be developed in Esslingen had to suffice, for Google Maps was not yet available in 1989. There was quite a bit of liberty that came with designing for a site that had not yet been visited, and the intellectual distance in this respect gave the designers much room for thinking outside the box.

    A novelty at the time, the competition brief asked that participants be as "environmentally conscious as possible" in their proposals for a complex of light industrial spaces and housing, as well as a train station and a post office, all to be integrated in the pastoral suburban community not far from the city of Zurich. The competition organizers also emphasized the importance of establishing an architectural dialogue with the natural surroundings. But for a design team working remotely, the only features of the environment that could be taken into consideration were those seen in the postcard. Thus, the winning entry that would come to be known as the 'Esslingen Triangle' began as an exercise in action at a distance,

Postcard of Esslingen on the periphery of Zurich, 1989

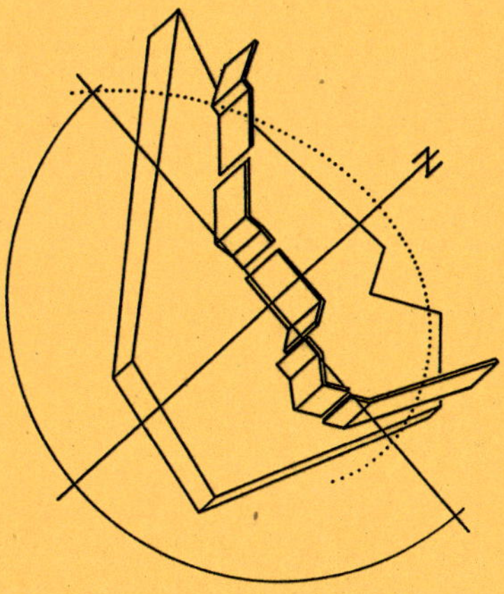

Solar orientation of the Esslingen Triangle

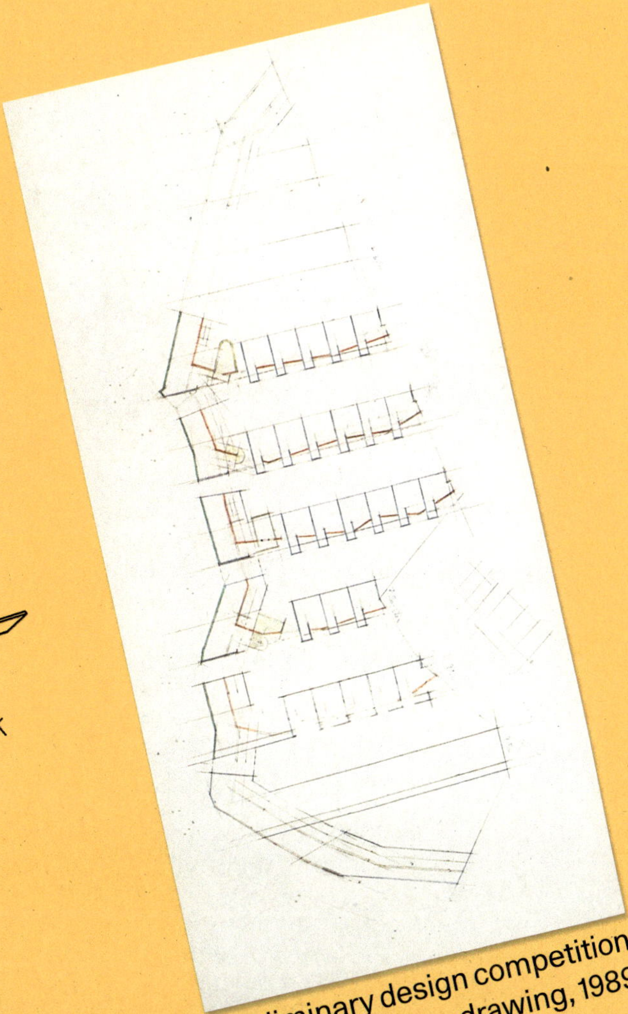

Preliminary design competition drawing, 1989

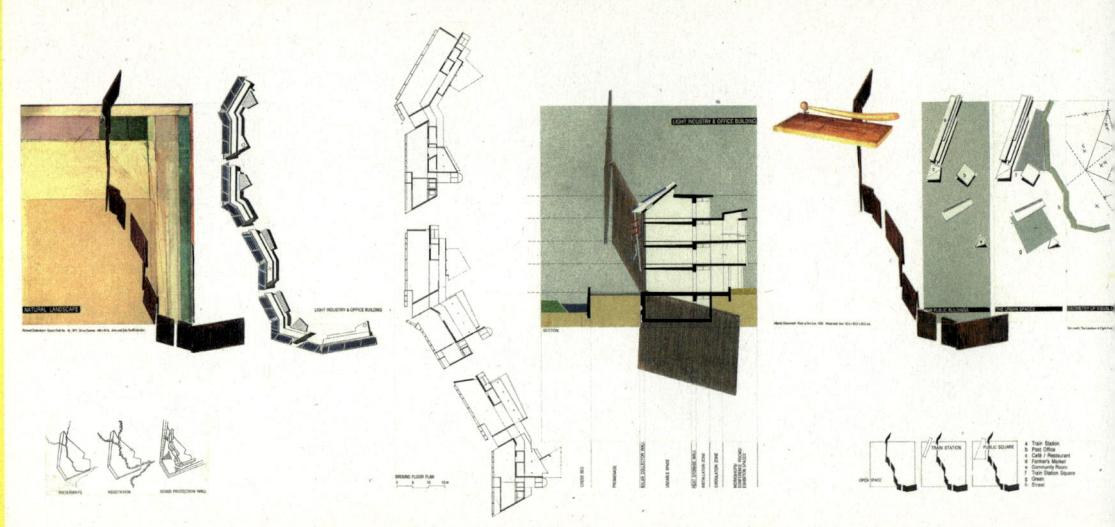

Collages exploring ways to translate existing site features into architectural propositions

Interior perspective of office spaces with views of the Alps

Basic site subdivisions: public-private, loud-quiet, open-dense

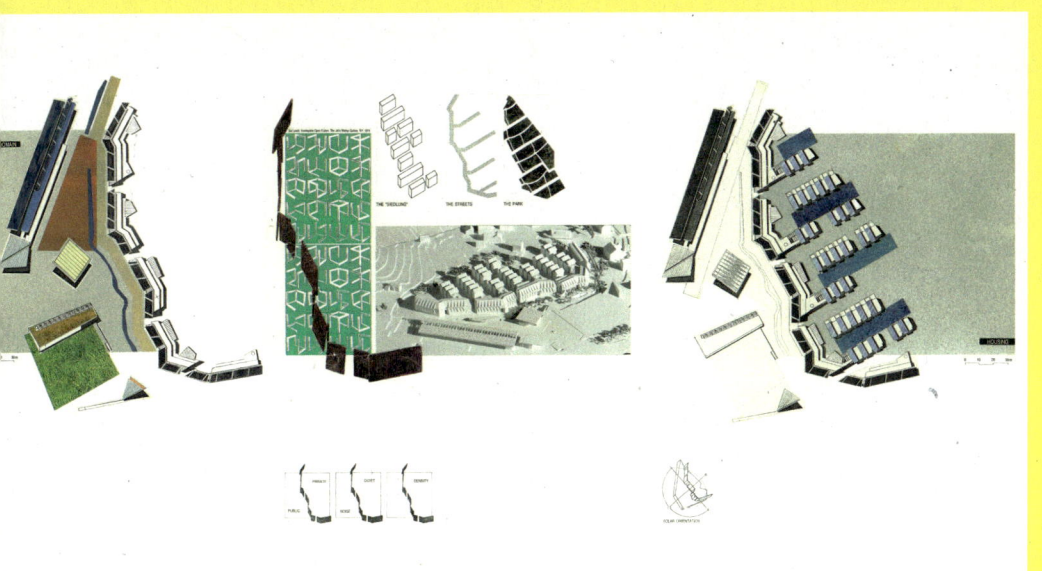

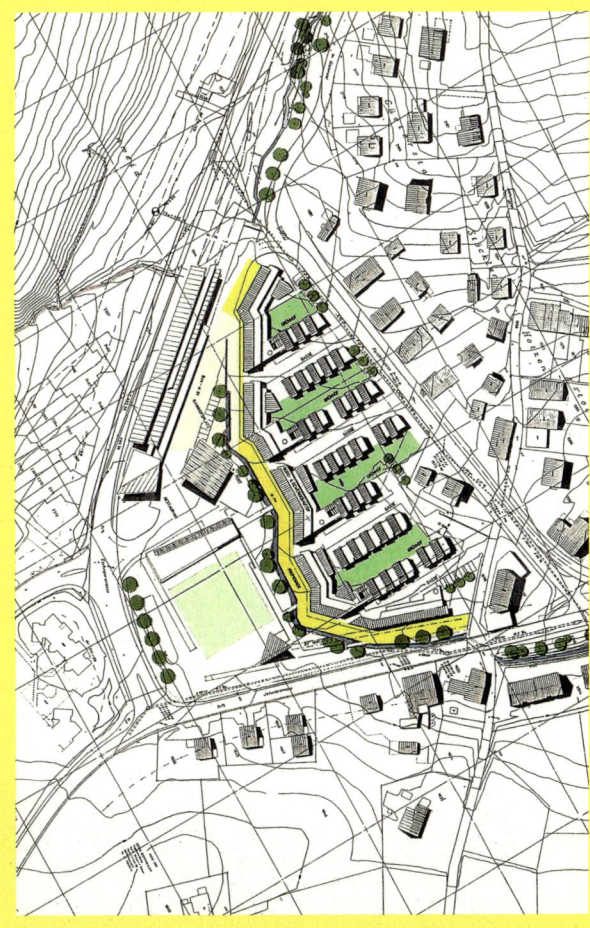

Site plan shown at the exhibition *Urban Revisions – Visions for the Public Realm*, MOCA, Los Angeles, 1994

Relief model of public buildings forming the town square

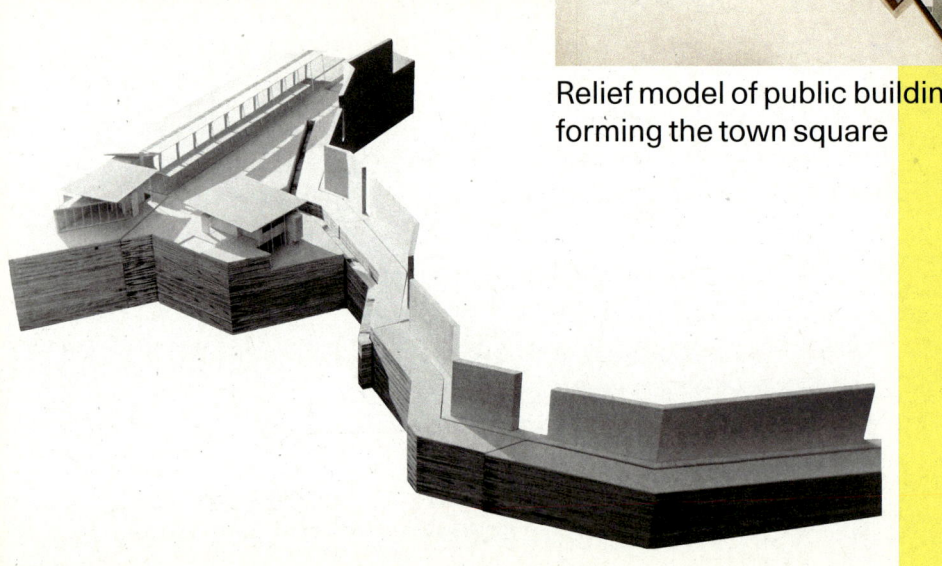

Wall of office, retail, and light industrial spaces along the creek, and public buildings defining the square

Square framed by roofs of train station, post office, and bicycle stands, 1994 (Reinhard Zimmermann)

literally drawn out of an interpretative process of projection upon projection made to take in the characteristics of the natural and built environments.

Drawing from the Site

With the call for environmental consciousness in mind, the initial design considerations were primarily determined by the nature of the landscape itself, with its rolling hills, agricultural fields, patches of forests, meadows, and waterways lined with trees. The town is nested within these elements and in the near distance were the first signs of sprawl already encroaching on the otherwise bucolic scene. So much could be read from the aerial view of Esslingen.

The first drawings made were of the stream running through the site, which would become the organizing element for distinguishing public and private domains in the proposal. Inspired by land art, this waterway was interpreted via collage as a prominent line traversing a field of color that in turn was translated into a tectonic wall. This element would subsequently become the string of office, retail, and light industrial spaces that snake their way across the site, while offering views of the Alps in the distance. Their southern orientation would eventually play a key role in the development of an integrated energy concept for the entire scheme premised on the use of renewable resources.

With a first structuring principle identified, the next question was how to integrate public space within a rural/suburban setting devoid of such an amenity. A series of discrete objects were set against the backdrop of the winding wall along the creek, each placed in such a way as to collectively form a new town square for the community, as if to define a newfound empty space within an empty space. The strategy was to concentrate new built fabric in tight clusters to create 'voids' in designated locations across the site. Environmental awareness was central, insofar as the new square was meant to promote the use of public transportation, comprised of a light rail connection to Zurich and a regional bus service to nearby villages. A village green for special activities, an enclosed farmer's market, and an all-purpose community space were provided to cultivate social relations as another facet of environmental awareness.

In contrast to the open arrangement of public buildings on the south side of the site, a cluster of row houses was situated to the north, with the linear band of light industrial buildings providing privacy for the new neighborhood. The east–west oriented housing units sit within a garden landscape, the lanes between them intermittently puncturing the band of buildings and providing access to a promenade along the stream. The compact organization of the housing units exemplified – at least at the time – how to densify a suburban context and thus optimize the use of land as a limited resource.

Together, these considerations took account of the contextual realities of the natural and human-made environments in an attempt to strike a balance between them. The team explored ways of incorporating such concerns as design catalysts from the outset, rather than as supplementary afterthoughts. In drawing from the specific attributes of the site itself, the ambition was to devise an overall strategy for reorganizing what was quickly becoming just another resource-intensive stretch of suburbia by making it instead a case study on redefining the relationships among city, town, and countryside.

Surprisingly, just a few years after the competition, when the project was still in development and being negotiated among local and municipal stakeholders, the Esslingen case study caught the attention of The Museum of Contemporary Art (MOCA) in Los Angeles, where design for the project had begun. In the early 1990s, the MOCA curators were organizing an exhibition featuring exemplary work that, with a critical attitude toward conventional urban design and planning practices, aimed to rethink accepted strategies of architectural form-giving. Positioned along these lines, the Esslingen Triangle fit into their show entitled *Urban Revisions – Visions for the Public Realm*, inasmuch as the rural/suburban town served in the scheme as a testing ground for the physical and social shaping of a new community commons.

Experimenting with Sustainability

Having established the main organizing principles of the project at the scale of the town and its surrounding landscape, the team began to develop the project components at the architectural scale. An early discussion with Konrad Basler and Ernst Hofmann – main clients and engineers of the project – entailed a lively debate about the terminology appropriate for designing *with* and *for* the environment, keeping in mind that 'sustainability' was not then a household term. In one of the first of the "Sunday meetings," as they would come to be known, the engineers and architects (though struggling for words) agreed upon an "ecologically minded approach" to realizing the Esslingen Triangle with respect to optimizing the use of

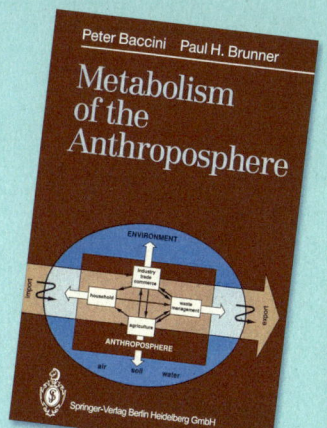

Peter Baccini and Paul Brunner, *Metabolism of the Anthroposphere*, 1991

Hovering roof of the train station in the landscape, 1993

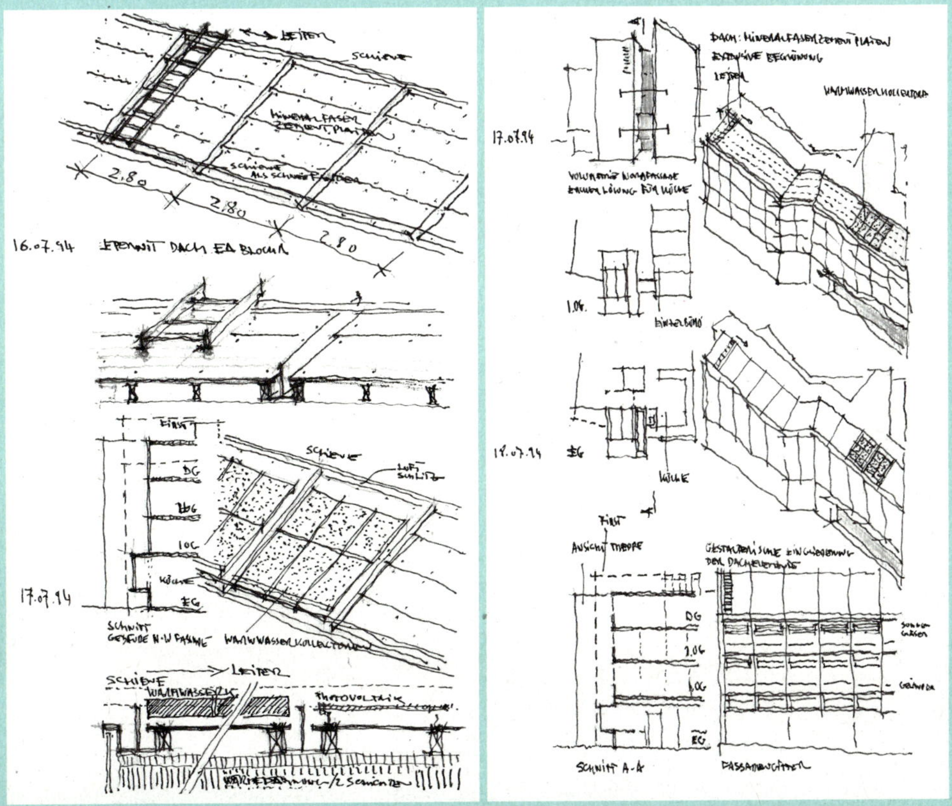

Sketches of the south-facing facade showing various construction layers, 1994

Layered facade construction

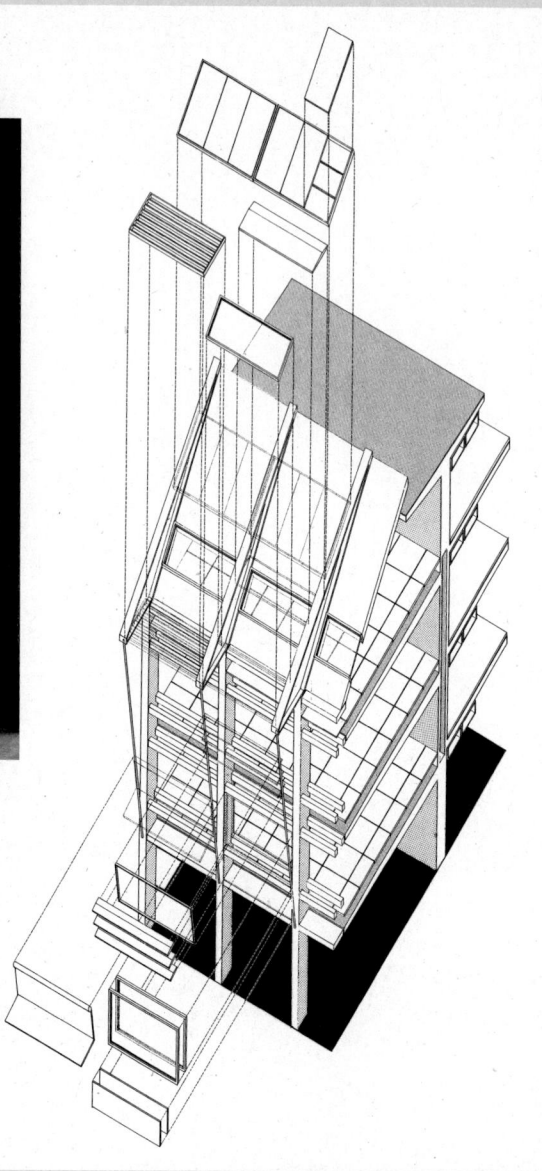

Layered construction with sun-shading screens, photovoltaic panels, and air-flow windows

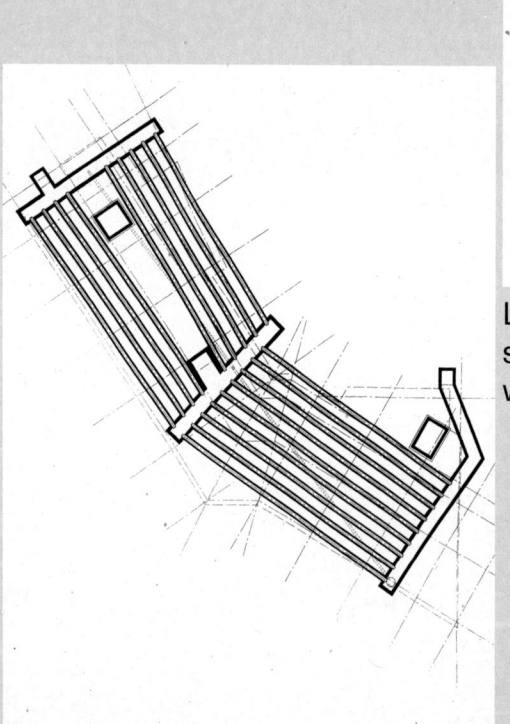

Horizontal geothermal energy collector

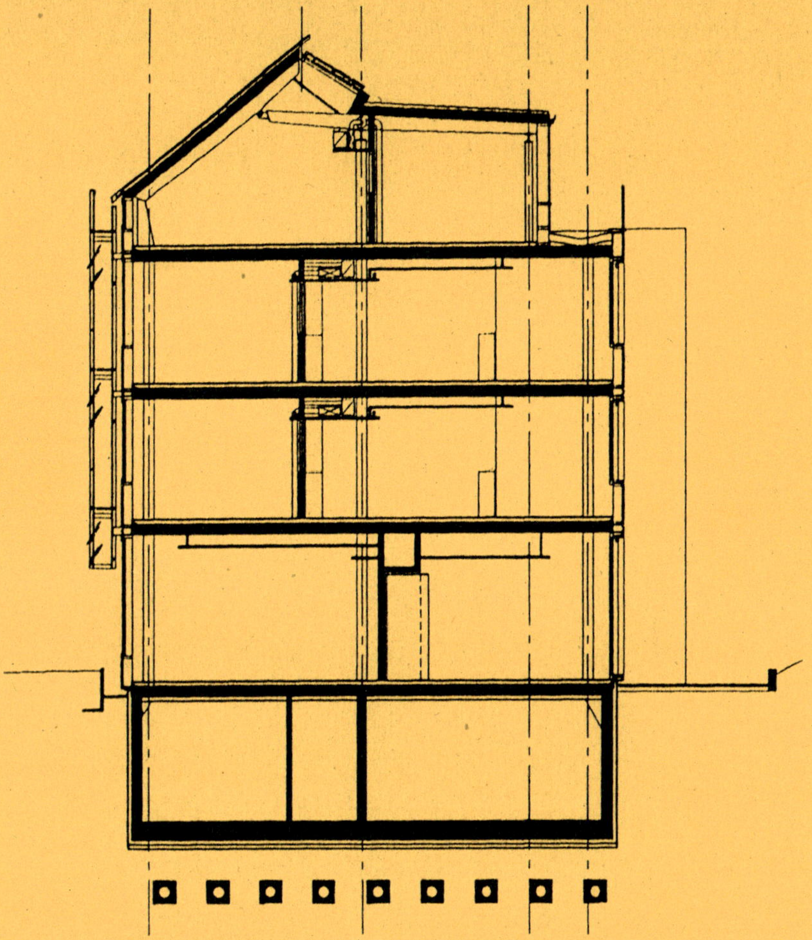

Cross section of office building with horizontal geothermal energy collector

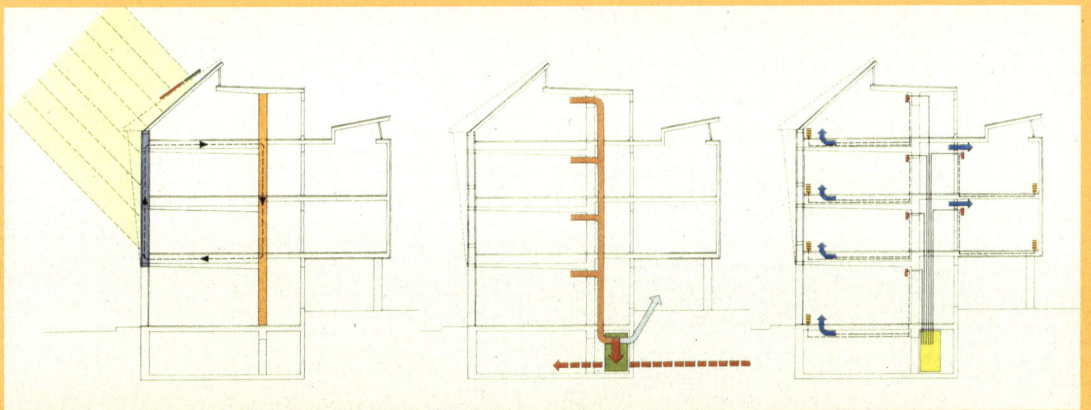

Technical systems for energy generation, heat recovery from exhaust air, and air-quality control

available resources – as the prefix *eco* denotes 'house' or 'household management,' in German the phrase became "haushälterischer Umgang mit Ressourcen." The project was becoming a study in how to make architecture sustainable before understanding exactly what this would entail – a way of doing without knowing, so to speak, but at least with an intuitive hunch.

As the Sunday meetings continued, the engineers pushed for more clarity on the issue of resources, specifically in terms of how the project's performance could set a standard in what would later be termed 'sustainable construction.' For the architects, it was becoming clear that the two engineers sought in the Esslingen project nothing less than to pioneer the building sector by treating the human-made and natural environments as an integral system of mutually reinforcing metabolisms. They were aware of the Swiss environmental scientist Peter Baccini's groundbreaking work on resource management. Baccini would soon publish his seminal book *Metabolism of the Anthroposphere* (1991), which addresses material stocks and flows of human settlements in space and time. So a project that began somewhat intuitively was being recast within engineering discourse as a visionary study in system interfaces – at its most basic, how the human-made meets the natural environment.

But such thinking, while valuable, was too broad for the task at hand. For the first office building, considered in this context a prototype, the three criteria of *optimized land use*, *energy conservation*, and *reduced material flows* were specified in order to make an ecologically minded approach to design more tangible. To these ends, the two clients initiated the practice-oriented research project Building 2000, in which their consulting firm would collaborate with the architects in devising a list of concrete action-points pertaining to the environmental challenges of the coming millennium, all of which were to be taken up not only in the design and construction of buildings for Esslingen, but throughout the building industry as well. Moreover, each action point was further assessed relative to the factor of time in a matrix charting the entire life cycle of buildings and of their constituent components. In hindsight, this research on the dynamics of building-environment relations could be viewed as a study on circular economy before the concept of 'closed-loop resource use' became widely known through publications like *Cradle to Cradle* that appeared a decade later in 2002.

Taken together, the list of objectives and the time-based matrix would inform the project's environmental directives, bearing on both the performance and the form of the architecture in its interactions with natural systems. To disseminate the findings of this internal research collaboration, two lectures were organized: the first, a presentation by one of the architects made to a group of consulting engineers from the firm Basler & Hofmann, who would become increasingly involved in the preparation of construction documents; the other, a keynote address delivered by Ernst Hofmann at the 1991 annual conference of the International Federation of Consulting Engineers (FIDIC) that situated the work in a broader discourse on sustainable practices (see the chapter "An Engineer Reflects").

In both lectures, the more abstract design objectives on the list were referenced to concrete examples to demonstrate how they could be implemented in the case study project. In terms of *energy use*, for example, the south-facing facade of the buildings along the stream was presented as a symbiosis of component functions: solar collectors for producing electricity, air-flow windows to capture heat for the offices and housing beyond, well-insulated envelopes and sun-shading screens to reduce undesired thermal flows, and integrated sensors to regulate system operations.

Regarding *material use*, what was presented amounted to a catalog of non-toxic, durable, and recyclable products: natural paints instead of synthetic finishes, non-composite materials, alternative insulation material in place of fossil fuel-based compounds, timber framing where possible, and road substrate made from recycled concrete. Construction assemblies would follow the logic of building in layers according to a product's durability, to facilitate the repair and replacement of component parts throughout the building's life span.

Both lectures took place at a crucial moment in the project's evolution – after schematic design, but before design development. The goal of the presentations was to promote what was considered to be a pioneering venture and galvanize excitement among colleagues about experimentation for the essential cause of sustaining our habitat. The lectures also aimed to demonstrate that research could be brought to bear on practice in view of expanding the overall environmental mandate of design professions.

An Architecture of Trial and Error

Once the broad environmental agenda for the Esslingen case study had been established, the more difficult task came with negotiating the terms of how the first office building would be constructed, especially considering that it would be used by the engineers themselves. This was made even more complex due to the three tiers of stakeholders within the company of Basler & Hofmann: the two senior

Production and assembly of prefabricated timber facade and roof panels partners or aforementioned 'pioneers,' the firm's executive committee in charge of the budget, and the corps of consulting engineers specialized in a broad range of disciplines – ranging from structural and mechanical engineering to material sciences and building physics. Though lively and enlightening, the ensuing discussions had their fair share of contradictions, with pros and cons weighing in on nearly every issue as to when to be pragmatic and when to be visionary. At times, costs would decide the matter at hand; at other times, a particular technology would resolve a dispute; and just as often, functional or spatial considerations would take the lead. But no sooner would a topic be agreed upon, than a plethora of others would come up in new rounds of bargaining.

Perhaps the most taxing of these sessions was the one in which the consulting engineers intensely scrutinized the original proposal. Here, words were not minced. They immediately questioned whether the Esslingen site was appropriate for the scheme, arguing that it would make more sense to build in the city rather than in the countryside that was already facing the prospect of more sprawl. And if the project would indeed be built on the site, then it should be denser than proposed. Additionally, in order for the project to really be ecologically minded, the buildings would have to be significantly bigger in terms of their height and depth, the argument being that the ratio of enclosure to useable space was inadequate as planned. Just as problematic for the engineers was the placement of the office and light industrial buildings, which in their view would have to be moved to give the housing units the preferred southern orientation. There were also concerns about security with respect to the multipurpose spaces meant to accommodate both pedestrian and vehicular traffic. All in all, the design team was given an earful. And just when it seemed that the proposal was doomed, the two senior partners, though attentive to the participatory debates, ultimately overruled the criticism for the sake of keeping the project on track. There would be no going back to the drawing board at that point in time, so the project would go forward in Esslingen more or less as drawn.

With all of that settled, at least momentarily, the focus was on how to construct the first prototype building in accordance with the energy and material objectives outlined in the earlier research. The main criteria for decision-making were the engineers' own stringent comfort requirements for work environments and their comparatively high standards for construction, even in Switzerland. At an executive committee meeting, the architects brought with them two miniature cars, a Rolls Royce and a Citroën Deux Chevaux, to prompt a decision on how high the standards should be on both fronts (workplace climate and construction quality). With the options of high-tech and low-tech up for discussion, the committee opted for a position between the two extremes, one less pretentious and costly than a Rolls Royce solution, but more technically and qualitatively sound than an off-the-shelf Deux Chevaux approach.

Numbers, metrics, and quantities are the currency of engineering and in this case would determine all parameters for construction. As engineers are typically prone to do, all elements – whether load-bearing or integral to service systems – were specified for maximum loads (Q_{max}), with a reserve capacity ($Q_{max, max}$), plus a precautionary backup for a worst-case scenario ($Q_{max, max}$ + catastrophic event). But of course, all of these factors in the end mean more material and more costs, thus raising the question as to the limits of sustainable practices. At this point in the process, the real debate boiled down to identifying what was really needed, which compromises would be acceptable, and how best to tweak dimensions, materials, elements, and systems to optimize their performance.

Although there were plenty of top engineers available, the work from this point on would proceed by trial and error, with enough successes and mistakes to go around. To begin with, the building envelope had to be super-insulated to minimize heat loss, which, although commonplace today, was not standard practice at the time, nor was conserving energy for that matter. However, by hermetically sealing the interior environment and considering the southern orientation of the offices, concern was raised about the prospect of overheating, not only due to the sun, but also due to the occupants and machinery inside. Therefore, the original idea for using air-flow windows to heat the buildings was scrapped. And with that, so too was the idea of using these windows to heat the housing units as part of an integral district heating concept (in any case, the housing would be delayed by some 25 years). Shading devices or brise-soleils were mounted on the facade to reduce excess thermal gain, as was already common practice. To cool the office spaces, a horizontal near-surface geothermal energy collector (approximately 5m below grade) with a heat pump was installed, as was a low-velocity fresh air supply system. Sensors would ensure the optimal functioning of these interrelated components with regard to energy savings.

With these measures, the matter of heating was apparently resolved without the need for additional equipment. Still, subsequent heat load calculations showed that for one week in the year, typically

Exterior and interior facade components, including daylight reflectors, 1996 (Reinhard Zimmermann)

First building along the creek facing the train station, 1996 (Reinhard Zimmermann)

Brise-soleil with daylight reflectors, 1996

in early January when occupancy is low, the workspaces would be too cold. In this rare instance, either the occupants would have to wear a sweater or a conventional heating system would be required in addition to the other measures already taken. The client/engineers decided on the latter and installed a small oil furnace that would later be replaced with a wood chip heating system – a textbook case of a Qmax solution winning out over a low-tech option.

Externally mounted daylight reflectors were proposed for minimizing the use of electricity by increasing the amount of natural light in the workspaces, a costly measure that, while making more sense in a thicker building, was realized nevertheless with experimental zeal. There was just as much enthusiasm about the roof becoming an energy generator via an array of photovoltaic panels for electricity and solar thermal collectors for warm water, a sensible idea that was nonetheless abandoned in part, inasmuch as the PV panels, at least for the client, were not viewed as cost-effective. This bit of environmental awareness would have to wait for the second office building that would be realized a few years later.

Though the project had been initially conceived holistically in view of satisfying a broad range of interrelated environmental measures, it was basically being resolved piece by piece and issue by issue. Each problem had its own solution, which was premised primarily on the performance of a particular component or system, thereby resulting in a rather haphazard accumulation of ideas. With this fragmented approach to design development, the ambition that the whole should be greater than sum of its individual parts was being compromised by the segmental thinking that comes with disciplinary specializations – the expert for heating, the expert for lighting, the expert for electricity, and so forth.

But as with any experiment, some things are more successful than others. The choice of materials and the way they were assembled would prove to be more attuned to environmental concerns than those worthy, yet sometimes ungainly tests with energy-saving measures. Realizing that there was great potential in using wood construction to reduce the building's environmental footprint, Hermann Blumer, *the* authority on timber technology in Switzerland at the time, was invited as an outside advisor to one of the project meetings to discuss the latest innovations in his field. Somewhat daringly, he proposed to build the entire building – basement included – out of wood, which came as a shock to the engineers present at the meeting. Although this proposal was intriguing, it was decided instead that the prototype would be built using a combination of different materials and techniques, a hybrid assembly in which each

Farmer's market, front and back, with the wall plate serving as counterweight for the cantilever, 2000 (Reinhard Zimmermann)

Housing units and community kindergarten for the Esslingen Triangle, 2018 (Reinhard Zimmermann)

component satisfied specific requirements. For the structural skeleton, reinforced concrete with recycled aggregate would be used to provide the necessary thermal mass, and a lightweight prefabricated timber frame would be used for the enclosure.

In place of fossil fuel–based foams, compacted paper and mineral wool would serve as insulation material and, in the same vein, the outer membrane would be made of mineral fiber cement boards to further reduce the building's ecological impact. Again, all materials and products would be applied according to their respective life cycle, assembled in such a way so that their maintenance or eventual replacement (and recycling) would not hinder the functioning of other component parts, thereby making even the construction details integral to larger ecological cycles.

Just as the first phase of the Esslingen Triangle was being completed in the mid-1990s, the project – to the team's surprise – received public recognition in Switzerland and the United States. Its trial and error origins aside, the first office building was accredited with the Minergie label because it complied with the newly established Swiss standards for minimal energy use, and that without even having applied for the certification. At roughly the same time, the project was also recognized by the American Institute of Architects for its environmental contributions, setting a standard for a context just beginning to put ecologically minded practices at the top of its agenda.

From Prospect to Project

Over three decades since the project began back in 1989, the overall scheme has yet to be completed as originally envisioned. As is common for an entry in a design competition for multiple public and private functions, the buildings and spaces were conceived as a unified ensemble that, in an ideal case, would be built as such. But the reality of such projects, then and now, is marked by fragmentation and heterogeneity. Taking into account changing interests over time and the *longue durée* of the work for the Esslingen Triangle, still underway as of 2023, there were numerous unexpected breaks and changes in what was optimistically foreseen as a continuous, undeviating process in which one phase would lead directly to the next. After the first buildings were realized, the project lay dormant for years, only to be picked up again later with different clients, developers, architects, engineers, and countless project managers, not to mention with new density requirements, new environmental standards, new programmatic prerequisites, and new construction technologies.

A case in point is the farmer's market that, when subsequently built, had to be awkwardly cantilevered because it was situated on top of a half-completed public parking garage. For the neighborhood of row houses, a new design competition was held that called for a significant increase in the number of units, parking spaces, and overall density of the complex – a competition incidentally won by the same architects of the original scheme. As for the creek, it became a two-phase project, the first complying to specific flood-control standards and the second to even stricter requirements accounting for a more extreme case of flooding. The band of buildings winding along the creek that first showed up in early conceptual collages would remain incomplete, with only three of the five actually realized to date. Rather than completing this band, the next generation of clients/engineers decided to add a wing to the first office building, a project also undertaken as an experiment of sorts, only this time not so much with regard to environmental concerns, but rather in pursuit of ever more efficient project management via the use of the latest update to Building Information Modeling software.

As for the context itself, that picture-perfect small town surrounded by rolling hills and agricultural fields has, in the meantime, given way to a sprawling agglomeration in which the Esslingen Triangle figures as but one fragment among many. Still, life here continues as it does. And it would seem that disjunction has an everyday charm, planning visions to the contrary notwithstanding. How could it be otherwise in those piecemeal habitats that we inhabit, all generated for the most part through bricolage and ad hoc growth? Whatever the answer, those disjunctive environments that we have produced constitute the real project – by no means ideal and far from unified – on which any practice will have to operate to be environment-compatible in the fullest and most effective sense.

An Engineer Reflects

Ernst Hofmann

An Engineer Reflects
Keynote address, FIDIC annual conference
Ernst Hofmann, 1991

Something was in the air at the gathering of engineers in Tokyo for the 1991 annual conference of the International Federation of Consulting Engineers (FIDIC) that supports the profession in supplying technology-based solutions for the built environment worldwide. The discussion on how best to align the construction sector with growing concerns about the state of the environment situated the event within a broader discourse on sustainable development, which at the time was gaining momentum. Among colleagues, a pioneering spirit prevailed not unlike that of the Brundtland Report published just a few years earlier that had set out to raise awareness of mounting ecological problems, while underscoring the urgent need for action – a call that would be taken up just a year later at the 1992 UN Conference on Environment and Development (Rio Summit).

    In his keynote at the FIDIC forum, Swiss engineer Ernst Hofmann used the occasion to outline measures for integrating ecological concerns into practice. On hand from a project in Esslingen, Switzerland, for which he and his partner Konrad Basler were the consulting engineers and main clients, Hofmann addressed the issues of optimized land use, energy conservation, and reduced material flows in an effort to reorient the engineering profession. In preparation for the lecture, Hofmann and Basler collaborated with the project architects to formulate a series of design tenets that, in promoting environment-conscious practices, would be as influential at the gathering in Tokyo as for the project in Esslingen. In addition to these tenets, which were intensely debated during the design phases of the so-called Esslingen Triangle, a matrix was made showing environmental criteria placed in relation to different stages in the life cycle of buildings. This checklist enabled the team of architects and engineers to cross-reference the sum of actions taken at the urban and architectural scales and ensure that the proposed measures did indeed optimize the use of land, energy, and materials.

Looking back at Hofmann's speech, his call for reconciling the imperatives of development with the imperatives of sustainability was put forth at a threshold moment in time when it was becoming apparent that our ways of life were incompatible with our ability to support them, thus putting our common future at risk. His lecture can be read as a debate on sustainable construction *avant la lettre*. Hofmann tackles this theme from two perspectives, oscillating between a practice-oriented reflection on technical solutions drawn from research conducted via the Esslingen case, and a speculative reflection on the challenges of making development sustainable in the context of a growth-based economy.

The following is a transcript of Hofmann's keynote address entitled "The Integration of Environmental Considerations into the Design Process – A Consulting Engineer Looks at Daily Practice," delivered at the FIDIC conference in Tokyo in September 1991.

> Reflecting on a recent and still ongoing project, my partner Konrad Basler and I had the unique opportunity to develop a parcel of land in the dual roles of consulting engineers and main clients. Working together with local authorities, we organized a design competition for the small community of Esslingen that lies in a rural landscape of open fields, waterways, and woods some 20km from the city of Zurich.

The condition of the global environment was a key issue addressed at last year's annual FIDIC conference in Oslo, where we collectively discussed the interventions necessary for achieving sustainable development. We were critical of a "wait-and-see" attitude toward new initiatives in energy and environmental policy and insisted that "the time for action is now." The audience of practitioners were summoned to "do a better job of environmental planning," implying that not enough was being done to engage with the real-world challenges of mitigating the detrimental impact of the building industry.

I still share that vision, being convinced that the environment must be central to architectural design as well as the pivotal focus of our work in the engineering profession. This very ethos was at the core of the brief for the competition in Switzerland, in which we asked the participating architects to be as conscious of the environment as possible with their proposed solutions.

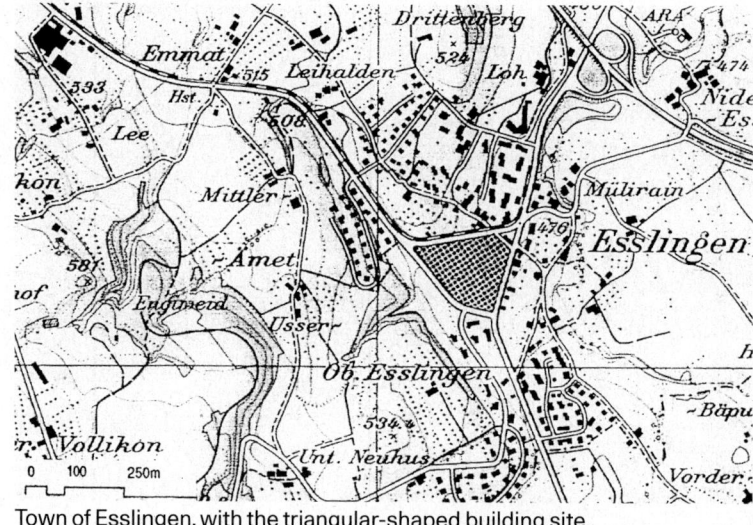
Town of Esslingen, with the triangular-shaped building site

The winning proposal shows how the architects used the land in an ecologically mindful way, insofar as the required buildings are carefully integrated into the built and natural landscape. Public buildings are organized around a new town square, while the private office and light industrial buildings that flank a creek running through the site serve as a buffer for the housing units beyond. With the provision of a train station with direct connections to Zurich as well as additional bus lines linked to the local transportation network, the Esslingen Triangle, as the project is called, essentially turns a remote village into an integral hub of an emergent metropolitan region.

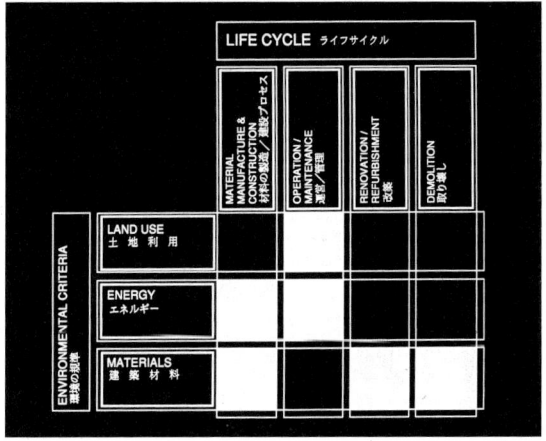

Matrix showing the life-cycle phases of a building (x-axis) and environmental criteria (y-axis)

As engineers, we closely collaborated with the architects to identify key environmental issues that had to be accounted for in the project's development, focusing particularly on the categories of land use, energy conservation, and material flows. Admittedly being new territory for us, we then defined specific tenets in correlation to these issues, which in turn were considered relative to the entire life cycle of buildings – from material production and building construction to operations and maintenance, and from renovation to dismantling in view of product recycling.

Environment-conscious land use: Three decades ago (in the early 1960s), only three billion people inhabited the planet. A decade later, this number doubled. Currently, the global population increases by a rate of 7.5 million people per month, which is more than the population of Switzerland. Incidentally, this small country has an annual growth rate of 40,000 people, which corresponds to a mid-sized European city. Of course, this number is negligible in comparison to that in developing countries (in Africa, Latin America, or Asia), but the issue here is not the discrepancy in population growth among world regions alone. Rather, this issue becomes all the more challenging when compounded with the reality of ever more people demanding higher living standards, with the desire for a better quality of life requiring more land, energy, and material. This is the real challenge at hand that now bears on the global environment.

Today in Switzerland, a country known for its high living standards, we consume twice as much space per capita as a generation ago, and this trend shows no signs of abating. Keep in mind that built land area, including the space for infrastructure, increased in the country by 43% from 1950 to 1980. The building stock from this period of accelerated economic growth was often constructed with insufficient care and with little respect for the natural environment. This material legacy remains a liability, economically and ecologically, and impacts our quality of life by default, not to mention that of generations to come. It is thus no wonder that large segments of the population are opposed to new construction and the reckless consumption of one of our most valuable and limited common resources.

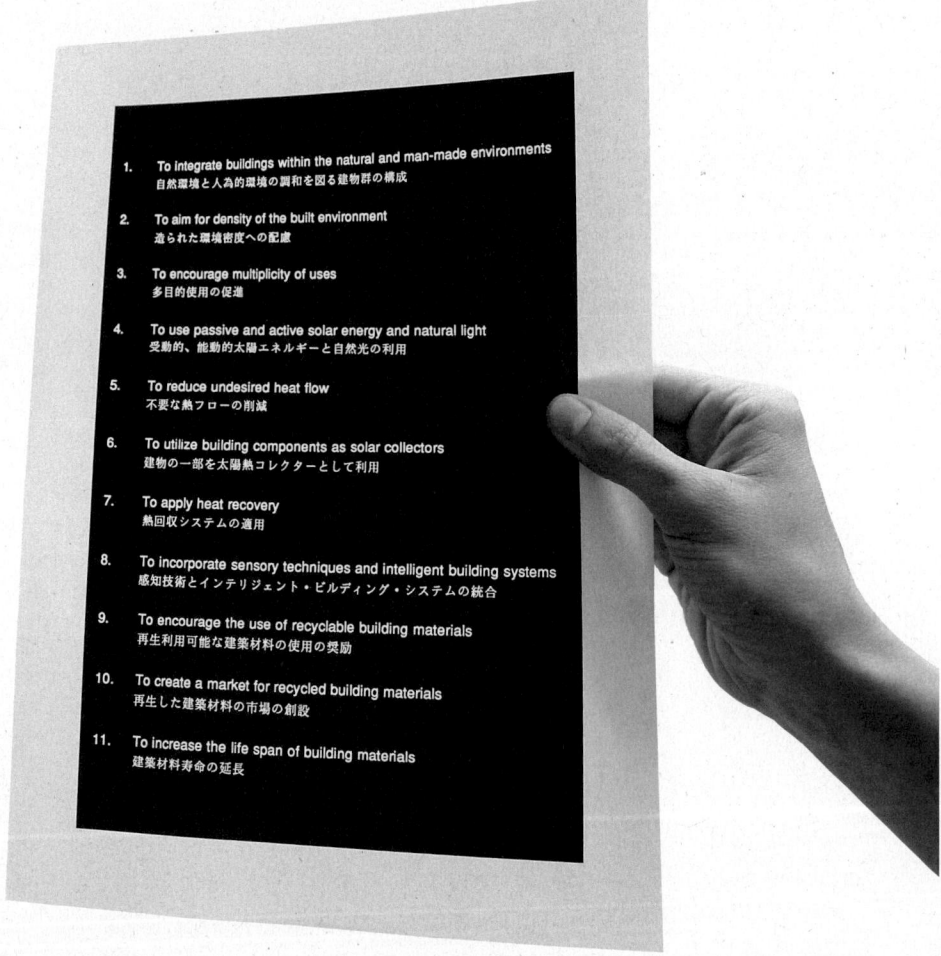

Tenets for the project in English and Japanese; prepared for Hofmann's lecture at the FIDIC forum, Tokyo, 1991

In view of the above concerns about land use, the following objectives were defined for our case study project in Esslingen: (1) to integrate buildings within the natural and man-made environments; (2) to densify the built fabric; (3) to encourage multiplicity of uses on the same parcel of land.

A series of thumbnail diagrams was prepared to show how the project was generated, taking into account features of the existing landscape such as topography, waterways, and vegetation. Additional vignettes highlighted the organization of the main built elements and how they optimize, for example, the use of land, solar orientation, sound protection, and views to distant mountain ranges. Another figure that became decisive in the project's approval in a local referendum was the one drawing attention to the new public square conceived as a collectively shared amenity. The added value of the overall venture in terms of land use is the integration of living and working functions in the same place that are linked to this nucleus of community life.

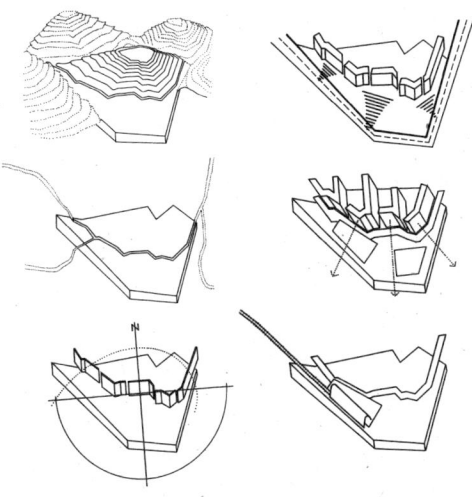

Integration of the proposed scheme into the natural and built environment (topography, waterways, solar orientation, sound protection, views, and light rail link to Zurich)

Concerning the density of the built environment, the winning scheme went beyond the requirements of the program brief by including a number of outdoor spaces like a promenade along the creek, a village green for special activities, and the above-mentioned public square, all enriching town life by engendering

An Engineer Reflects

a newfound collective realm. The concentration of buildings in clusters of varying densities freed up space for such amenities.

Moreover, the scheme was selected because it proposed multiple uses for these spaces that, in effect, called into question the conventional separation of functions – vehicular traffic here, buses there, bicycle lanes and pedestrian activities somewhere else. In the proposed project, all share the same surface, a design

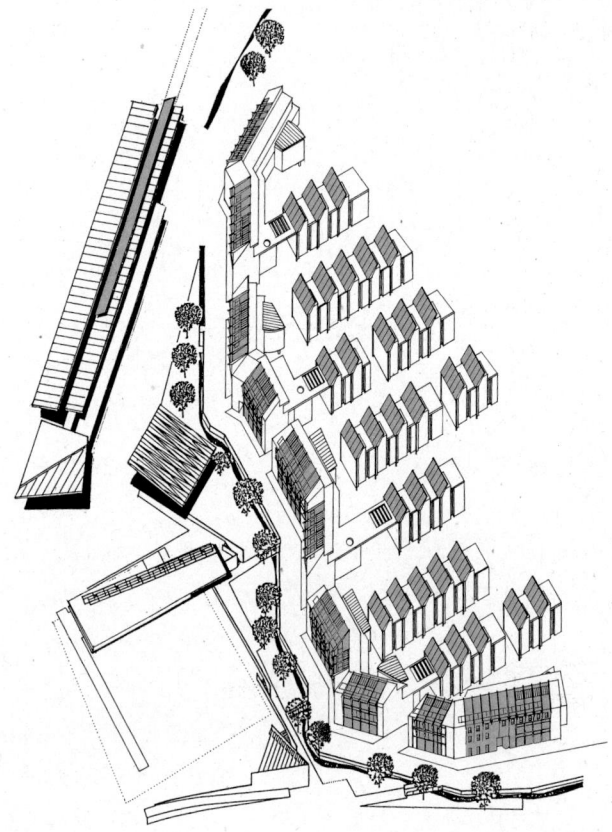

South-facing facades and roofs used for energy production

move, by the way, that required considerable negotiations before it was approved. Following the same logic, the roof of the partially submerged parking garage can accommodate a village green as well as a covered farmer's market. The waterway promenade doubles as a forecourt to the light industrial buildings, while providing access to the lanes that – acting also as children's playgrounds – lead to the housing cluster. In addition to optimizing land use, the multiplication and overlap of functions is a principle applied to the buildings as well in view of their environmental

Competition model: (sq) town square; (1) train station; (2) post office; (3) restaurant; (4) office and light-industry buildings; (5) housing units; (6) village green; (7) existing creek

performance. The light industrial buildings not only provide a sound buffer for the housing units, but their south-facing facades and roofs also act as energy generators.

Environment-conscious energy use: At last year's conference, we were told that "one of the greatest engineering challenges of the future will be to develop less environmentally damaging sources of energy, while reducing total energy consumption through better energy efficiency in the home, in transportation, and in industry." Taking this call for action to heart, my partner and I have investigated where the biggest potential lies in terms of energy savings in our own country. It is estimated that in Switzerland 44% of the total energy used goes to the construction and operation of buildings. We as engineers have a significant influence on energy consumption and it is precisely here where we need to leverage that influence.

Energy consumption in Switzerland (1990): 32% transportation, 24% industry and agriculture, 4% construction, and 40% building operations

Accordingly, supplementary planning goals concerning energy conservation in the case study project were identified: (4) to use passive and active solar energy and natural light; (5) to reduce undesired heat flow; (6) to utilize building components as solar collectors; (7) to take advantage of heat recovery; (8) to incorporate sensory techniques for optimizing operations.

The urban design layout of the project facilitated the environment-conscious use of energy, with a premium placed on renewable resources. The southern orientation of the buildings ensured the maximum usage of sunlight. The internal zoning of the buildings responds to different parameters for internal climate control, with the functions situated relative to their respective thermal and lighting requirements.

With respect to undesired heat flows, optimal insulation and impermeable building envelopes are essential, keeping in mind that thermal insulation is the most significant factor in energy savings. While desirable in terms of utilizing daylight and generating energy, south-facing facades must nevertheless be shielded to avoid overheating.

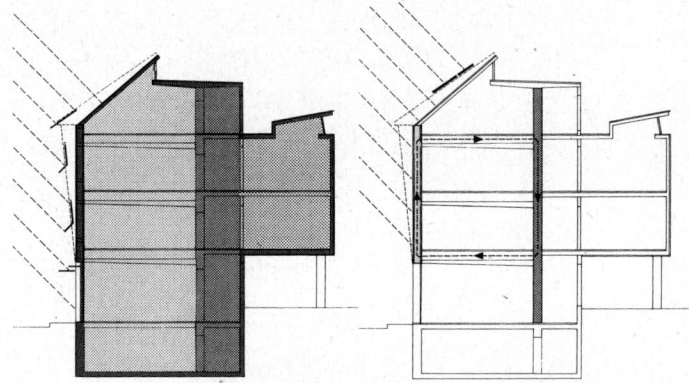

Thermal zoning and solar installations, the latter using air-flow energy capture and photovoltaic panels

In terms of energy generation, the building envelopes (including roofs) function as a power plant, so to speak, at least as envisioned. We are currently considering the advantages of using the Trombe wall principle, whereby south-facing facades capture solar energy within the layer between the external and internal membranes. The thermal energy is then stored within a massive wall inside the building and gradually released over time. Two types of roof-mounted collectors are being considered for heating water and producing electricity. When a surplus is produced, it is fed into the public utilities network, itself treated as a storage reservoir of sorts.

Heat recovery from exhaust air is also a significant aspect in energy planning for working environments, considering the substantial amount of heat generated by machines, installations, artificial lighting, not to mention the occupants themselves. In our case, this surplus can be used to heat the project's housing units – an integral concept involving the redistribution of energy across the site. To coordinate these measures, an intelligent control system is needed for regulating heating, lighting, and ventilation. This integrated digital system responds to real needs rather than to a predetermined schedule, inasmuch as the number of occupants as well as interior and exterior climate conditions vary continuously. In addition to the use of thermostats, ventilation can be regulated with air-quality sensors, whereby the concentration of carbon dioxide can be measured to modulate the supply of fresh air.

As important as such measures are, we cannot overlook the overall quantity of fossil fuel–based energy consumed in the building sector. Accordingly, a diagram was made comparing three metrics: status quo consumption, Swiss target standards, and sought-after benchmarks for our project, the latter being pursued along two trajectories, one predicated on reducing the quantity of energy needed, the other on specifying the quality of the energy produced. Concerning quantity, the Esslingen project has the potential to reduce the use of fossil fuels by approximately 40% due to energy-saving measures. Concerning quality, renewable energy sources can reduce the use of fossil fuels by as much as 70% compared to the already stringent Swiss standards. Achieving these ambitious goals, however, will take more than only innovative engineering; it will require energy-conscious officials, developers, and users as well.

We must be aware that any new building brings with it an additional energy load. There is also the conundrum that any energy-saving goals are offset by the imperative for growth.

However, the embedded energy in our existing building stock is significant, as are the potential savings afforded by tapping into this abundant reservoir. If we were to fully comply with our own tenets while also renovating as much as possible, the amount of energy required for the building sector could be reduced by 40% by 2020, thereby returning us to the level of the 1960s, at least in Switzerland.

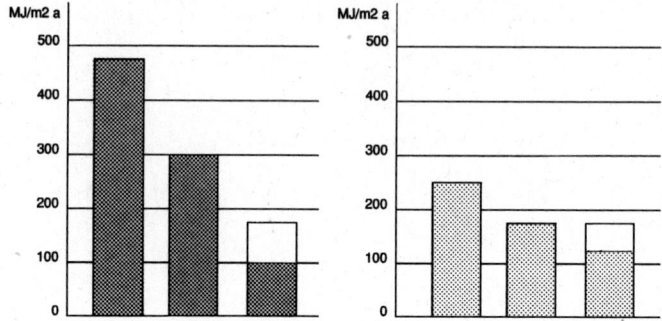

Energy use in Switzerland as of 1990 for heating (left) and electricity (right) on the basis of three metrics: status quo consumption (left columns), professional targets (middle columns), and project benchmarks (right columns, solar gains in white)

Coming back to our project and with the measures for energy savings in mind, the bottom line is that the total consumption for its operational phase can be considerably reduced. Yet this gain will most likely be annulled by the additional amount of energy needed for the fabrication of building components such as additional insulation, high quality windows, and photovoltaic cells used to make the project more environmentally sound. Such is the situation in which we find ourselves – a vicious circle that makes the enticing prospect of a 'zero-energy building' a demonstrably unrealistic one. That said, the demanding task of achieving optimization through smart land and energy use must include innovations in material use if we are to have any impact on resolving the current impasse.

Environment-conscious material use: As was made clear in our Oslo forum, the principle of using environment-concious materials essentially implies that the material flows required to sustain our standard of living cannot be open-ended. Therefore, as many products as possible should be recycled after their use, and we must go from waste-based to reuse-based technologies. How does this mandate affect the engineering profession?

The building sector requires the largest flow of materials of all industries in our country. The construction industry (buildings and infrastructure included) has utilized in the last ten years an estimated average of 9 tons of materials per capita per annum for new construction, yet only half a ton per inhabitant per year has been demolished. The annual net growth of 8.5 tons per inhabitant significantly increases the total volume of material stock. Acknowledging that new construction creates waste, it is safe to assume that with an increase of material flows, there will be a drastic increase in the amount of discarded material. In the long term, we will have to strike a balance between material use and material waste.

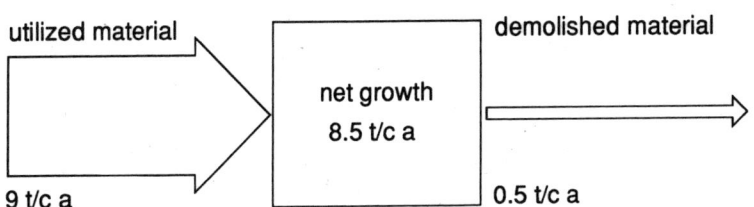

Material flow diagram (per capita and annum in Switzerland, 1980 to 1990): 9 tons new construction, building stock increase 8.5 tons, 0.5 tons demolition (P. Baccini and P. Brunner, 1991)

To transition from waste-based to reuse-based technologies in view of reducing material flows, our planning goals must be expanded to include the following directives: (9) to encourage the use of recyclable building materials; (10) to create a market for recycled building materials; and finally, (11) to increase the life span of building materials.

These demands will be central to the upcoming planning phases of our project with respect to determining the products to be used, which will require consultation with recycling experts in the construction sector. We now know that buildings erected prior to World War II were richer in reusable building components than contemporary buildings, insofar as plastics, composite materials, and toxic chemicals were not in widespread use at the time. For our case study, this means that (a) natural paints and lacquers will replace hazardous synthetic paints; (b) a substitute material will be used in place of hydrochlorofluorocarbon-based insulation; (c) additives will be selected accordingly to avoid complications in the future reuse of concrete; (d) composite materials will only be used if they can be separated into their constituent parts; (e) plastic laminates will be avoided due to the large amount of energy required to separate their component materials.

At the Oslo conference, we were advised that "engineers should become expert green consumers when specifying their procurement of materials." To help with our work, the ecological profile of any given material can provide valuable input concerning its environmental impact throughout its entire life cycle. In Europe, for example, material manufacturers are attempting to determine the constituent components of their products. And it seems only reasonable to prioritize the use of such certified building materials. But for recycling to become a widespread practice, not only do we need a market for recycled materials, but also quality standards concerning their reuse.

For our project, we intend to identify where recycled materials could be implemented. Concrete made from pea gravel, for instance, can be utilized for street substrates or aggregates for non-load-bearing elements. Similar considerations will have to be made concerning the load-bearing elements, thermal insulation, external cladding, interior finishes, and so forth.

We also intend to account for the varying life spans of different products, while taking every effort to use more durable ones, considering that the removal and preparation of materials for reuse is energy intensive. Materials should remain in place as long as possible. Life span in this case is generally determined by aging as well as by technical obsolescence. It might be helpful here to distinguish materials according to their longevity: primary structure (150 years); enclosure (60 years); mechanical systems (30 years); paint, awnings, and solar collectors (15 years). Just as important is to layer components within the construction assembly according to life span so that their replacement does not impair the functioning of others. This logic has ramifications for the work of engineers and architects alike, expanding their practices by including the imperative to design with time in mind.

The economy of the environment: In this presentation, I have addressed those areas where we must become more environ-

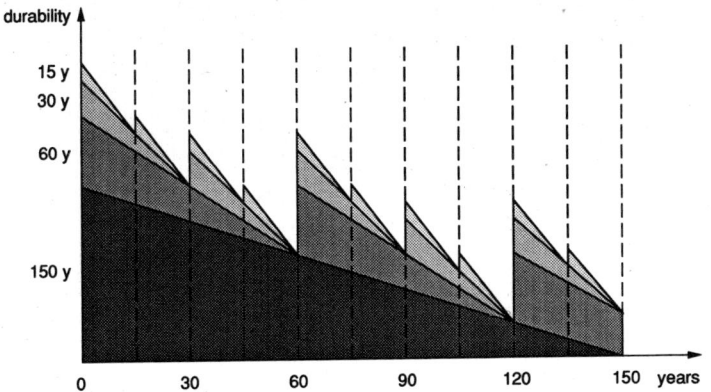
Life spans and replacement cycles for building materials and components
(P. Steiger, "Bauen und Oekologie im Dialog," *SIA-Dokumentation* 46, 1990)

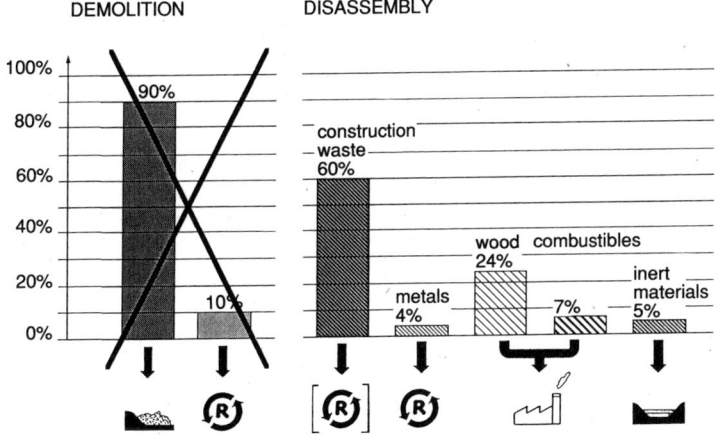
Material volume of demolition and disassembly, showing that most construction materials could be recycled

mentally conscious. The issues of land use, energy conservation, and material flows, though presented here independently, are in reality interrelated and become even more complex when considered relative to the bigger picture of population growth, the demand for higher living standards, and the imbalance between gains made in optimizing construction and the additional resources required to do so. To engage creatively with these challenges, we can no longer rely on analytical reflection alone, for we must enhance our intuitive capacities as well.

To this, I must ask: Can our society afford an environment-conscious technology? To be candid, we have no choice. Contemporary short-term thinking stands in contradiction to the aspiration of sustainable development. Yet the damage already done should remind us of the future consequences of our actions if we do not change our ways. But this is easier said than done. To build today in accordance with more environment-mindful standards is more expensive than to build with conventional technologies, at least for the time being. What is even more expensive in the long run is to continue building unsustainably.

We are convinced that more can be achieved with economic incentives than with mere recommendations and restrictions. As environmental leaders, we must invest our efforts on all levels so that the price paid for our resources corresponds to their limited availability. This is a long-term task worth its ultimate costs. But to get there, we must first learn how to build with the environment in mind and demonstrate its value before the market follows suit. For it is the environment that must determine the course of the economy and not vice versa.

Stripped Down

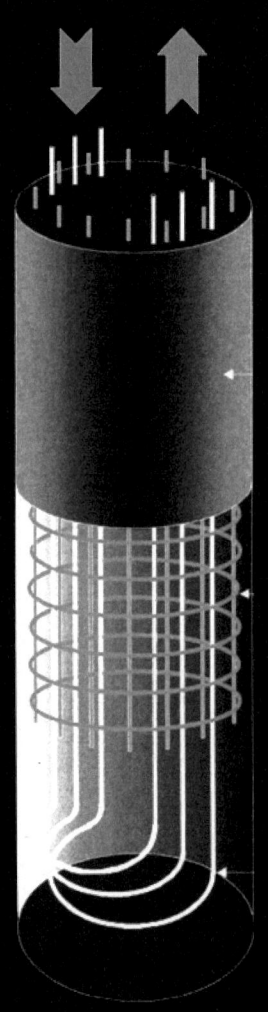

Zurich Airport Terminal

	Designing the Process		Everyday Poetics

Discourses

Manuel Castells, *The Rise of the Network Society*, 1996

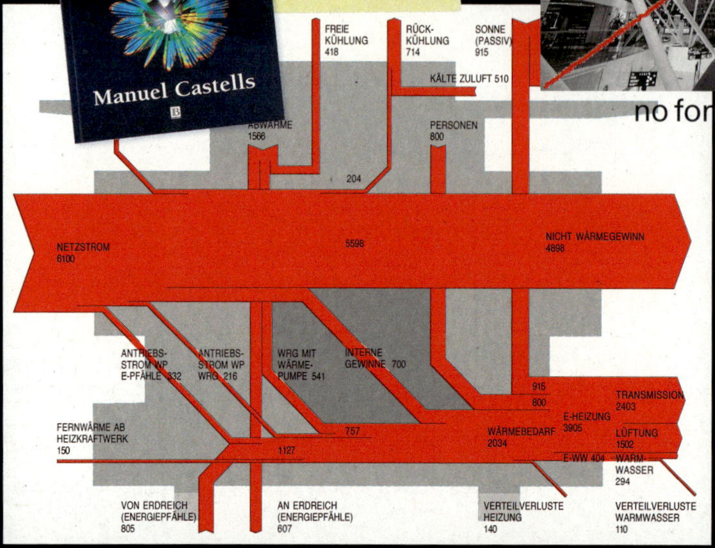

Use

Energy

no formal exuberance

Materials

what you see is what you get

energy flows

all materials exposed
no mechanical systems

Economy

low cost

strategic reduction of components
reduce to the max

Technology

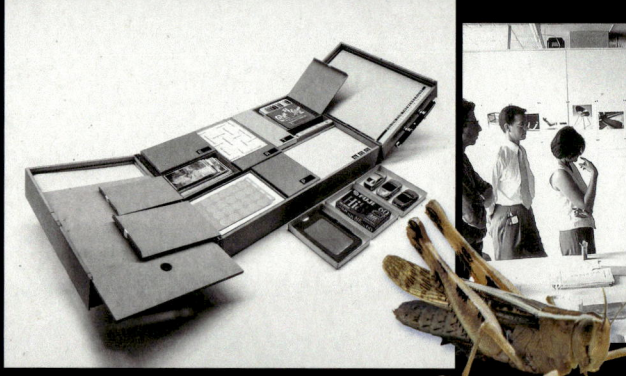

Methodology

Saul Steinberg, *The Labyrinth*, 1960

designing the process

interdisciplinary team

Zayetta (team name)

Policy

research project

moderated workshops

working with images

Commission for Technology and Innovation (CTI)

Lean Technology

The Undecorated Shed

do more with less

Peter Fischli and David Weiss, *Airports*, 1990

8,000m² PV panels (264,000 kWh per year)

300 probes @ 35–70m

economy of means

no commercialization

freeway construction

lean tech

architect as general contractor

Kyoto Protocol, 1997

communication tools

privatization of airport authority

Swissair grounding

Stripped Down

Stripped Down
Midfield Terminal, Zurich International Airport
1995–2003

Passengers come and go. They arrive, they depart. This is the basic operational diagram for any airport terminal wherever it may be. These facilities are essentially processors of people and things on the move. As 'spaces of flows' for information, resources, and money, they are premised on big numbers, routine, and efficiency, while rarely viewed as places in and of themselves.

The design competition brief for a new midfield terminal at the Zurich International Airport in the mid-1990s was no different, inasmuch as it too was predicated primarily on quantitative parameters. The program read like a manual on designing by numbers: 27 gates for planes of different sizes; peak passenger capacity of 5,000 per hour and 40,000 a day; and 80,000 m² of usable space broken down into precise area specifications for every last function. This had to fit on a roughly 750 × 200 m parcel of land surrounded by runways and taxiing lanes. Not surprisingly, the proposal had to be cost-efficient in terms of getting the maximum performance with minimal investment, affordability being a decisive factor in choosing the winning entry. But there were other key metrics as well. The energy load for operations of the entire airport, including the new terminal, had been capped at 1994 levels, meaning that optimizing the sum of resource flows for the new building as well as the existing facilities would also be a determinant issue in the deliberation process – never mind that a 'sustainable' airport is a contradiction in terms. So, the high ecological performance of the terminal had to be achieved with a minimum of economic resources.

While satisfying all of the quantitative prerequisites, design proposals had to be formally expressive as well in order to satisfy the airport authority's wish for a representative structure of symbolic significance. This identity-making proviso was, at heart, a desire to raise the airport's international ranking via place branding. In striking a balance between quantity and quality while fulfilling multiple desires, the "gateway to Switzerland" – as the project was advertised in the national press – would most likely need to be divined from an Excel spreadsheet on which numbers served as both judge and jury.

Designing the Process

How does a team qualify for such a high-profile competition with no experience in airport design whatsoever? The architects who eventually won had assumed from the outset that they would be the underdogs in a field of quite experienced competitors. When preparing the pre-qualification package required for prospective participants, the rookie team opted to present a design process rather than, as is typical, showcasing their previous work. This strategy was born of necessity considering that there was no comparable project of this type or size in their portfolio.

At the time, the architects were engaged in practice-oriented research at ETH Zurich, focusing specifically on the early phases of design to improve the quality of decision-making among all stakeholders involved in complex projects. This research was conducted under the auspices of the Swiss Commission for Technology and Innovation (today Innosuisse – Swiss Innovation Agency), a federal institution supporting knowledge transfers between academia and industry. The findings, still in development at that time, would make their way into the formal pre-qualification submission and would inform the entire process from design to completion after the competition had been decided. In short, a design process conceived in the abstract would become the procedural underlay for designing a concrete project, in this case, a new airport terminal.

Faced with the challenge of scale, the architects drew on their ongoing research when assembling the team and devising the overall approach to the task at hand. The team would have to be heterogeneous in its makeup (multiple disciplines, different levels of experience, varying ages, comprised of men and women) as well as

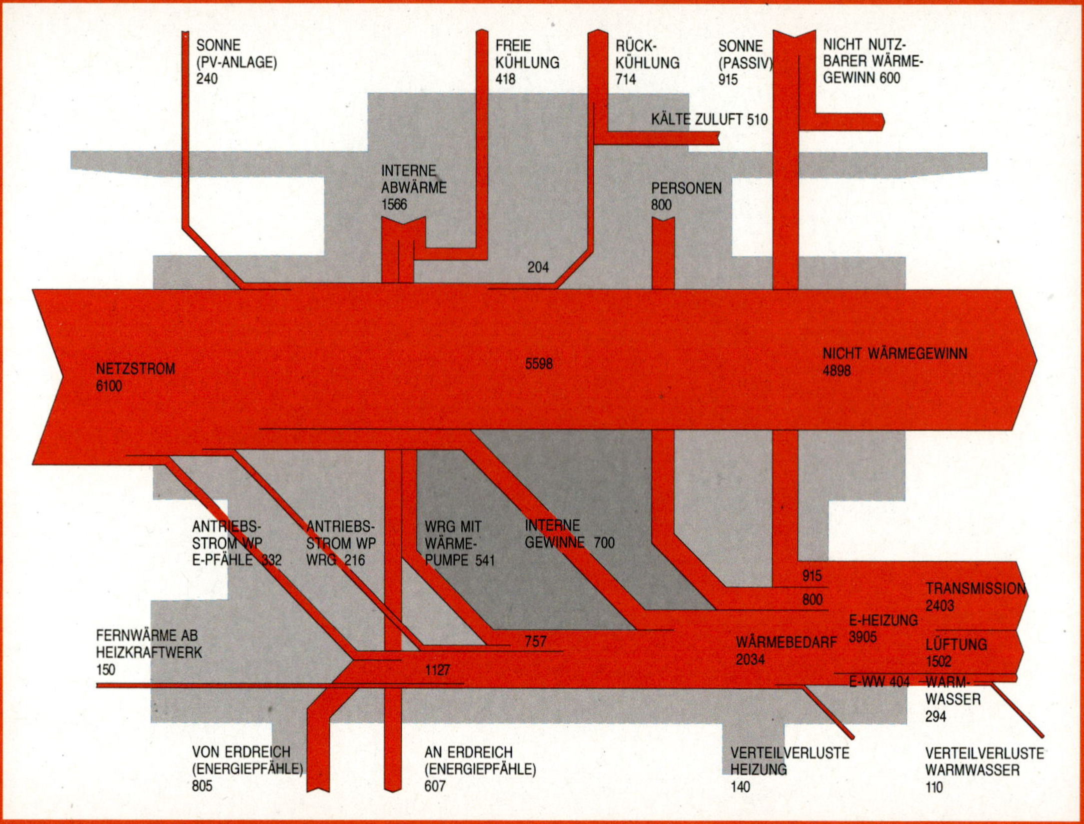

Energy and electricity distribution throughout the terminal conceived as a "space of flows" – a phrase coined by Manuel Castells in *The Rise of the Network Society* in 1996 (Amstein + Walthert, Zurich)

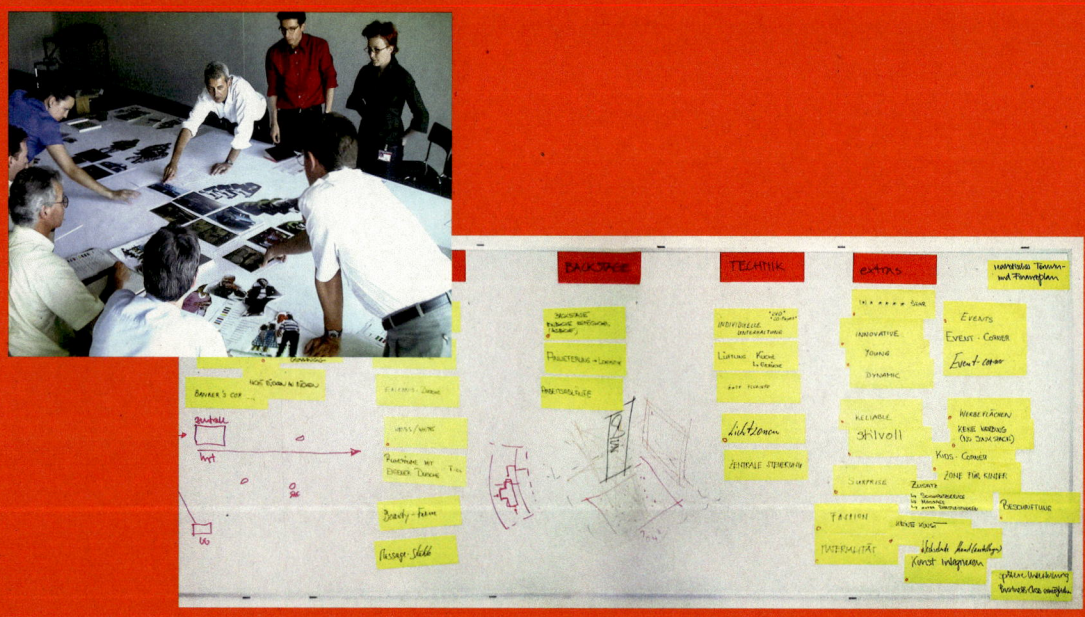

Interdisciplinary team workshops using images, diagrams, and sticky notes highlighting discussion topics

Saul Steinberg, drawings showing various ways to go from A to B (*The Labyrinth*, 1960)

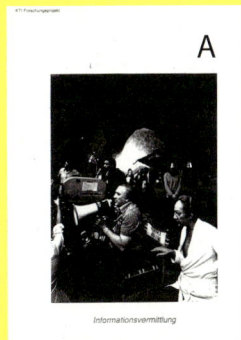   

Overhead projector transparencies for design workshop moderators, 1995–1997

Toolbox used by the team coach; research on decision-making in the early design phases (ETH Zurich and Swiss Commission for Technology and Innovation, 1995–1997)

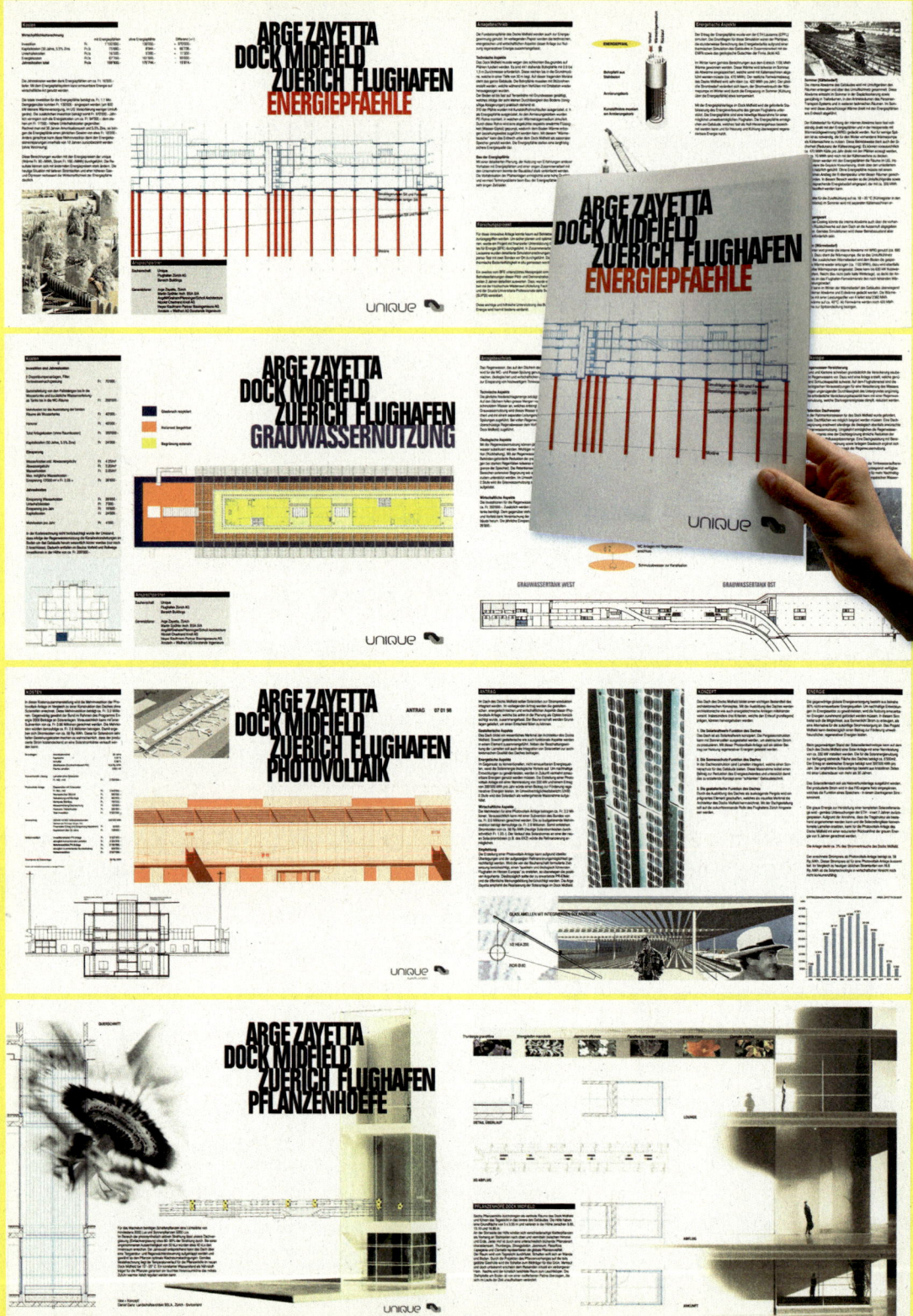

Flyers showing milestones in the design process – energy piles, gray water use, photovoltaic array, and courtyard vegetation in its inclinations (rational, intuitive, critical, playful, pragmatic). In addition to the architects, there were structural and mechanical engineers, energy experts, cost estimators, construction managers, and a young graphic artist who, in the role of joker, visualized one proposition after another to make the discussions more tangible.

Yet such a mix of people could prove explosive, especially when working under pressure. Accordingly, a coach – a group psychologist – was brought on board immediately in the first workshop in early 1996 to steer discussions, monitor conflicts, and ensure a sense of cohesion. She acted as an intermediary among group members to shift the focus from individuals to the project itself, while keeping everyone on the same page when oscillating between strictly disciplinary and transdisciplinary work. Not only was a name given to the group as a bonding gesture of sorts, but also a new atelier was set up at the airport where all were asked to work collectively on a project that demanded collective authorship.

Just as the team makeup was a matter of design, so too were the methods to be deployed. The only thing certain was that the approach to designing the terminal would not be any linear progression from A to B, bearing in mind the sheer number of interests to be accommodated, not to mention the plethora of unanticipated setbacks or detours that would inevitably occur throughout the process. In the preliminary as well as subsequent design phases, regular workshops were held to encourage dialogue among the different professionals who suddenly found themselves face to face and tasked with solving increasingly 'wicked problems' on a daily basis.

It is one thing to get a diverse group of people in the same room, but it is another thing altogether to get them communicating with each other effectively, their own disciplinary idioms notwithstanding. The coach, who incidentally was involved in the ongoing university research on early design phases, would come to the airport workshops with an elaborate toolbox devised specifically to facilitate decision-making, albeit in a playful way. There were compartments in the box with miniature cars to prompt debates about different standards of construction: Would it be high-tech or low-tech? Monopoly money was used to thematize budget issues: Would the proposed solution be affordable, including hidden costs? There were also several magic writing pads that could be passed around to encourage people to draw out their ideas as they were being discussed: Is this what you meant and might that work better?

As it became apparent, especially to the coach, that multidisciplinary collaboration could quickly devolve into a babble of rival languages, she suggested to work more with images as a common medium of communication to overcome, or at least highlight, misunderstandings. Any concept or proposal had to be visualizable. This stipulation would later give rise to a series of flyers produced quickly and cheaply – as illustrated minutes of workshop meetings – to disseminate relevant information concerning design decisions on important milestones: spatial sequences and routes of passenger circulation, renewable energy measures, itemized cost estimates for construction, choreography of material use, and so on. This straightforward mode of communication was crucial, not only to keep the ever-increasing number of team members informed, which in time would grow to more than 50 people, but also to keep the ever-shifting and restructured client committees of the airport authority up to date. The design process would thus become a project as frenzied in its flows as an airport itself.

Everyday Poetics

One of the first sets of images discussed in a workshop with the engineers showed two freeways under construction that brought up the idea of treating the new terminal as a utilitarian piece of infrastructure rather than an architectural icon. Civil engineer Marilyn Reece, seen in one of the images in front of a freeway interchange in Los Angeles in 1965, had approached her project with aesthetics in mind when vowing to put her "heart and soul into it." In so many words, infrastructure has its own formal appeal, even though it is seldom assessed in terms of how it looks when performing its function. Another image of a freeway in San Francisco shows a fragment of a double-decker structure alluding to the possible stacking of airport decks to separate departures from arrivals. On the basis of these images alone, the general concept of the new terminal began to take shape by way of skeletal organizational diagrams that could almost be read as pieces of a highway. As an infrastructural work, the building would operate as an integral part of the larger airport infrastructure, its stripped-down aesthetic a conscious product of standard civil engineering construction techniques.

By coincidence, Swiss artists Peter Fischli and David Weiss had published their book *Airports* just a few years earlier, foregrounding the commonplace banality of those non-descript places that we have all passed through en route to another place. There are no flying roofs or undulating planes here. Rather, the metallic bodies of the aircraft, the odd machinery on the ground, and the emptiness of the tarmac all add up to everyday qualities devoid of superlatives,

Photographs of freeways under construction used in a workshop with engineers – Santa Monica Freeway Interchange, Los Angeles (1965) and Embarcadero Freeway, San Francisco (1968)

Peter Fischli and David Weiss, *Airports*, 1990
(© Peter Fischli David Weiss)

Polaroid photograph of model at 1:2000 prepared for the first workshop, 1996

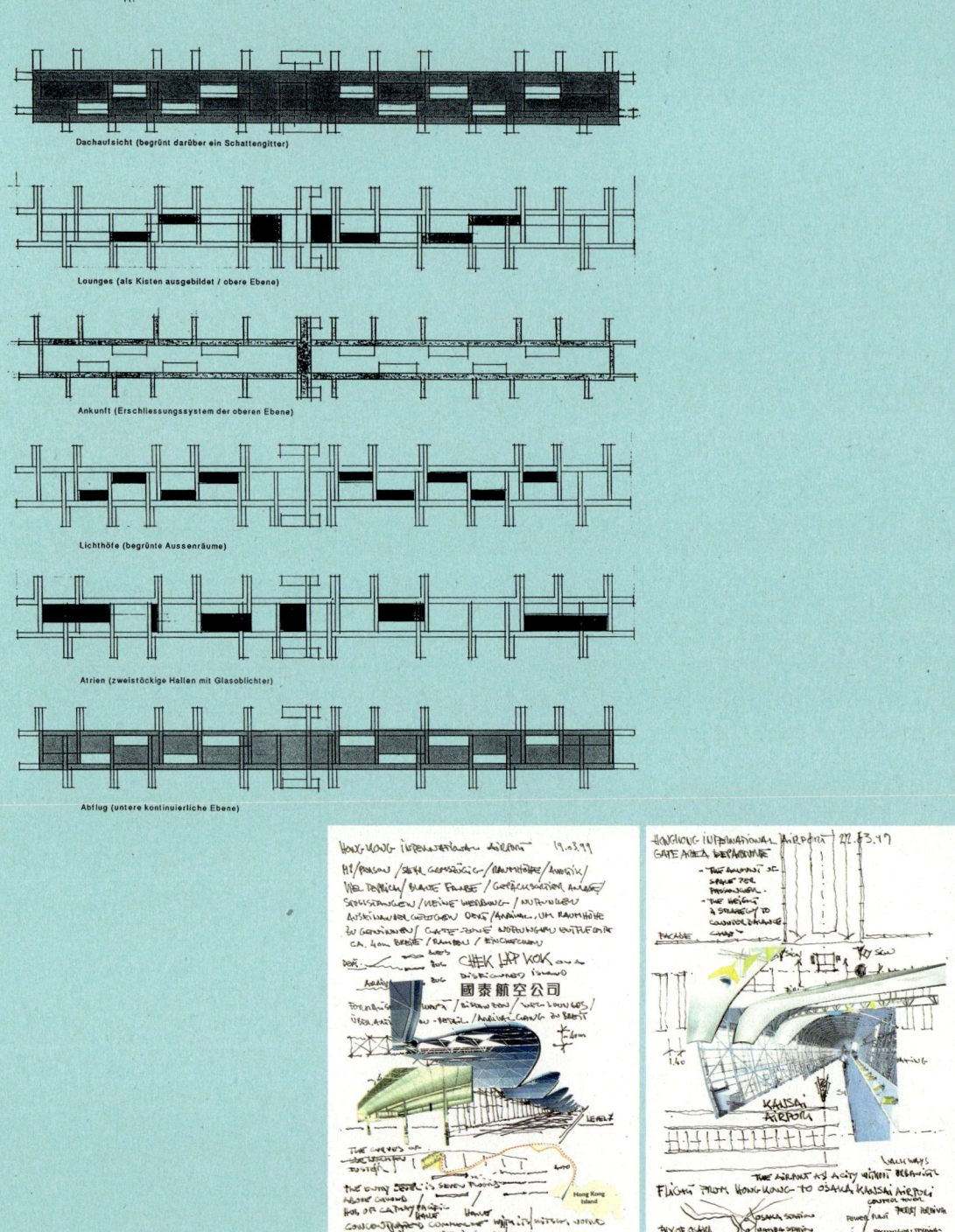

Diagrams of arrival and departure levels, 1996

Architect's travelogue made during field trips to airports in Southeast Asia save for the bare-bones technologies that make an airport work. It was certainly this unadorned aesthetic that had prompted Le Corbusier many years earlier to claim that an airport should remain as "naked" as possible, its brute concrete structure set against the biomorphic forms of the planes. It was this very sentiment that would be carried through in the design of the new terminal – naked, stark, robust, restrained, and derived from everyday experience.

Even though it had been generally decided that the project would not be distinguished by its formal exuberance per se, but rather by how much could be gleaned from an economy of means, the architects took it upon themselves to visit renowned airports of the world to see firsthand how they operate. Having toured terminals in Bangkok, Singapore, Kuala Lumpur, Hong Kong, and Osaka, they returned somehow disillusioned by the rather meager state of airport architecture – poorly constructed, disorienting in its organization, formally superficial, over-scaled, overly commercialized. In fact, all of the airports visited began to look the same, despite their pretense of being uniquely spectacular and out of the ordinary. If nothing else, this trip (via airports, to airports, for an airport) confirmed what *not* to do when designing a contemporary terminal.

Instead, the design team sought a way to give a face to those things that are usually hidden by habit; namely, to the poetics of everyday experience when traveling from A to B. The building itself would step back, as it were, with 'design' becoming effectively invisible. The architectural qualities would come forth by way of a network of relationships, whether determined through sequences of movement and rest, visual connections near and far, daylight distribution for orientation, and varying intensities of spatial awareness. The structure would be exposed and materials shown for what they were even when aged, with no cladding used throughout. The building's internal organization would be self-evident in its clarity and ease of use. Construction details at all scales would be straightforward, but no less tectonically developed. All of this would take place in a structure that does not announce itself when functioning as both common tool and precise instrument.

In order to carry through on these design intentions, the team would have to thread the needle, operating somewhere between conflicting requirements of a client's desire for representation, which in airport design often results in excessive formalism, and cost constraints that usually leave designers no other recourse than to settle for a generic solution. The attempt to draw a poetics from everyday circumstances provided a possible way out of the trap of having to choose between a big form or a banal box.

Lean Technology

The issue of balancing economic concerns with the desire for formal identity – while also adhering to ecological benchmarks – came down to how technology is deployed. Although not only a technological object but also a place in and of itself, the new terminal evolved as an interface of different disciplinary competences and techniques coming together in punctual synergies to find the optimal way to materialize a particular design proposition. These synergies of disciplinary knowledge would help the team transition from multidisciplinary to transdisciplinary approaches to the work. But even this convergence of expertise required a common orientation to channel the stream of ideas.

"Reduce to the max" became the maxim when putting high-tech, low-tech, and no-tech options on the table. With the logic of minimal resource-use up for debate, it was decided that the project would be stripped of any unnecessary space, system, or component. One proposal, for example, was to get rid of the basement; another, to do away with dropped ceilings and wall coverings; still another, to eliminate mechanical systems altogether. Although not all such suggestions were heeded in the end, they were on the right track to doing 'more with less' as opposed to doing 'less with more.' For the sake of reducing the environmental impact of the building, the less, the better. Less is less – less form, less technology, less matter, less emissions, and so forth.

One need only recall all of those airports that use exaggerated forms to make a statement, but in fact needlessly waste material and energy resources in the effort to do so. This issue was taken up by a keynote speaker at an industry-sponsored conference in New Orleans in 2000 when comparing the sectional drawings of the new airport terminals for Madrid and Zurich. Both projects were in development at the same time for the same program and passenger capacity, yet the midfield dock in Zurich has half the volume of the one in Madrid, the message being that bigger is not necessarily better.

When it finally came to translating good intentions into practice for the terminal in Zurich, the mechanical and structural engineers at one of the early workshops agreed on a logic of augmented performance, whereby the foundations, for instance, also serve to transfer geothermal energy to heat or cool the building depending on the season, thus avoiding the need for a costly supplementary system. Some 300 such energy piles were cast in situ (measuring between 90 and 150 cm in diameter with varying depths of 30–70 m due to the uneven bedrock) to draw on the thermal storage capacities of nearly 500,000 m³ of earth via roughly 12 km of coils threaded through the foundation piles.

The architects responded with visualizations of their own, first with the analogous image of a millipede crawling across a rock, and then with a collage of a beach house on stilts multiplied as an extended structure on many legs. For the architects, the combined structural and energy concept also had spatial implications, the number of pilings determining the rhythm of columns throughout the building above. Yet for all that they do, such piles are excessively expensive. With optimization in mind, one of the engineers suggested using integrated beams on the underside of the slabs, which would allow the span between columns to be increased from 8 to 10 m. This seemingly small adjustment significantly reduced the number of piles and, in so doing, saved a considerable amount of money and material, while enhancing the spatial qualities of the terminal as well.

Following the same logic of the multiple functionality of elements, another workshop discussion among the architects and energy consultants led to the idea of a double facade that provides space for the boarding ramps and forms a thermal buffer to minimize heat loss. The glazed facade maximizes the amount of daylight in order to reduce the electricity needed for artificial lighting and provides passengers with views of the planes and the landscape beyond. The roof of the buffer zone serves as a shading device to lower heat gain in the interior spaces. A 4,200 m² array of photovoltaic panels is mounted on the cantilevered roof plane, which likewise provides additional sun protection. Even though this was the largest integrated renewable energy generator of its kind in Switzerland at the time, its maximum capacity of 264,000 kWh per year amounts to only a fraction of the electricity needed for the terminal. A decentralized system of monoblock heat pumps installed along the north face and on the roof assures a steady flow of conditioned and recovered air without the need for extensive ductwork, with the space of the building itself used for air circulation instead. Rainwater is collected in large tanks and used as grey water throughout the facility. All the vital resource flows coursing through the terminal – air, water, electricity – are sensor-regulated to make it as fine-tuned a machine as possible, one that, although lean, admittedly relies on a significant amount of technology.

The same types of considerations applied to the choice of material for the overall structure. The main goal was to keep the embedded material stock to a minimum: as little material should be

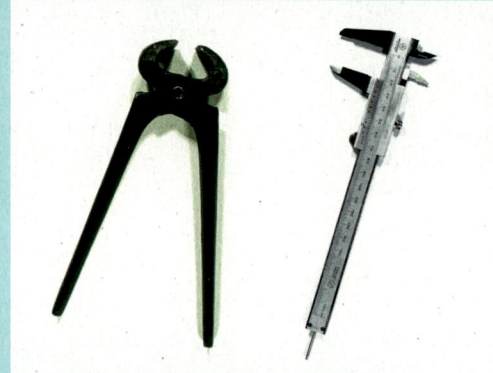

Workshop image highlighting the dual quality of the terminal as common tool and precise instrument

Collages showing relationships among materials for floors, ceilings, and walls

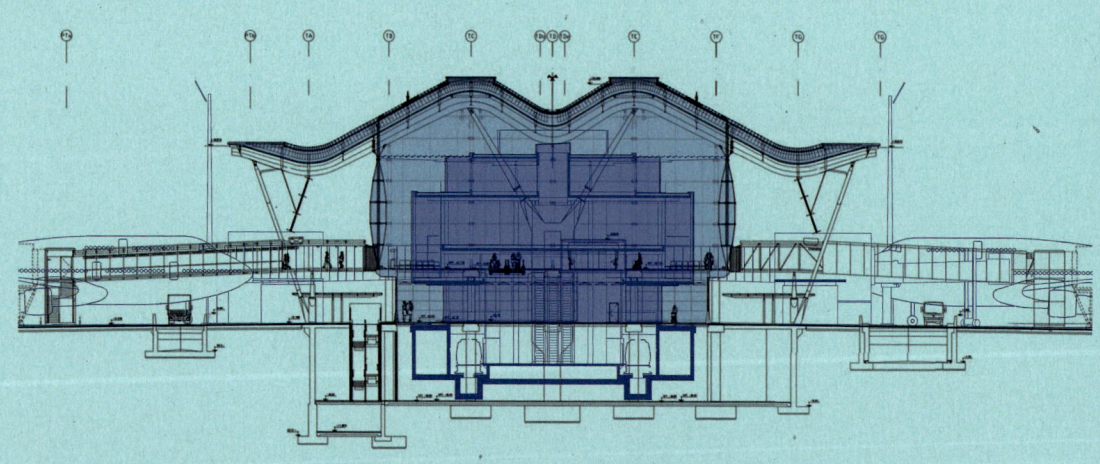

Sectional overlay of the Madrid Airport by Richard Rogers and the Zurich Midfield Terminal; presented at the Passenger Terminal Expo, New Orleans, 2000

Workshop slides showing well-known adages from architectural discourse (Mies van der Rohe, Robert Venturi, and Rem Koolhaas) to which "less is less" was added

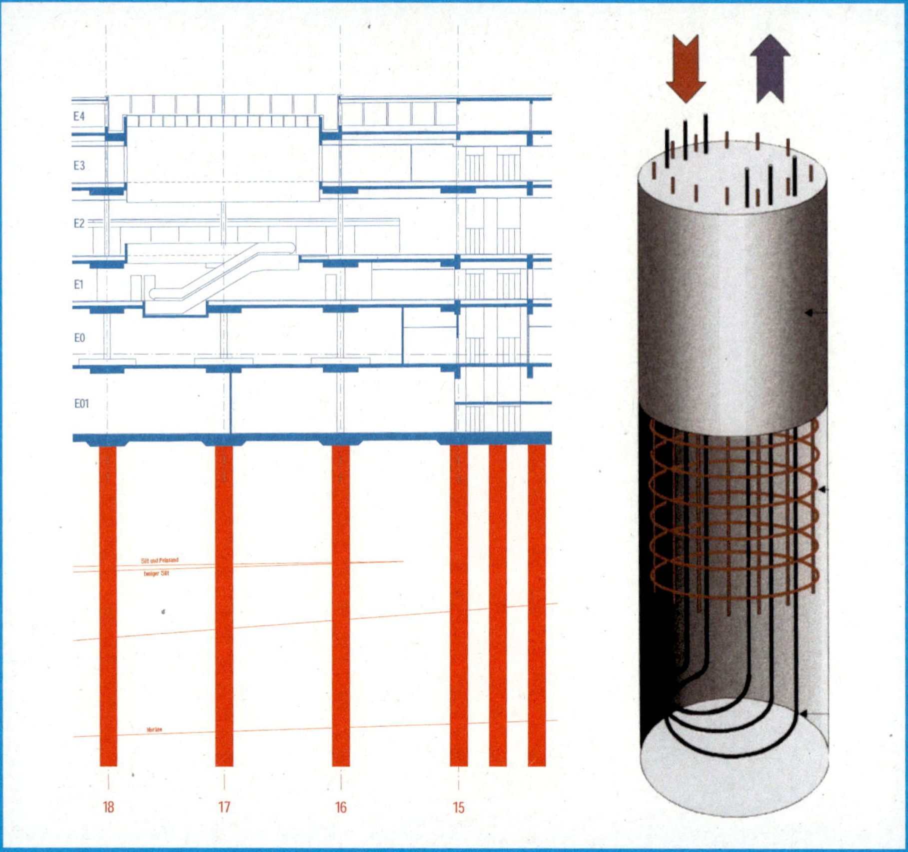

Detail showing water coils threaded through the energy piles

Model of the building, with energy piles anchored in bedrock

Serial montage of a beach house on stilts used in a discussion on the impact of the structural system on spatial organization used as possible. Moreover, all materials had to be robust, durable, and easy to maintain, particularly on account of what they must endure in a high-use setting such as an airport. The exposed concrete decks – recalling the highway section – act not only as expansive platforms on which passenger flows take place, but also as a thermal mass that absorbs and stores heat energy to level out temperature fluctuations over a 24-hour cycle. Here again, structural and energy considerations worked hand in hand to enhance the building's environmental performance.

In the bigger picture, these design measures were in line with the Kyoto Protocol's mandate to reduce CO_2 emissions and resource use in general by transitioning to renewable energy sources. This broad environmental contract was ratified in 1997, coincidentally just when the terminal was in the design development phase. Coming back to the related mandate of the competition program limiting energy consumption of the entire airport to 1994 levels, numerous calculations were made on spreadsheet after spreadsheet for how the new building compared to the existing ones in terms of its energy performance. By all measures, the new midfield terminal outperformed the others in terms of energy consumed for lighting, ventilation, cooling, equipment, and heating. With this, the project resonated with larger environmental concerns in the air at the time.

With construction fully underway, the overriding concerns quickly shifted to speed and efficiency, as is most often the case in the industry. For a building half a kilometer long, the flows of incoming and outgoing materials were exorbitant and the assorted activities on site became ever more frenzied as work progressed. What was unusual for a project of this scale was that the architects also took on the role of general contractor, meaning they had a say in the day-to-day operations as the project was being built: so many cranes installed, so many cubic meters of soil moved, so many tons of material lifted, so many workers per team, so many containers on site, and so forth. As general contractor, the architects could control the quality of work and ensure that solutions inferior to those proposed would not compromise the project's environmental performance and architectural integrity.

At peak hours, however, the scene resembled anything but an orderly construction site, thus flying in the face of any sustainability mandates, despite efforts to manage stocks and flows here as well. Indeed, mountains were moved. Yet there was nearly as much waste generated as there was new substance built. The gains made on those experiments conducted for the new terminal building to make it more sustainable were offset to varying degrees by the losses accrued in its construction – a catch-22 situation if ever there was one. Moreover, these collateral losses were never calculated and, because they seldom are, remain a costly externality to what is often considered to be environmentally sound construction.

The Undecorated Shed

As it goes, things can often take an unexpected turn, and not necessarily for the better. For one thing, the airport authority (the client) became a partially privatized entity operating under the name Unique in early 2000 and was intent on maximizing its profit margin. It was within this context that the architects received a rather vulgar promotional brochure from a commercial planning firm commissioned by the client to design scenic pockets for retail and food concessions throughout the building. Predictably, this theming of space drew on stereotypical images meant to convey an aura of 'Swissness' – the Alps, alphorn players, waterfalls, clocks and watches, traditional clothing for service staff, regional food, and the like – to give a more popular face to the undecorated shed of the terminal by way of kitsch imagery.

For another thing, the national airline Swissair, for which the new terminal was being built, went bankrupt in late 2001 as construction was almost completed. The suddenly grounded fleet was docked behind the nearly completed terminal, kept out of sight to soften the blow of a national embarrassment. The work would be delayed by a year, and when it resumed for the newly named airline Swiss, the hard-won balance struck between economic and ecological concerns was further jeopardized by mounting costs and the ever-increasing amount of resources used to restart the project.

The client, Unique, was understandably concerned about the prospect of their investment going to waste, and so the issue was how to make the terminal even more lucrative when it finally did open. Predictably, managers wanted more surface area for advertisements as well as more commercial spaces and rentable lounges to generate additional revenue. Since the terminal had been honed down to its essential capacities, however, it proved to be a challenge for both the client and the architects to accommodate the supplementary spatial accessories in an integral way. The design scheme had already carefully incorporated dedicated commercial zones within space-defining elements concentrated around the main entry points of the departure level. It would take rounds of give-and-take negotiations to identify where more such zones could be introduced discreetly as interventions punctuating

Model of boarding ramps in the facade buffer zone

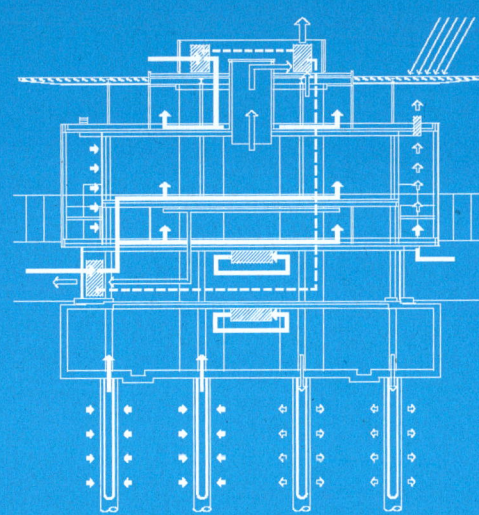

Diagram of energy flows and mechanical systems

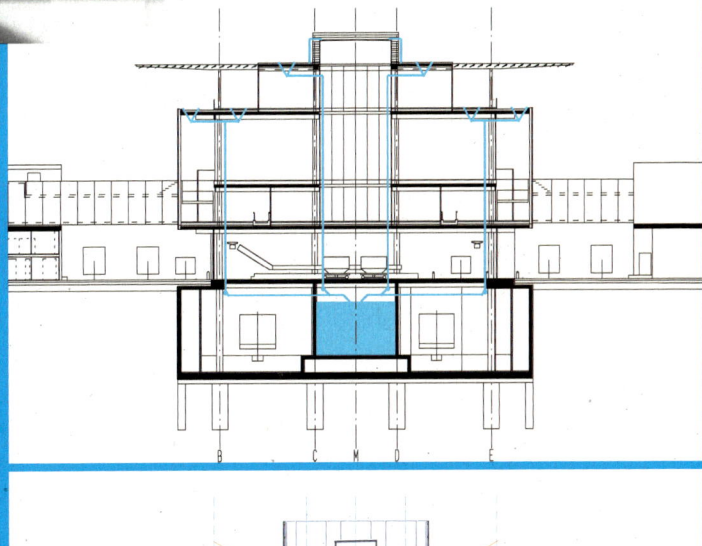

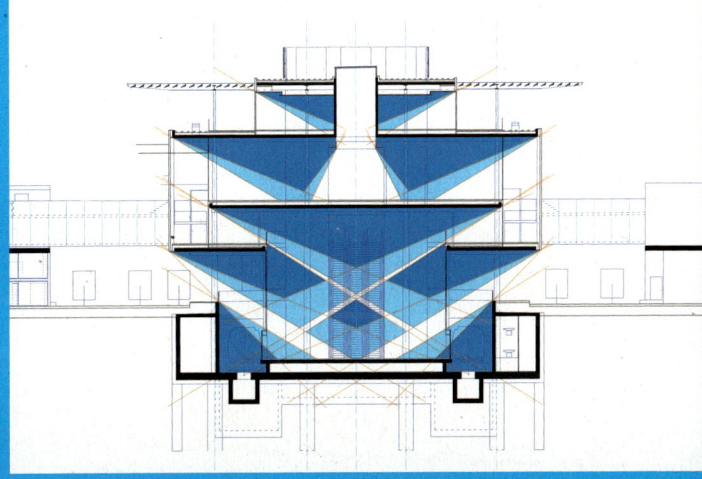

Diagrams showing gray water storage and daylight distribution

Energy consumption in MJ/m² per annum for lighting (yellow), ventilation (light blue), cooling (blue), equipment (green), and heating (red) of different Zurich airport buildings

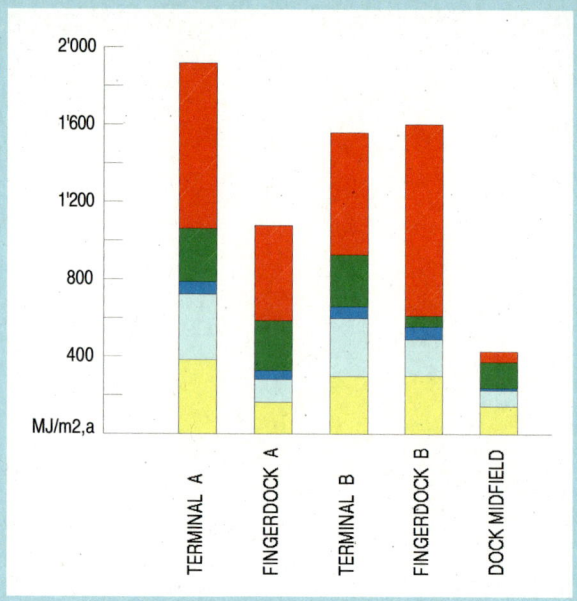

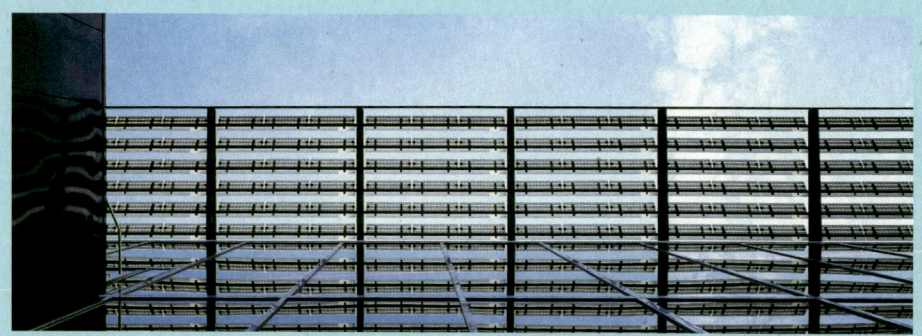

Photovoltaic installation (Christian Oberholzer)

Exposed concrete structure and buffer zone with boarding ramps

Construction site photographs, 1999

Sample pages from a commercial brochure for retail spaces, 2000

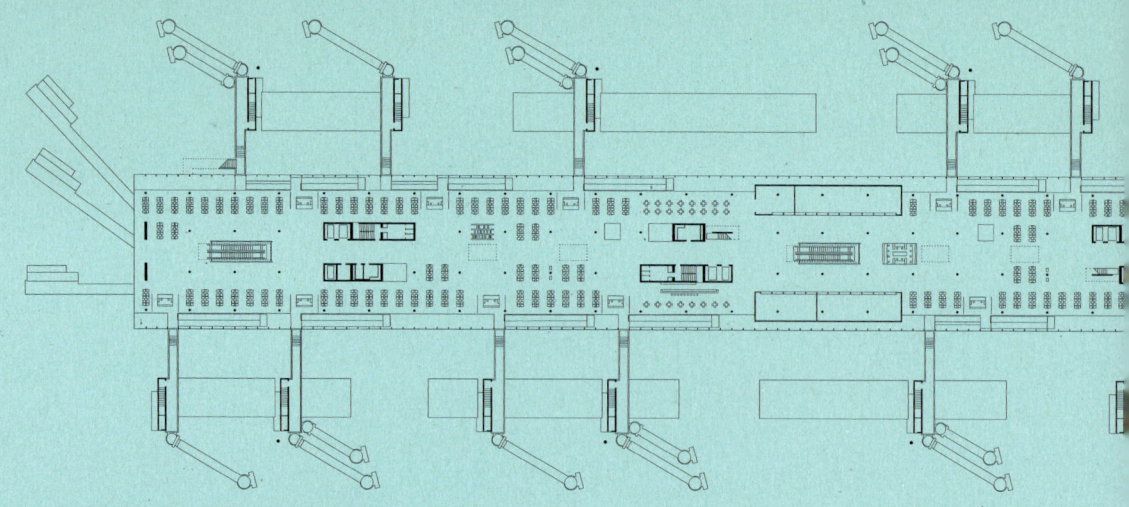

Plan of the departure level

Interior views of the departure level (Ralph Bensberg)

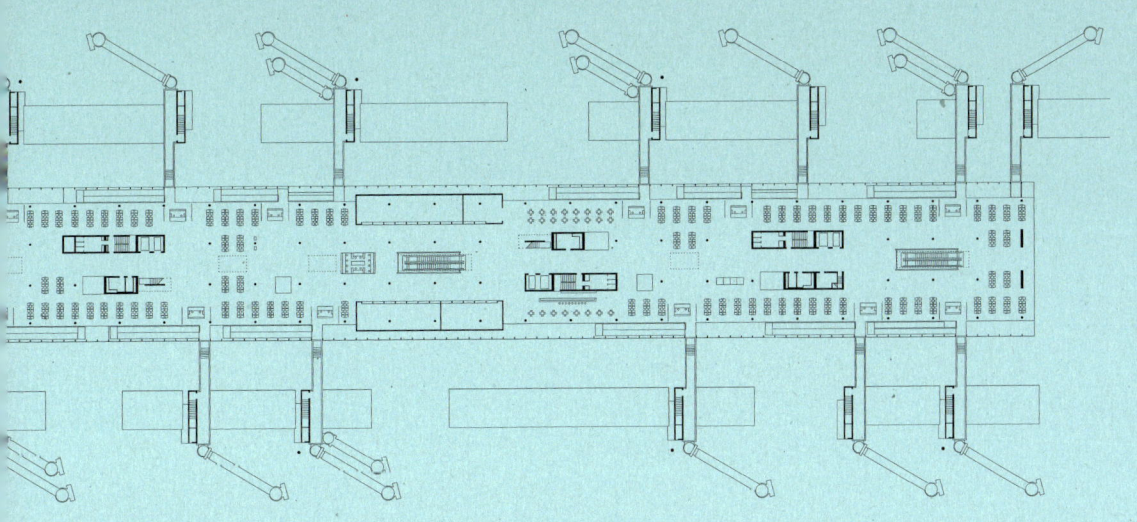

Exterior view of the facade with fire escape (Christian Oberholzer)

Swissair planes docked behind the terminal after the company's bankruptcy, 2001

the space of the terminal. In these discussions, sustainability was on the side of the architects. The extra energy load of all those add-ons – electricity for waterfalls, blinking signage, or theater spotlights – exceeded the original calculations, and thus undermined the performance targets for the entire airport. The pivotal question here was whether economy would trump ecology.

Realizing the true economic and environmental costs, the client settled for a more restrained solution to integrating the extra income-generating enhancements into the terminal's architecture. Perhaps just as influential in keeping the new midfield terminal from becoming just another anonymous last-stop shopping spot on the way to somewhere else was that the design had already provided an identifiable aesthetic that was arguably quite apt for a small Alpine country renowned for its restrained ways. Here, the question was whether the everyday poetics of forthright materiality, modestly generous spaces, varied choreographies of daylight, unencumbered flows of movement, and lean technical systems did not already suffice in giving an identity to the airport as a place in its own right. Even though compromises had to be made, the strength of the original vision largely holds in the completed terminal. And while it is indeed a 'space of flows,' it is just as much a 'space of places' stripped of the unnecessary to provide moments of respite from the hustle and bustle of travel. As if to proclaim that there is no evidence like self-evidence, what you see in Dock E is what you get.

Stripped Down

Minor Architecture

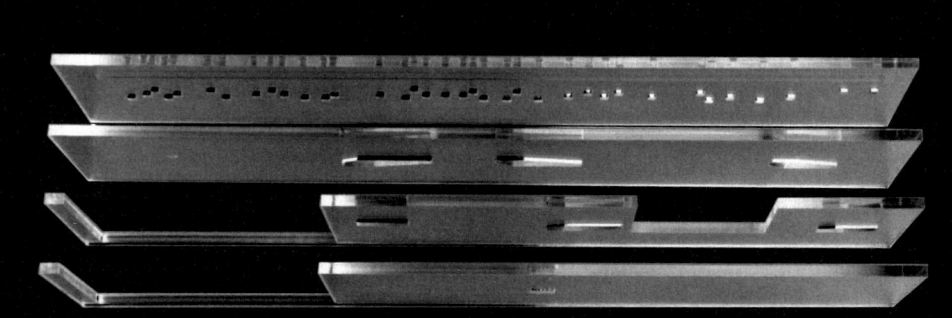

Zurich International School

Discourses

Use

Energy

compacted campus typology

Roland Barthes, *Writing Degree Zero* (1967) and "The Death of the Author" (1967)

Materials

no money ...

Economy

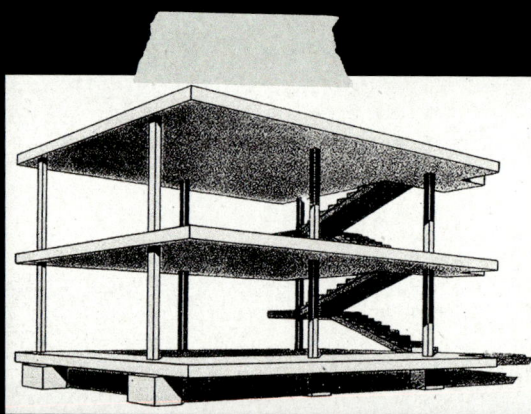

Le Corbusier, *Maison Dom-Ino*, 1914–1915

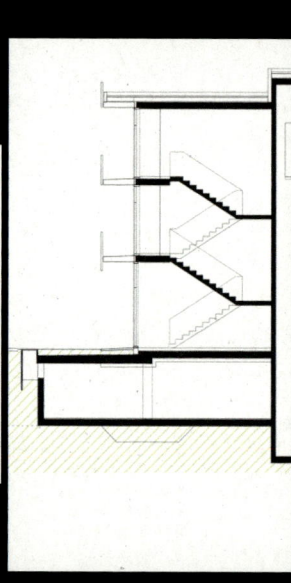

Technology

... geothermal probes ... heat pump ... decentralized airboxe

"emptied typology"

surplus space/free space

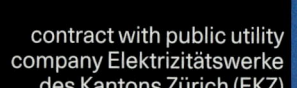

no architecture ...   no technology ...

Methodology

no energy labels ...

Policy

contract with public utility company Elektrizitätswerke des Kantons Zürich (EKZ)

92

Zero-Degree Technology   Zero-Degree Economy

Gilles Deleuze and Félix Guattari, *Kafka: Toward a Minor Literature*, 1985

"The birth of the reader must be at the cost of the death of the Author."
Roland Barthes, 1967

WHAT IS MINOR LITERATURE? →

no PV panels ... missed opportunity!
`30 probes @ 150m`

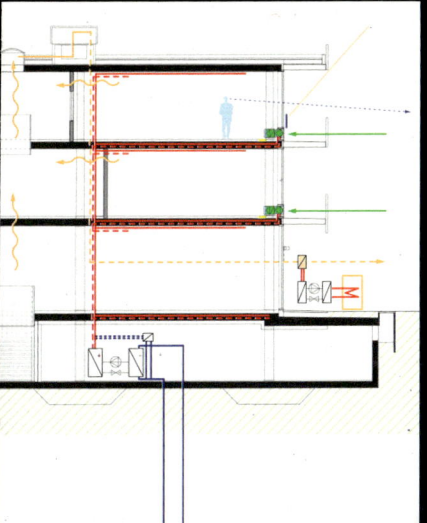

community flea market

no hidden systems

directly attached to floor slab

acoustic panels with thermal conduction elements ... air-recovery heat exchanger ...
clip-on technical installations

capital 'A' vs. small 'a' architecture

Leutschenbach vs. Zurich International School (ZIS)
(Dario Pfammatter and Reinhard Zimmermann)

Minor Architecture
Zurich International School
2003–2008

Any design competition brief is an expression of desire. In wanting to realize a project, a client has a vision, albeit vague, of what a future building should be. Of course, when it comes to design briefs, not to mention desire, there is as much left unsaid as there is said. For every quantitative item on a wish list (functional requirements, surface areas, budget constraints, environmental targets, etc.) there are assumptions and expectations to be read between the lines that remain unspoken but are no less formative for the design process. When participating in a competition, the real work of any architect is essentially to distill potential from the gaps between what is stated and what is implied. Though often presented objectively, competition briefs leave much to be designed, beginning with the brief itself.

    In the case of the design competition for a new facility for the Zurich International School (ZIS) in late 2003 (a private-sector entity legally organized as a nonprofit foundation), the client's program called for a cluster of buildings loosely assembled around a collective open space, very much in the tradition of an Anglo-Saxon campus in a bucolic setting. The ensemble of freestanding 'houses' on a 'commons' was to accommodate 500 high school students of diverse nationalities, all of whom were to be brought together in a representative school community. In keeping with the client's vision for a campus-like cloister, special functions such as a library, theater, and gymnasium were to be housed in dedicated buildings among those for classrooms, a cafeteria, and administrative offices, with sports fields and outdoor recreational spaces nearby. The preference for this particular spatial arrangement, one rooted in tradition, reflected the school's educational ambition to prepare students for university in an enlightened, contemporary way. The flexible curriculum allowing students to devise their own course of studies would promote independent learning; small study groups would foster in-depth dialogue among students and teachers; and the inverted classroom format putting students and teachers 'at eye level' would prompt a more participatory form of schooling. At least for the client, the campus as a tested typology was the appropriate form for expressing such pedagogic aims.

So much could be read from the competition brief. But a closer reading disclosed a potential mismatch between the client's stated desires for a new school and the client's projected budget for building one. Needless to say, any design solution had to be affordable, and demonstrably so, with all competition participants being asked to provide a detailed cost estimation of their respective schemes. Yet when trying to accommodate the functional program within a campus layout of multiple buildings, the numbers simply did not add up. Hardly an oversight of the client, such a discrepancy could be alleviated by phasing the project, that is, by building it piece by piece, a rationale which further reinforced the desire for a campus layout. As it turned out, the nonprofit foundation would have to raise the funds campaign by campaign to even afford the school. So the project for ZIS could only be sustained if the winning proposal was affordable and if the school's representatives were successful in their fundraising efforts.

With the economy of the new facility central to the client's call for entries, environmental sustainability was mentioned only in passing throughout the competition brief as an issue to be addressed, but again, only if affordable. Any measures taken to reduce the project's ecological footprint would be appreciated or nice to have, as it were, but at what price? Accordingly, newly introduced energy or building performance codes at the time would play little or no role in assessing the entries, despite the fact that the Swiss Minergie-P label, for example, had just been instituted and had become the standard for public schools throughout the country. As desirable as label-compliance may have been for the client, economic performance would be decisive in the end.

Study model of a five-building variation forming a campus-like layout

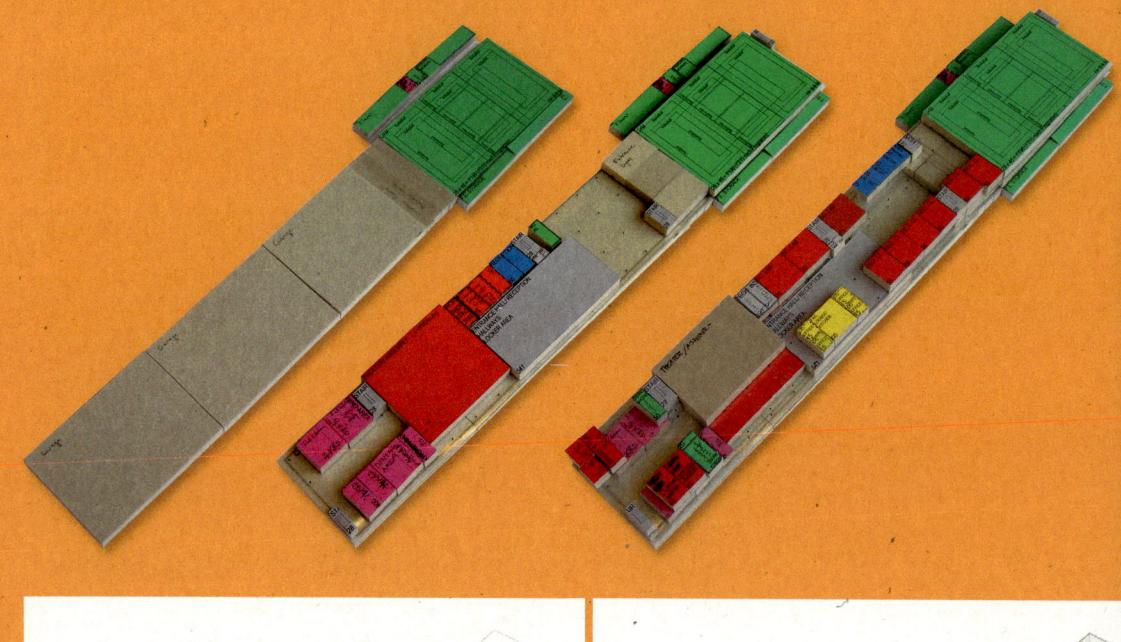

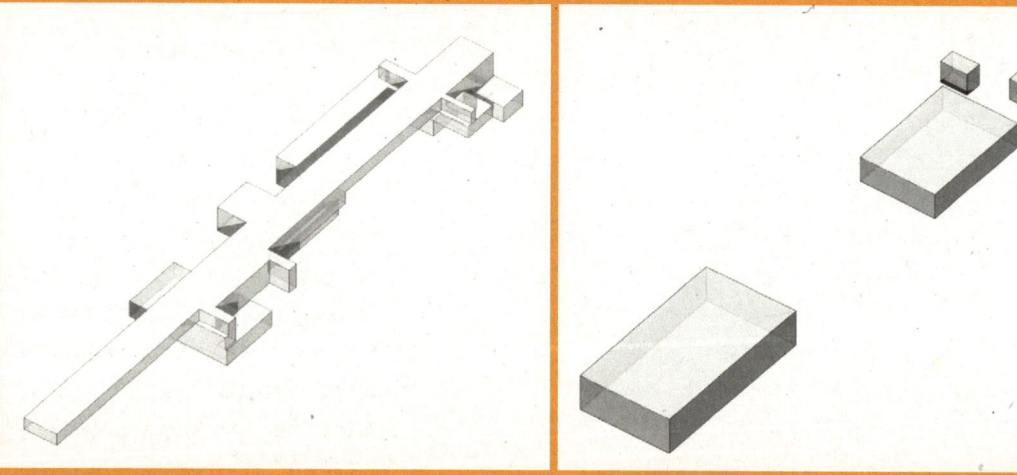

Sequence showing spaces for circulation, collective uses, classrooms, and 'free space' for future extensions

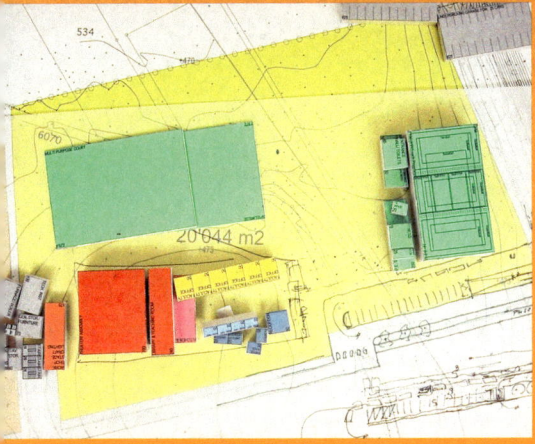

Study for a two- or three-building variation

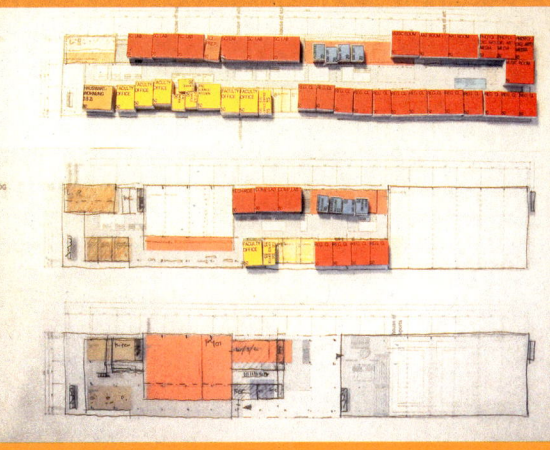

Study for an all-in-one structure on three levels

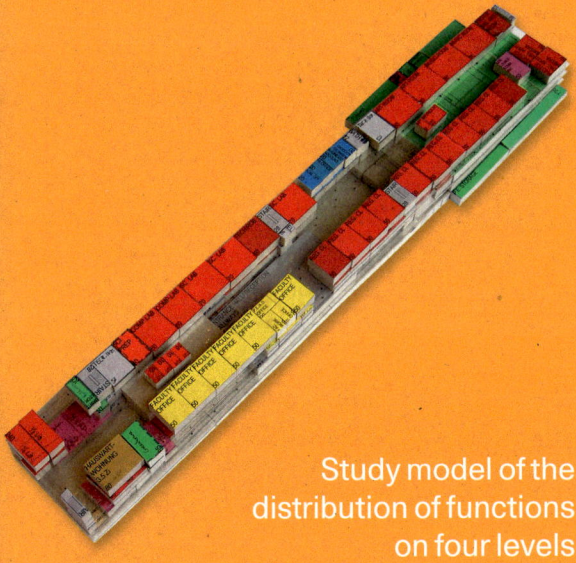

Study model of the distribution of functions on four levels

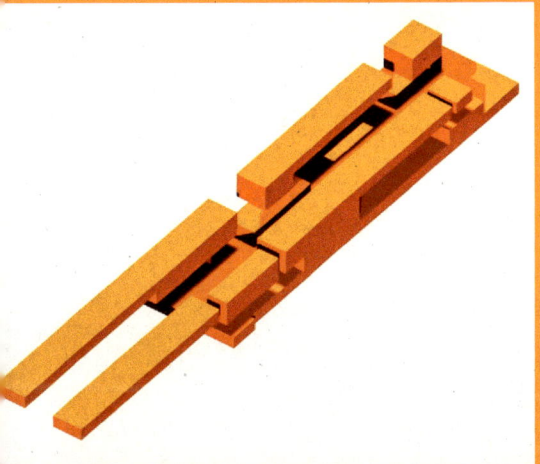

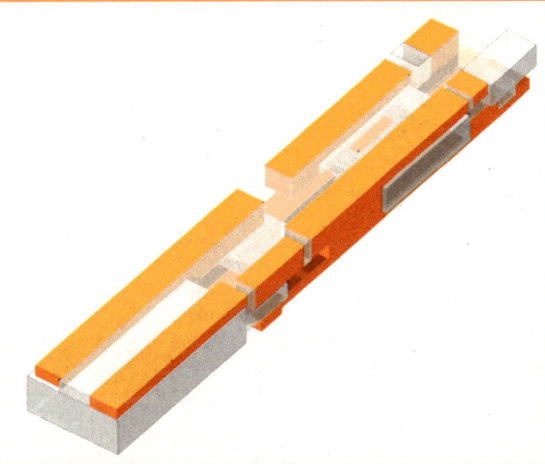

Minor Achitecture

Site plan of the design proposal

Exhibition photograph showing the site of the new neighborhood, 2007

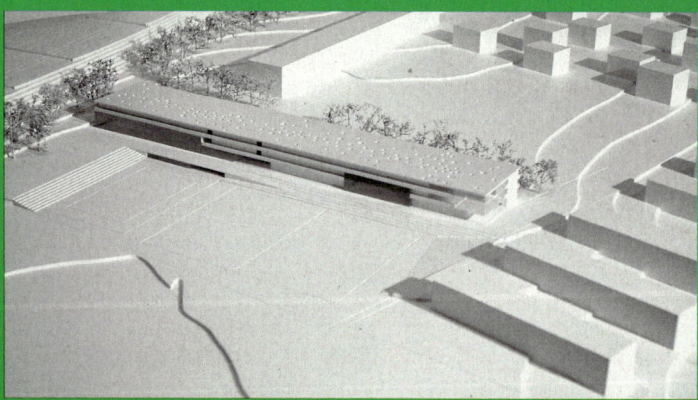

Competition model, with the public park on one side and sports fields on the other, 2003

The site for the new school is on the outskirts of Zurich in the rapidly growing suburban community of Adliswil, some 20 minutes from the city center. Anything but bucolic, the parcel is adjacent to a freeway, which effectively blocks any view of Lake Zurich below. A new land-use ordinance for the community had already been passed stipulating the development of a housing district. At its core would be plots dedicated to a communal park as well as public buildings like a school, a library, or sports facility. Considering, however, that ZIS wanted to build a new school on this very site and, in so doing, initiate development of the neighborhood, a touchy political question arose as to how a private facility could be made public and thereby comply with the new zoning ordinance aimed at community-building in the most literal sense. While relevant, this issue was only implicitly addressed in the competition brief, insofar as the primary focus was on the requirements of the new school itself. Nevertheless, all competition entrants did look for synergies between the public and private domains by trying to make the amenities of a privately owned school available to the public and thereby make the Zurich International School an anchor of the new neighborhood.

Zero-Degree Architecture

Trying to unravel the brief, the design team who eventually won the competition made numerous attempts to arrange the myriad functional requirements of the school by testing various constellations of spaces. Via a commonplace method among architects, color-coded models were used to playfully explore the potential of the campus typology on the site, with individual blocks accommodating the respective functions. At times, there were variations for five buildings, for four buildings, and then three, but it would not take long for the architects to arrive at what would eventually become the proposed scheme of a single 'house' for the entire school.

Though risky as a proposition, the main idea was to compress the programmatic spaces into a compact linear volume (160m long, 28m deep, 3 stories high) made up of several integrated 'houses' that form a campus in one structure situated between the park on one side and sports fields on the other. Apropos affordability, the team settled for the concept of a concentrated entity – the more compact, the better, and, by extension, the cheaper. The footprint, the volume, and material deployment would be minimized, while various functions could be arranged next to or on top of each other. This design strategy would allow for a flexible assemblage of modules that form a spatially enticing learning and teaching environment, or what the architects referred to as "a campus within."

With the siting of the building resolved, the next round of decision-making concerned the internal organization of the variegated school functions, ranging from very large to very intimate spaces. The favored solution came in the form of 'stacked plateaus' on which the spaces could be distributed. Three types of spatial clusters were distinguished: the concentrated classroom clusters of rooms treated as individual 'row houses'; the large public spaces such as the library, theater, greenhouse, and gymnasium treated as the 'public buildings' within the volume; and the circulation zone treated as a 'commons' meandering throughout the structure that would serve as lobby, cafeteria, teaching forum, and informal gathering space all in one, in essence becoming a crossover of marketplace and internal street decks. To free up this internal collective zone and reduce fire loads inside what are effectively the school corridors, the emergency egress would partially wrap around the building outside and provide balconies overlooking the park.

While working through the implications of this differentiated but compacted architecture, it became apparent that the internal commons could be oversized to create a spatial surplus large enough to accommodate not only the immediate requirements of the school, but also those not yet known. In other words, though the school program was compacted into one building, the building itself was de-compacted from within by making the circulation space more generous than required. This solution would also solve the phasing issue by offering ZIS an in-built reserve for future expansion inside the school, offering 'free space' much like Lacaton & Vassal's School of Architecture in Nantes that would later open in 2009.

What was beginning to emerge in the design process was a generic type-form or "emptied typology" (a term later coined by Michael Meredith and Hilary Sample from MOS Architects in New York) that, in being repetitive and flexible, would make the school adaptable to evolving needs. Although at its core nothing more than a standard Corbusian "dom-ino frame" (as used for, say, a parking garage or factory), the reduced structure would be gradually filled in with the school's functional amenities over time. The idea was that this empty scaffold could be used, in the words of MOS Architects, "for something else, imagined by someone else, to happen," unfinished and left open for interpretation.

In the case of a school, the generic armature of the load-bearing frame could accommodate the serial components of the program like classrooms, while also being sufficiently adaptable to

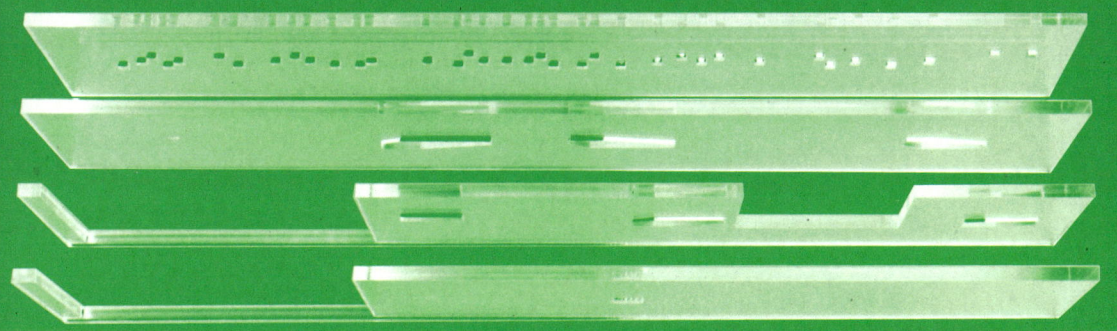

Plateaus or levels of the Zurich International School (*agps clues*, Aedes Architecture Forum, Berlin, 2012)

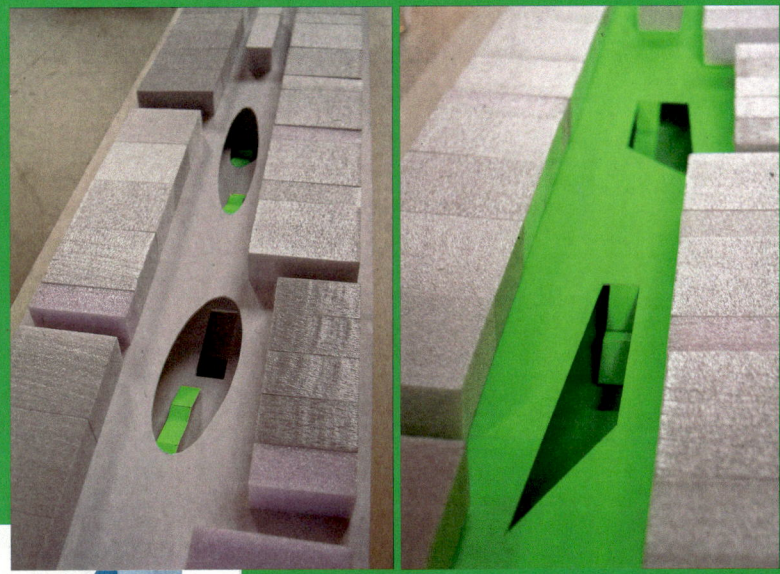

Vertical connections between plateaus, with oval and trapezoidal openings

Perspectives exploring the spatial characteristics and uses of the central zone

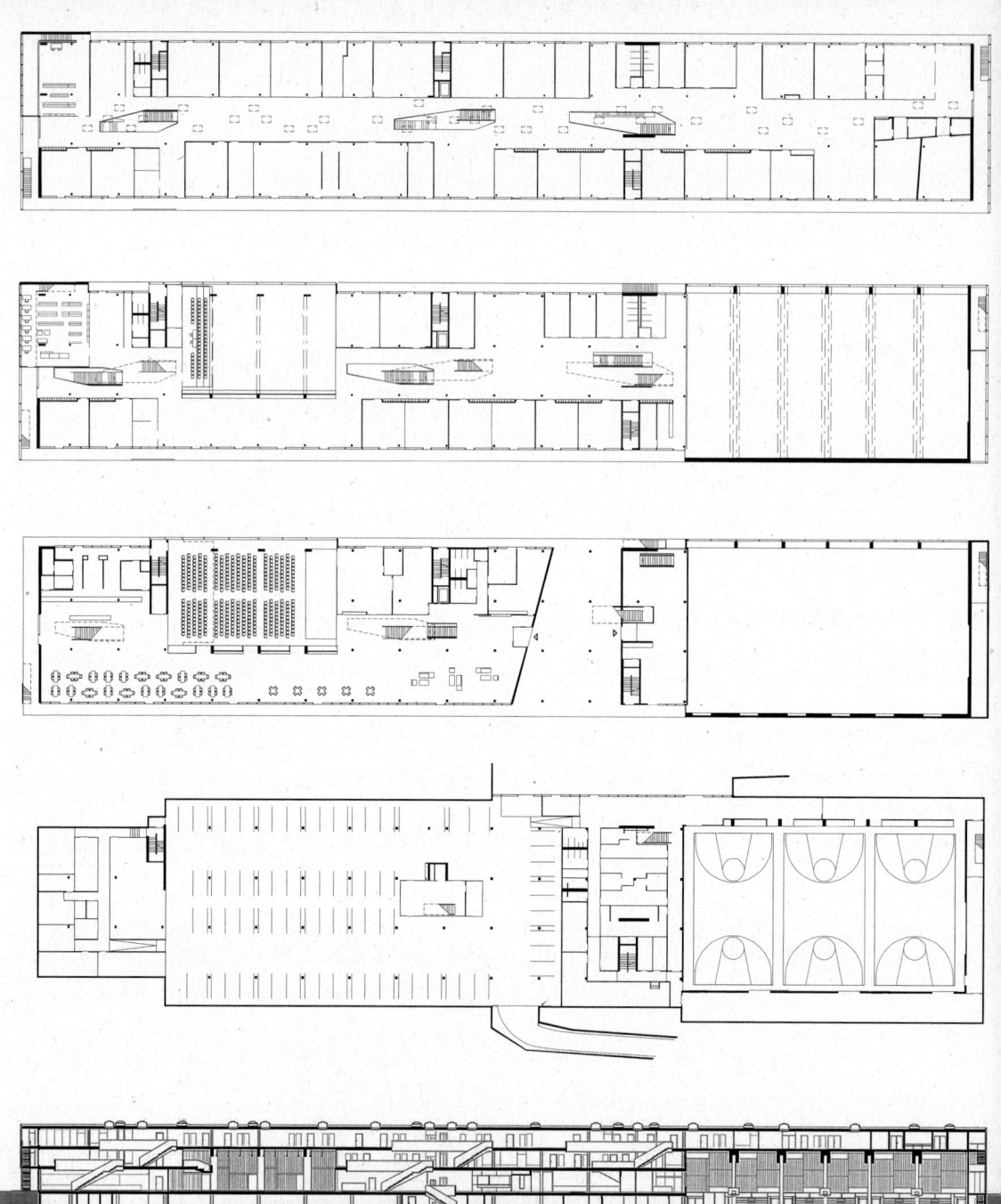

Plans of the four levels and longitudinal section

Structural frame under construction – gymnasium, cafeteria, circulation zone, and stairwell opening

accommodate the larger spans required for the gymnasium and theater that would cut through the three levels (plateaus) of the building. Other elements meant to break the repetitive rhythm of the frame are the staggered, open stairwells that provide spatial continuity to the internal commons across the plateaus in the modernist spirit of the *plan libre*, or free plan.

Throughout the process, team discussions centered on how little had to be designed and what would constitute, in effect, a 'zero-degree' condition of architecture, whereby form recedes to free up the potential of use. The team was aware that the term *degré zéro* had been introduced in literary criticism by none other than French philosopher Roland Barthes some time ago to describe a neutral mode of writing, colorless and devoid of particular stylistic references. When applied to architecture, 'degree zero' meant that the users of the school (or readers in Barthes's sense) would be the active agents in making the school what it is. The architects as conventional form-makers would cede to the background, providing only the necessary infrastructure for ZIS to evolve as a work in progress. Essentially, the team engaged in the design of the 'unfinished,' without compromising the refined production of buildings *as* architecture.

Zero-Degree Technology

In the effort to design the least amount of architecture necessary for the school's program, the question came up as to whether the same could be done with the requisite technology for the project. In the age of well-tempered environments in which building interiors are completely controlled by technical services, was a 'zero-degree technology' even possible? The design objective to achieve zero emissions and deploy a minimum of materials in the process, of course, made sense environmentally. And in view of the short life span of technologies in general, it seemed reasonable to bring the same logic of programmatic flexibility to bear on the building's mechanical systems, which are nonetheless needed to create fit environments for human activities.

Consequently, technical components would be not only minimized but also attached to the basic structural framework and left exposed as wall- or ceiling-mounted appliances rather than being concealed within the architecture. Literally applied onto the structure as clip-on devices, the technical systems would be concentrated in designated locations, coordinated with the structure where possible, though in some cases even clashing with it and left as is.

As realized in the project, zero-degree technology finds its expression in a rough, straightforward mode of implementation. It is neither overly designed nor is it fetishized as an emblem of progress. Whereas the structural armature is built on site with industrial-grade concrete and is left in its brute state, infill elements like walls and facade panels, for instance, appear as an untreated amalgam of off-the-shelf catalog products. The mechanical systems themselves are likewise left as they are and installed in the most direct way possible to allow for unhindered repair and replacement when necessary, accepting that technology inevitably breaks down and must be replaced.

As if designing before the advent of air conditioning and, in any case, being somewhat suspicious of technology, the architects tried to eliminate technical systems wherever possible and instead use the building itself to passively moderate the school's environmental performance. Fire escape balconies could also serve as brise-soleils or sun-shading elements to reduce heat gains; openings in classroom walls facing the internal corridor space would facilitate natural cross ventilation; windows in the gymnasium would improve fresh air circulation; and the chimney-effect of the stairwells could be used for passive cooling and night-flushing to further lower the building's temperature after hot summer days. With such measures, the school would not have to rely on a barrage of costly technologies to perform sustainably, for that capacity would already be built in.

A consequence of this vigilantly pragmatic approach is a considerable reduction of shafts and ductwork required for moderating the building's indoor climate. The primary energy required to do so comes from the ground itself, with the geothermal mass providing an abundant, CO_2-free source of energy. Thirty geothermal probes or borehole heat exchangers extending 150m into the earth are connected to a heat pump, a technical option taking advantage of the mere 10-degree differential between the temperature of the ground and that needed for heating the classrooms in winter.

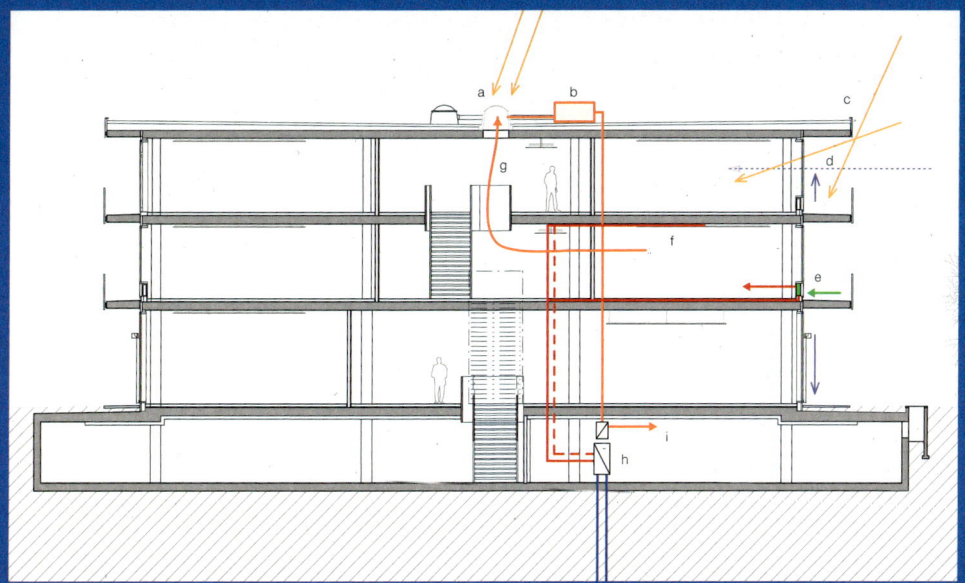

Components: (a) air exhaust; (b) air return; (c) summer shading and winter passive heating; (d) shading screens; (e) airboxes; (f) acoustic panels with thermal conduction; (g) air overflow; (h) geothermal probes and heat pump; (i) air-recovery heat exchanger

Assembly of prefabricated frames and robotic glass installation

Surface-mounted systems attached to floor slab (to be partially covered by ceiling panels)

Radiant floor coils for large spaces installed prior to sub-floor pouring

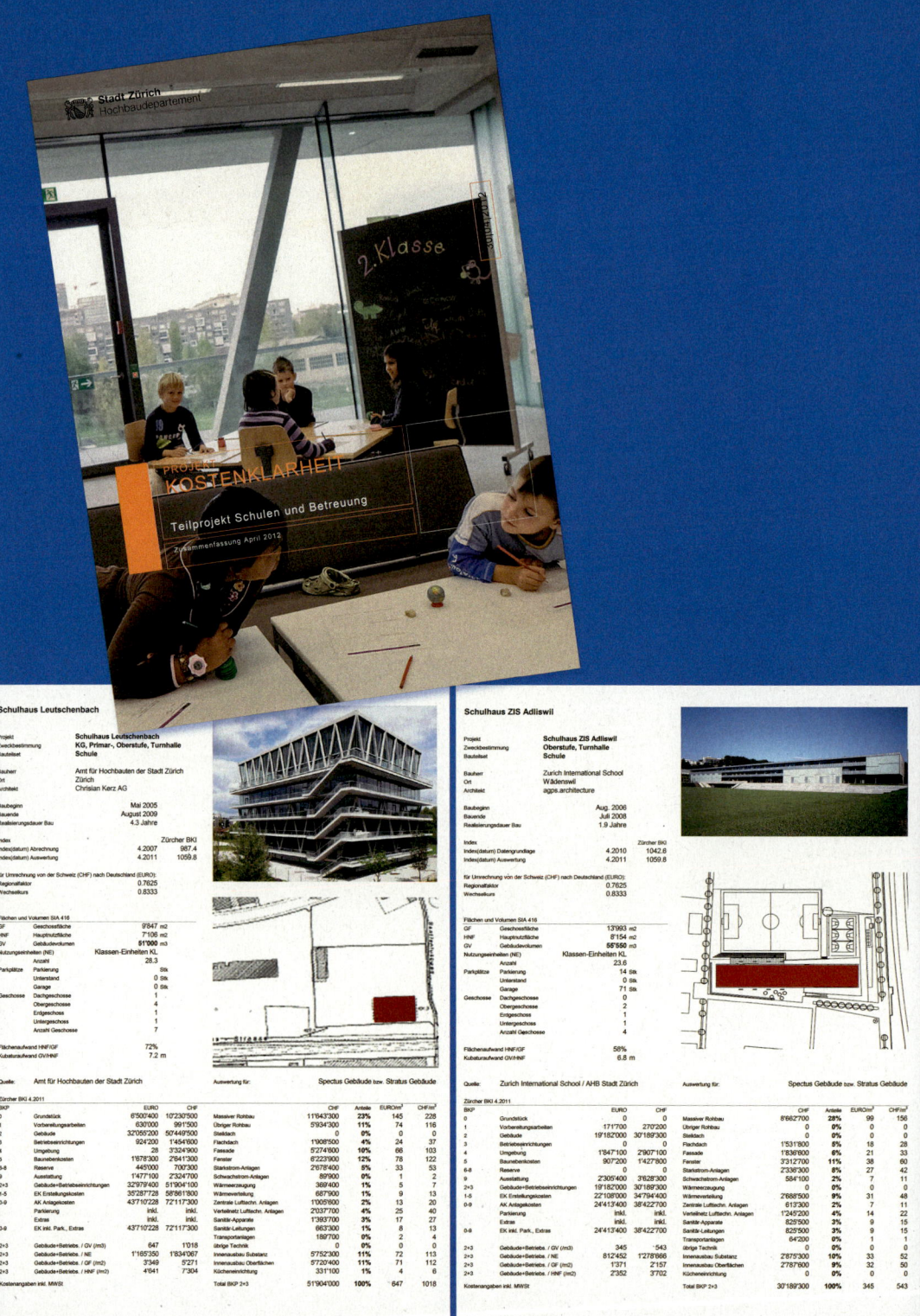

Cost-Clarity Report comparing the Leutschenbach School with ZIS, 2012

Cooled or heated water from the heat pump is transferred by way of three loops throughout the building. The first is through pipes leading to airboxes in the facade that condition incoming air to the desired temperature; this solution allows for a decentralized and locally specific ventilation system, an innovation at the time born of on-site trial and error. The second loop is via coils in the subfloor that are used in the large spaces of the gymnasium and theater where airboxes are not sufficient for conditioning the volume of air. The third loop allows spaces to be heated or cooled by way of acoustic ceiling panels that transfer thermal energy to the concrete slabs, thereby effectively capitalizing on the heat-storage capacity of the building's structural frame.

In addition to such measures, the architects and engineers proposed a photovoltaic installation on the roof to further enhance the school's energy performance and reduce its ecological footprint. Though cost-effective in the long run, the client nonetheless turned down the option of using free solar energy, citing budgetary shortfalls just when construction began. In hindsight, this would prove to be a missed opportunity, particularly considering that ZIS had already been approached by the local utility company (Elektrizitätswerke des Kantons Zürich, EKZ) to enter into a novel public-private partnership. EKZ was willing to finance, operate, and maintain the mechanical systems in the school's equipment space in the basement, an amenity provided free of charge by the client via an easement in the property-use agreement. In return, ZIS would only have to pay for the resources used like any other customer, while EKZ could provide any surplus energy to other parties in the community. Needless to say, the client was more than willing to accept this innovative arrangement because it saved them money, at least in the short term. With this synergy between the public and private sectors, a part of the building becomes part of the public utility infrastructure for district heating and cooling, a setup which in time would become common and even applied to photovoltaic installations on buildings throughout the city as an incentive to pursue more sustainable practices in the construction sector.

Zero-Degree Economy

The design philosophy of a no-frills, understated building and the strategy of omitting whatever technical systems were deemed unnecessary led to an economy of means in construction and ultimately to lower costs when compared to other similar structures – much lower costs, indeed. In fact, the reduction of the school's requisite architecture and technology would not only reduce upfront costs, but also those for operations in the long run, thereby highlighting the potential of a 'zero-degree economy' in the production and use of buildings. But to achieve a budgetary leanness meant that every design move had to be checked and rechecked by cost estimators, who in time took on a more vital role in the design process. This also meant that there could be no value engineering after the fact, that is, no money-saving measures made by contractors on site. All design efforts to minimize expenditures would be discussed and agreed upon before work began. Above all, such precautions were taken to ensure quality, while moderating the costs for building the new school.

That was all fine and good. But as soon as the project was completed in the late 2000s, a controversy erupted over the issue of how much a new school should actually cost. Always on the lookout for a possible scandal, local and national press opened a debate pitting the new public Leutschenbach School in Zurich against the newly built private facility for ZIS, the former reportedly twice as expensive as the latter. Suddenly politicized, the issue made its way to the city parliament, where the heated question came up as to why public schools were generally more expensive than private ones. How could it be that two schools, both with the same number of students, both built at the same time, and both environmentally sustainable in their own right, could vary so drastically in terms of their costs?

To clarify the matter, Basler & Hofmann Engineers – with whom the ZIS architects had previously worked – were asked to conduct a benchmark cost analysis that was published a few years later in 2012. The study compared a range of recently completed school buildings in Switzerland, looking at everything from structural frames and the amount of glass in facades to technical systems used and sustainability measures taken. It became clear in the end that the press had somewhat exaggerated the cost differential between the two schools initially spotlighted in the debate, with the engineers' *Cost-Clarity Report* showing Leutschenbach to be 25–30% more expensive than ZIS rather than double the price.

The report went on to outline in detail the numerous reasons for this difference. Sure, Leutschenbach's sophisticated structure, the floor to ceiling glass of the facades, the highly developed secondary wall system, and the design decision to conceal all technical services within the architecture did indeed contribute to higher costs. However, it was the obligation that all new public schools comply with the Swiss Minergie-P label that made Leutschenbach

North elevation facing sport fields, 2008 (Reinhard Zimmermann)

Gym facade with escape balcony, 2008 (Reinhard Zimmermann)

Escape balcony (with windowsill sun shading) leading to the fire stair at the building's western end, 2008 (Reinhard Zimmermann)

Everyday life, 2011 (Andrea Helbling)

Community flea market, 2012

significantly more expensive, especially in view of the extensive ventilation system that the code mandated. So even though in this particular project design decisions could have been made differently by the architect, the legally binding environmental standards made the building more costly by default. As for the ZIS project, what confounded Basler & Hofmann in their comparative report was the 'free space' that was integral to the design. Not knowing how to quantify the spatial reserve afforded by the oversized common space, the engineers disregarded this surplus that the school basically received for free.

Price differences aside and with all pros and cons taken into consideration, the report ended on an upbeat note by citing the overall quality of school architecture in the country, be it Leutschenbach, ZIS, or other similar school buildings, for they all exemplified high-standard educational facilities. The report itself was hardly neutral in this respect, inasmuch as it encouraged politicians to recognize the centrality of architecture to the cultural value invested in the Swiss educational system.

This final assessment would spark still another debate, this time among architects, about the nature of architecture at its most fundamental level. At one extreme, there were those who argued in favor of 'authored' design, in other words, for one-off canonical works that embody the creative finesse of the designer. At the other extreme, there were those who advocated a more restrained hand in design, whereby architects, in pursuing an economy of form, produce an open framework in which uses and users can evolve. To all intents and purposes, the discussion weighed in on architecture with a capital 'A' versus that with a small 'a,' or *major* versus *minor* architecture.

Needless to say, the design of an open framework that is recessive rather than dominant requires nonetheless intensified authorship, albeit in a way that does not foreground the author as such. Coming back to Roland Barthes, it is worth recalling what he referred to as "the death of the author" in celebration of the reader's agency in making the work work, so to speak. In place of capital 'A' authorship, the author with a small 'a' takes a back seat "in the interest of writing," whether when producing a text or, for that matter, architecture.

In so many words, the Zurich International School is an experiment in 'minor architecture' that explores the potential of zero-degree design. Moreover, the concept of a minor architecture in practice unsettles time-honored conceptions of authored architecture both as an expression of a disciplinary stance and as a pure art form. Minor architecture is unapologetically open to the unfinished and often undecidable course of a building's life over time, accepting the unavoidable messiness of daily life and the disorderliness of our actual condition in the world. Design intent does not have the final say in ZIS. While the project does aim to give definition to the immediate needs of the school through its design, it also opens up space for drastically heterogeneous social and spatial circumstances to emerge however they will. And even though built, it is here where the project remains open-ended in its aspiration to house procedures in action with an architecture vitally dedicated to life proceeding by its own volition.

Minor Achitecture

Balancing Performances

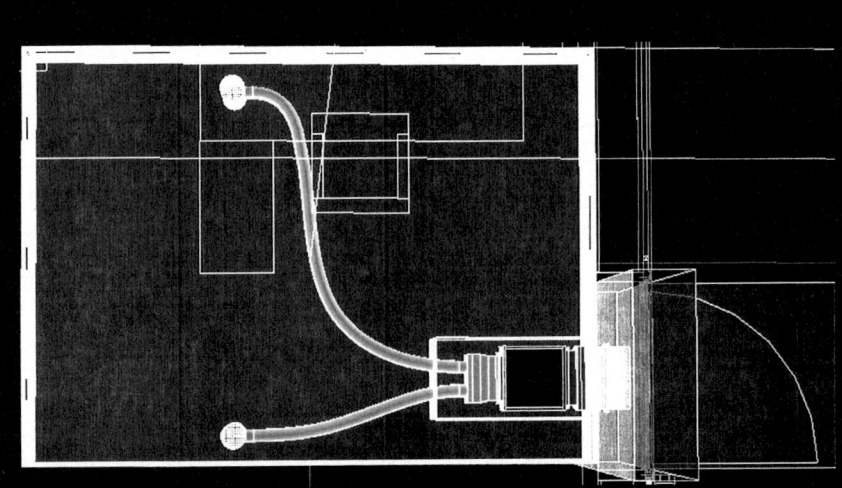

International Union for Conservation of Nature

Balancing Benchmarks

IUCN — The World Conservation Union

safeguarding the natural environment, founded in 1948

Red List of Threatened Species since 1966

William McDonough and Michael Braungart, *Cradle to Cradle*, 2002

mission: protect the environment via science and policymaking

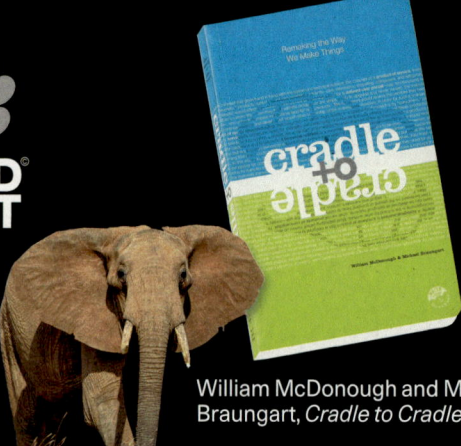

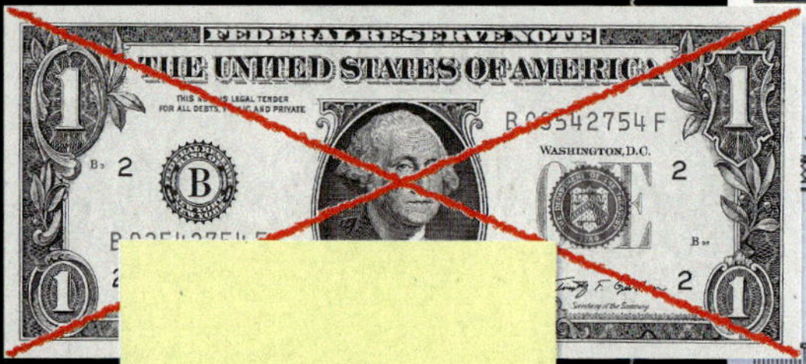

"elephants over architecture"

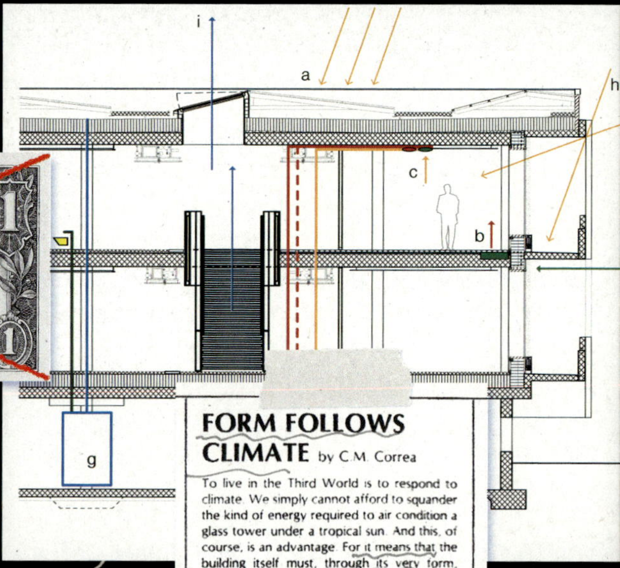

FORM FOLLOWS CLIMATE by C.M. Correa

To live in the Third World is to respond to climate. We simply cannot afford to squander the kind of energy required to air condition a glass tower under a tropical sun. And this, of course, is an advantage. For it means that the building itself must, through its very form, create the "controls" the user needs.

This degree of climate control involves much more than just sun angles and louvers; it concerns the section, the plan, the shape and the heart of the building. The Emperor

Charles Correa, "Form Follows Climate," 1980

go for labels, labels, labels

MINERGIE-P-ECO®
Mehr Lebensqualität, tiefer Energieverbrauch
Meilleure qualité de vie, faible consommation d'énergie

EU #EnergyLabel

environmental performance labels as benchmarks

Discourses · Use · Energy · Materials · Economy · Technology · Methodology · Policy

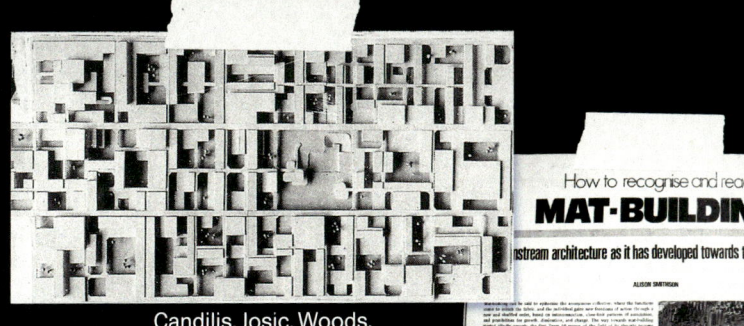

Candilis, Josic, Woods,
Free University of Berlin, 1963

Alison Smithson, "How to Recognise
and Read Mat-Building," *AD*, 1974

less and less operational energy ...

1,400m² PV panels

14 probes @ 250m

with more and more material deployment ...

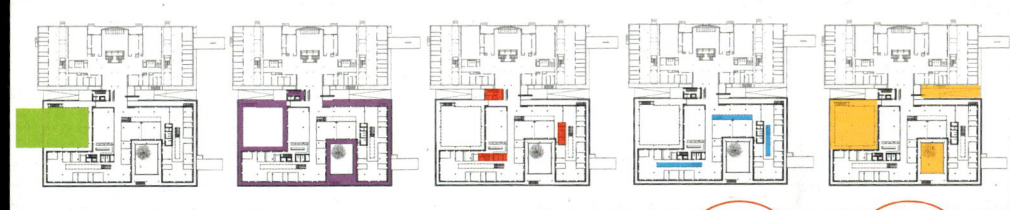

and more and more
technology ...

12.0 kg CO₂~eq./m²/a
excl. commuting

18.7 kg CO₂~eq./m²/a
incl. commuting

and more and more
gray energy ...

Environmental Impact
Assessment Report

UN 2030
Sustainable
Development
Goals, 2015

like a puppet on a string ...

———— change the policies

Balancing Performances

Balancing Performances
International Union for Conservation of Nature (IUCN), Gland-Geneva
2006–2011

How do you house an international organization dedicated to protecting the environment? Admittedly loaded, that was the question at hand when setting out to design a substantial addition to the existing headquarters of the International Union for Conservation of Nature (IUCN) in the Swiss town of Gland. Considering the union's global standing, not to mention the stakes involved in its attempt to conserve what remains of the natural world, its head office sits among the rather mundane, disjointed suburbs of the *métropole lémanique* stretching between Geneva and Lausanne. Just next door to the site is a gas station, a car maintenance garage, and a roundabout. There are also anonymous office buildings, apartment blocks, and assorted villas. All are interspersed randomly with patches of forest, vineyards, and agricultural fields. Nothing out of the ordinary here. For all intents and purposes, the rather environmentally indifferent setting for the new extension could not be further from the union's mission.

  A somewhat nomadic institution in the decades after being founded in France in 1948, with seats across Europe in the interim, IUCN based its operations in Switzerland in the early 1960s to reinforce ties with international policymakers stationed nearby at the United Nations headquarters in Geneva. This move made sense considering IUCN's objectives to promote sound environmental

Photograph of the IUCN grounds taken after the project received the Umsicht – Regards – Sguardi award, Swiss Society of Engineers and Architects (Jules Spinatsch, 2011)

IUCN's Red List of Threatened Species logo from 1966

Existing headquarters built in 1989

Views of the atria in the existing building, 2006

policies worldwide, and that at a time when the environment as a matter of collective concern was hardly an issue.

As the first global environmental union working at the nexus of science and policymaking, IUCN has brought together states, government agencies, and civil society organizations with a shared goal to safeguard all forms of life on the planet. It participated in establishing the World Wildlife Fund and created the now-renowned Red List of Threatened Species not long after relocating to Switzerland. In succeeding years, it would also facilitate the ratification of such key intergovernmental treaties as the Ramsar Convention on Wetlands, the World Heritage Convention, and the Convention on Biological Diversity. Still another milestone among the union's achievements is the 1980 publication of the *World Conservation Strategy*, a groundbreaking document – produced in collaboration with the UN Environment Programme and the World Wildlife Fund – that helped define the concept of 'sustainable development' and shape the global discourse on sustainability thereafter. Most recently, IUCN played a seminal role in pushing forward landmark international accords like the Paris Agreement and the UN 2030 Sustainable Development Goals or SDGs.

To say the least, this was no ordinary client for the architects asked to design an extension to the headquarters of the world's largest and most diverse environmental network. And housing it in a sustainable way would prove to be a matter of reconciling contradictory parameters, whether spelled out by code or laid out by the client.

Balancing Benchmarks

Whatever would be designed, of course, would have to account for what was already there. The existing building on the site in suburban Gland had been built in 1989, amounting to nothing more than a large, generic and rather introverted two-story box adorned with a few postmodern motifs for accent. But perhaps most surprising for the architects was not the lackluster building per se, but the utter lack of any consideration for its environmental impact. In fact, it was the epitome of unsustainable architecture. This was due in no small part to the communal zoning ordinance that limits the height of buildings to two floors plus an attic, which in turn yields an unfavorable ratio of enclosure to volume. What results is a low, fat box with a lot of surface area that is scandalously inefficient in terms of energy and material use. Despite having to adhere to the same two-story-plus-attic ordinance and with all calls to alter said ordinance falling on deaf ears, the extension would have to overcome this given shortfall in building performance, and that as a rather low, fat box itself.

The only notable quality of IUCN's existing head office was the rather messy way that its interior spaces were used, not to mention the unruly jumble of activities taking place in central atria, which left books everywhere, plants all over the place, copy machines and other technical equipment scattered throughout, and so on. Such disarray did have its appeal, most of all for those working there, despite the fact that the everyday clutter violated even the least stringent of fire codes. So first of all, the existing headquarters would have to be cleaned up to comply with the law. That part of the task was clear.

For its part, the new extension would have to balance competing demands from the outset. It would have to allow for the scientists and environmental policymakers to freely interact and informally go about their daily business with as much clutter as needed, but remain code compliant. The client was also fed up with being trapped in a closed box and thus wanted a building that was opened up to the surroundings, irrespective of their faceless attributes – as if turning a glove inside out. Above all and contrary to the existing building, the new headquarters extension would have to be a best-practice case in sustainable architecture, considering the repute of IUCN as a veritable guardian of the environment. As if that was not enough, a growing number of requirements at odds with each other would be added to these initial criteria, which, in sum, would make the design of the new extension a balancing act of give-and-take, and then some.

For starters, the project would have to satisfy two competing objectives by being affordable *and* sustainable. The client was adamant that the new headquarters be as economical as possible. Less money would go into the new building in order to have more for safeguarding endangered species, with "elephants over architecture" becoming something of a mantra in nearly all client-architect meetings. "A sustainable building, yes. But an overly expensive one, out of the question." So the task came down to getting maximum environmental performance for minimal costs, while also offering IUCN a new building more worthy of its cause. Whereas the economic benchmark set by the client stipulated a standard office building that would have to do more for the money, the environmental benchmark stipulated an office building that would have to outperform conventional structures of its kind across a broad range of metrics.

Bearing in mind that IUCN is primarily a policymaking organization, the client insisted that the measure of the new building as

Model of the extension in relation to the existing building, 2007

Glove turned inside out used in a presentation to highlight the opening up of the extension in contrast to the closed existing building, 2007

IUCN headquarters, with the new extension, in the context of suburban Gland, 2011

Logos of environmental performance labels by the Swiss Minergie association, US Green Building Council, and European Union

Measures taken to balance the performance of components in view of criteria set by certifying agencies

IUCN cooks and a sample of their locally sourced menu meant to reduce the footprint of daily operations

Scoresheet for the LEED Platinum rating, with itemized performance criteria, 2009

a policy-setter in sustainability be gauged by established national and international labels in the construction sector. But fulfilling all of the different criteria was easier said than done, especially considering the sheer number of indices that had to be accounted for. Among all the labels considered which certify the top achievement in material and energy performance for buildings, including the highest one of the European Union, the architects and their engineers decided to aim 'only' for the demanding benchmarks set by the US Green Building Council LEED Platinum rating and those of the Swiss Minergie-P-Eco standard.

Complying with the criteria of these two rating agencies alone made the design process an exercise in juggling hundreds of indicators to balance the environmental footprint of different building systems and components. Furthermore, this mode of designing by points, so to speak, whether determined by LEED or Minergie, reframed design as a rather bizarre bartering process of this for that, some trade-offs more common, others entirely unexpected. Transforming the roof of the existing building into a green roof for water retention, for example, offset the ground surface covered by the extension; recycling concrete from nearby buildings earmarked for demolition earned enough points to allow the use of a synthetic rubber membrane on the roof for waterproofing; planting an additional tree, even in the garage, would mean getting an extra parking space; the use of waterless urinals compensated for the ecological impact of appliances in the kitchen; using wood for the facade construction allowed for more glass in the enclosure, which in turn allowed for more daylight and thus reduced the amount of electricity needed to illuminate the spaces. So went the game of give-and-take.

Still other rounds of bartering for an ecologically sound building brought the architects into conflict with the client, who, at one point, insisted on single-occupancy offices despite convincing evidence that open offices translate into less space, less material, less energy, and, ultimately, less money. Such benefits notwithstanding, the users won out on that particular issue. Fewer LEED points for that one.

Another decisive yet unusual meeting, this time with the cooks of IUCN's canteen regarding the contents of the menu, had a more sensible outcome, in that they agreed to use predominantly regional products certified as organic. Perhaps seemingly trivial, this measure tremendously reduced the building's daily operational impact, though no points for such a proviso were awarded at the time by the certifying authorities.

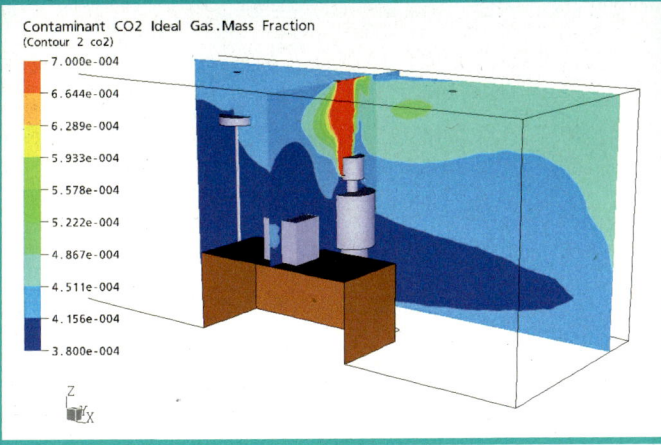

CO₂ content of air in a single-occupancy office, 2007 (all diagrams by Amstein + Walthert, 2007)

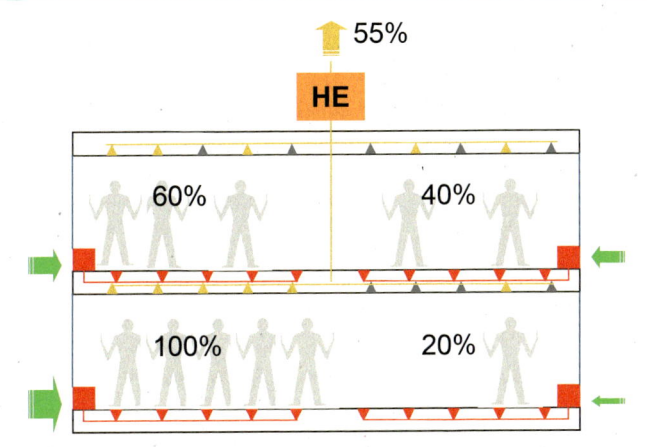

Ventilation needs in relation to occupancy, with CO_2 sensors determining the amount of air used

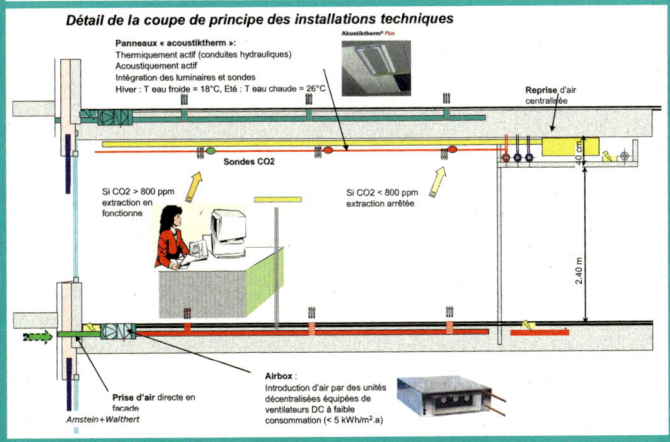

Mechanical systems interaction for a single-occupancy office

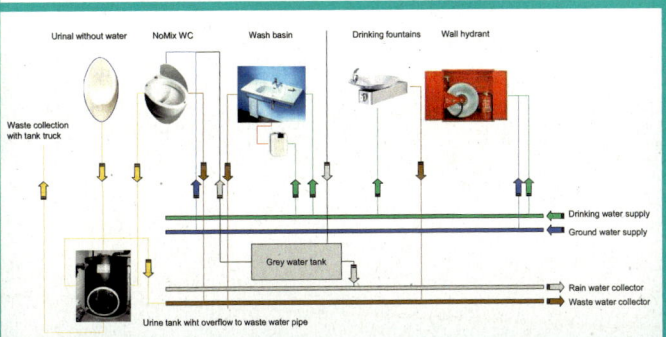

Systems for incoming and outgoing water flows

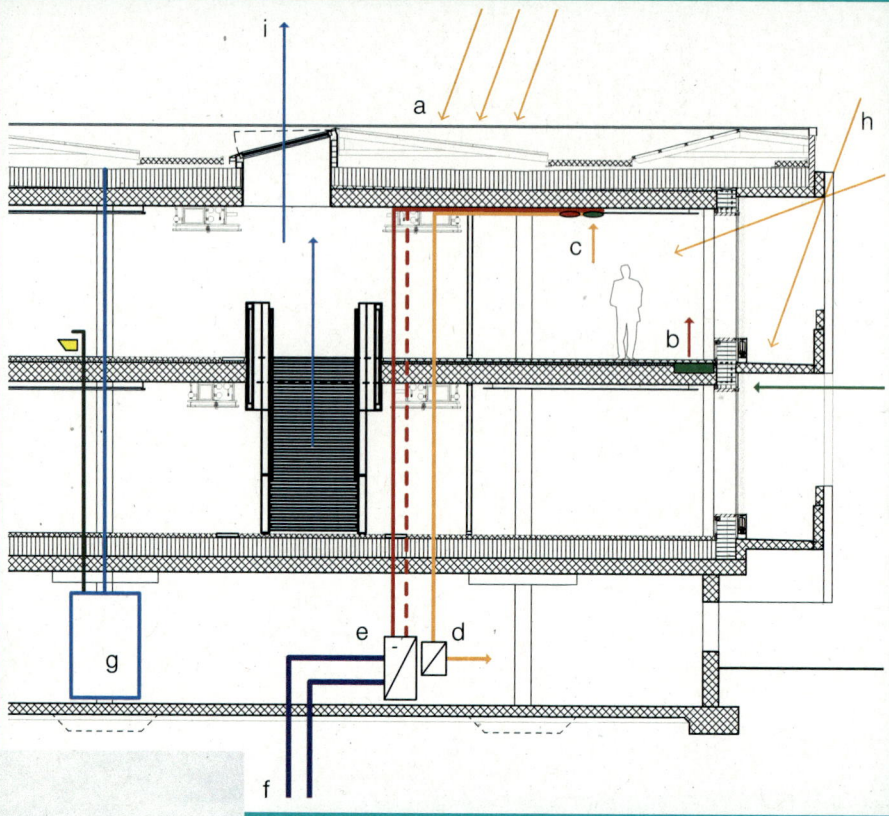

Mechanical systems: (a) photovoltaic; (b) airboxes; (c) CO_2 sensors and air exhaust; (d) heat recovery exchanger; (e) heat pump; (f) geothermal probes; (g) rainwater tank; (h) passive sunshading; (i) air exhaust (Amstein + Walthert)

Equipment used to drive the 14 geothermal probes 250m into the ground

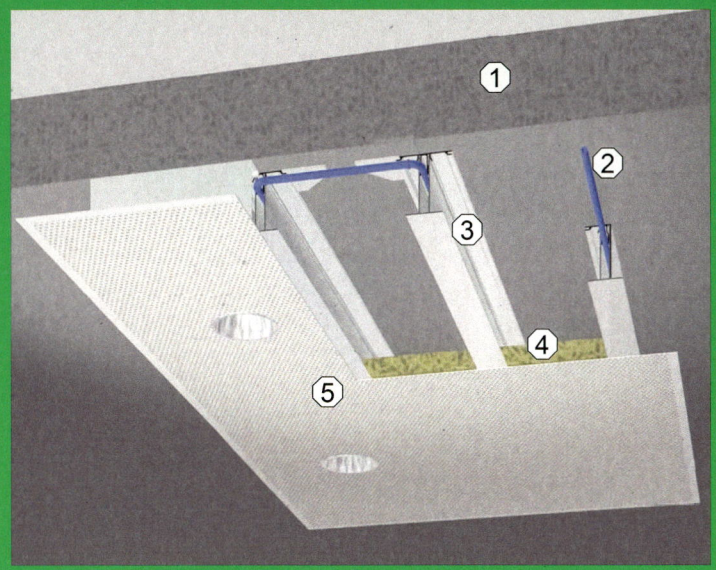

Modular ceiling panels: (1) slab; (2) heating/cooling pipes; (3) thermal conduction elements; (4) acoustic inlet; (5) perforated panel

Airbox ducts on formwork prior to pouring the slab and modular ceiling panels

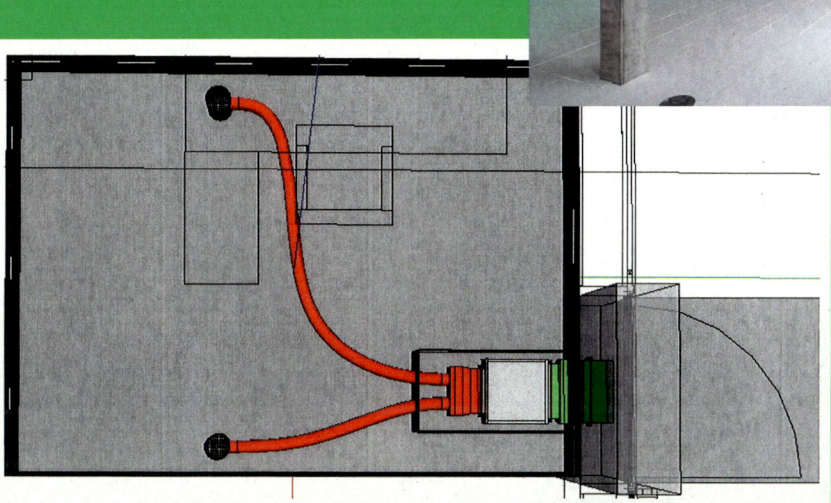

Diagram showing the placement of airboxes

129

With respect to landscaping, still other rounds of negotiations eventually prompted the client to bring their own in-house biologists into the discussion, who favored a just-let-it-grow approach in place of a 'designed' garden. There was even an argument that sheep could be brought in to graze the fields to avoid using machines to mow them. A related debate also arose as to whether the facade should have hanging plants, a feature that, surprisingly, the scientists categorically rejected, arguing that a 'greened' building was too literal a gesture for IUCN, not to mention too resource-intensive in terms of cost, water, and energy for upkeep.

Such bartering would go on as the design process progressed literally point by point, with every move weighed against another regarding its potential benefits and hazards. All in all, this approach essentially would make the building a patchwork of ideas, systems, and technologies that would be brought together in such a way as to increase its environmental fitness, even if this meant an inflation of trade-offs, *ad absurdum*.

Balancing Flows

The design of the IUCN extension proceeded early on by way of a dialogue among the architects, engineers, and client representatives regarding how to construct sustainably, a dialogue that would eventually involve product manufacturers and project contractors as well. Whereas the LEED and Minergie performance rating systems served as the basis for design discussions, the engineers took a systems approach in responding to the respective target points. Each point was translated into a correlating diagram of a system's performative capacity that in turn required a corresponding technology.

There were diagrams for the separate incoming and outgoing water systems, be it for groundwater supply, drinking fountains, rainwater collection, fire hydrants, wastewater, or urine tanks. There were diagrams for incoming and outgoing airflows as well as diagrams for energy transfers from underground earth tubes to heat pump to distributed airboxes to thermal storage in the slabs, as if delineating a complex chain reaction whose flows could be reversed when necessary (e.g., from heating to cooling and vice versa). Another diagram that the engineers were particularly fond of was for newly developed suspended modular ceiling panels that would cover 50% of the entire ceiling area. These so-called super-panels – tested in multiple prototypes, some of which failed miserably – would incorporate acoustic insulation, lighting fixtures, CO_2 sensors for monitoring air quality, and water pipes for heating and cooling, along with thermal conduction elements. By way of trial-and-error experimentation, the building's inner workings were plotted out system by system and one technical installation after another, all under the rubric of what the mechanical engineers termed a "lean technology approach" to the design of service components for the building, at least for them. Most important, the overall system would be engineered in such a way so as to maintain a constant state of equilibrium.

As the engineers became more and more emboldened by the prospect of a genuinely scientific design method, meaning that the performance of components could be calculated to the last value, it seemed that the issue of sustainability became more and more synonymous with technical prowess. The iterative process of trying to match performative parameters to operational diagrams and then to technical systems, though frenzied at times, essentially aimed at controlling energy and material flows, the architecture itself being the medium to channel them in the most environmentally sound manner.

With regard to energy, it was clear that the extension had to consume as little as possible, for this would at least satisfy the "P" of the Minergie-P-Eco label – "P" standing for passive buildings that use ultra-low amounts of energy. But to achieve this ranking required an exorbitant amount of thermal insulation as well as triple glazing, thereby making the extension a hermetically sealed volume with virtually no thermal transmission from inside to outside, or vice versa. So much for it being opened up to the surroundings, P-rating aside.

Still, the quality of energy flowing within and through the building was another issue altogether. The extension could only be considered a best-practice case in sustainable construction when the energy needed for its operations was renewable. When evaluating potential energy sources, the engineers briefly debated using Lake Geneva as a thermal reservoir but rejected that option because the pipes would be too long and too costly. They even suggested using heat from the municipal sewage system as a viable source, but this idea too was dropped as the temperature differential for cooling would be excessive. It was ultimately decided that the most reasonable option would be to use geothermal and solar energy for all building operations, the objective being that the extension would rely solely on CO_2-free sources. Any surplus energy generated could be used for the existing building and thereby reduce its own ecological footprint. Yet again, all such stipulations called for a significant number of technical installations, not least of which being 14 geothermal probes pounded 250m into the ground as well as 1,400m² of photovoltaic panels on the roof, with everything else installed in between.

With the P-rating criteria fulfilled, design efforts turned to the issue of optimizing material flows as stipulated by the "Eco" of the Minergie-P-Eco label. To qualify for this standard in full, the extension would also have to be built in such a way as to greatly reduce its material impact on the environment. Readily available raw materials like wood would have to be used, the potential toxicity of products would have to be considered, and a high proportion of recycled building materials would have to be incorporated where possible, with building components themselves also being easily demountable and recyclable in accordance with a 'cradle-to-cradle' sensibility.

Whereas the use of wood for the facade construction made sense, the more difficult part of the work came with finding environmentally compatible uses of concrete for the foundations and slabs. Fortunately, IUCN had already launched a worldwide initiative to advise major companies about how to make their operations more sustainable just a couple of years before the extension project was commissioned. The architects for the project took advantage of IUCN's "Private Sector Engagement Strategy" by bringing the Swiss concrete industry directly into the design process to explore different compounds and processing techniques for its product.

The rounds of experimentation and laboratory tests with material specialists – again, some succeeding, others failing – yielded variations of CO_2-reduced concrete, diverse ways to use recycled concrete, and more ecologically sound options for producing insulating concrete. This probing mentality concerning the role of materials in sustainable construction would be carried through to every component down to the last piece of furniture. Nothing was left unexamined with respect to what went into them, how they were made, where they were produced, under which conditions they were fabricated, and when they would need to be replaced. Here again, the work involved a balancing of material criteria to achieve optimal eco-performance.

This was all fine and good when trying to design a sustainably constructed building for a client concerned about sustaining the environment. Yet a striking imbalance was revealed in an "Environmental Impact Assessment Report" prepared to evaluate the project after the building had been built on the basis of scientifically assembled data available at the time.

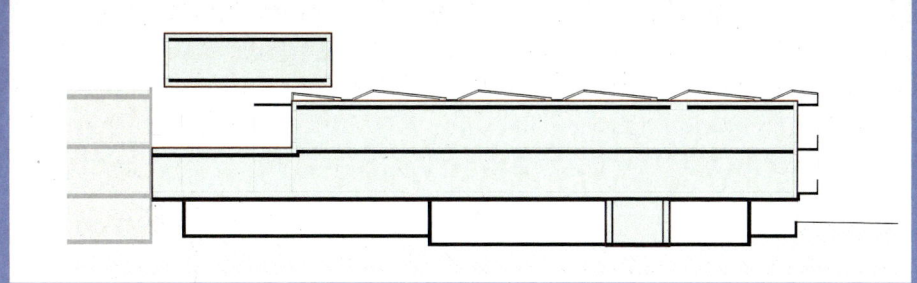
Section: IUCN extension in relation to existing building

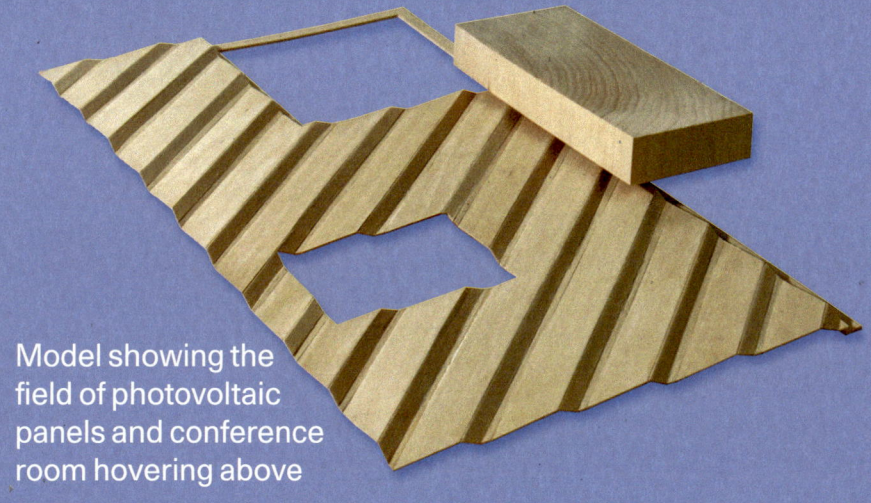
Model showing the field of photovoltaic panels and conference room hovering above

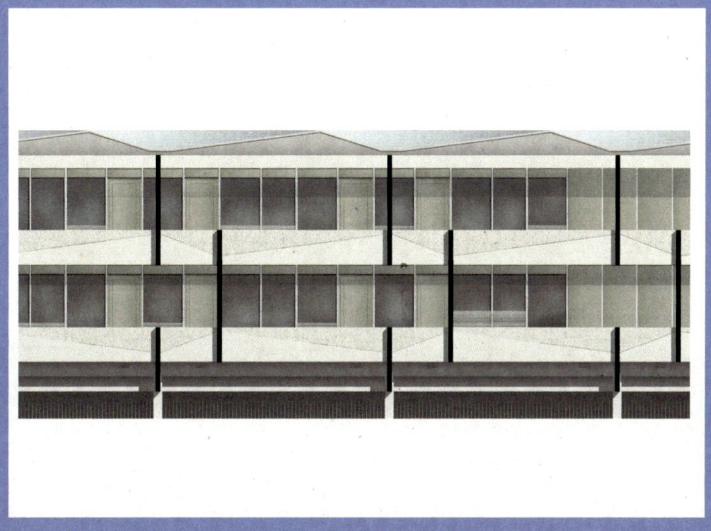
Facade study with the fire escape balconies and office fenestration

TEC21 featuring the IUCN project as an example of how to use recycled concrete, June 2010

Atria with skylights for direct air exhaust; all slabs built with recycled concrete

Material experiment using recycled concrete

Prefab balustrade elements

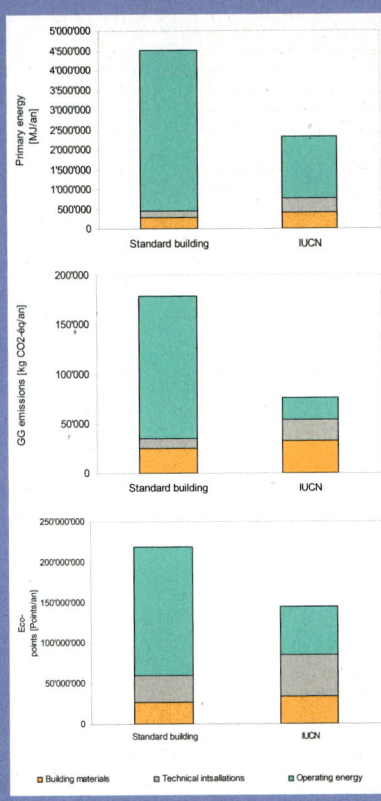

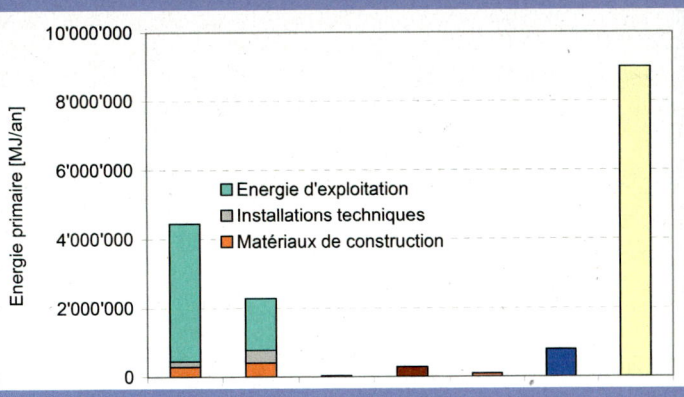

Energy use: operations (turquoise), installations (gray), construction materials (orange); standard building (left column); IUCN (right columns): energy for building, water use, furniture, IT equipment, commuting, and air travel (Environmental Impact Assessment Report, 2010)

Environmental Impact Assessment – standard building (left) and IUCN extension (right): energy for construction and operations (top), greenhouse gas emissions (middle), ecopoints (bottom); materials (orange), installations (gray), operations (blue)

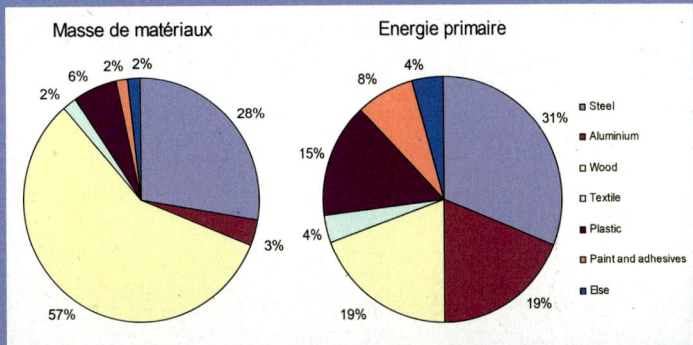

Types of furniture materials (left) and their embedded energy (right); 57% is wood, consuming only 19% of the total embedded energy; all in all, the furniture amounts to 38 tons of material

The report, which went well beyond the one prepared to qualify for the LEED Platinum label, had been commissioned by IUCN to learn from their 'experiment' in building construction and to guide them in future environmental policymaking. In short, the study compared a 'standard' office building – defined by the arithmetic mean of data obtained from a number of like office buildings built in Switzerland – with the new one in Gland. This comparative analysis focused on three indicators: energy consumption, including the gray or hidden energy of the building's construction and that required for operations (measured in megajoules or MJ); the amount of greenhouse gases emitted – CO_2, CH_4, N_2O, O_3, etc. – throughout the building's life cycle (measured in kg of CO_2 equivalent or kg CO_2-eq.); and the calculation of "environmental impact points" referenced to the official Ecoinvent database compiled from a broad range of resource sectors such as energy, agriculture, waste, transportation, and construction (evaluated in eco-points per unit of quantity). Interestingly, the assessment report adopted a 'cradle-to-grave' approach for the sum of calculations, essentially accounting for the performance of all building components throughout their entire life span, minus their potential recycled value due to the lack of reliable data.

  The results of the report were sobering. The IUCN extension, though extremely efficient in energy use for daily operations, required not only more technology to achieve said efficiency, but also substantially more materials compared to a standard building. The metrics showed, for example, that energy consumption was reduced by a factor of six, but the embodied energy in the initial construction was three times higher than that of conventional structures. In this case, 'lean technology' did not necessarily mean less materiality; in fact, it meant more of it. Even so, the IUCN extension balances out this discrepancy when considered in terms of the life cycle of its constituent components (building 80 years, photovoltaic panels 30 years, technical installations 20 years, furniture 10 years, IT equipment 4 years). The overall energy savings ultimately compensate for the surplus of embedded energy in the construction materials and in the technical components. Granted, the client does get more from the building than went into it in the long run but could have gotten even more if IUCN had not insisted on complying with LEED and Minergie policy benchmarks that, ultimately, required more materials and technology.

  Faced with the hard facts of its own report, IUCN conceded that future building construction policies would have to be reworked to truly balance performance and impact. But there was more in the balance from the lessons learned. Based on the data, the union realized it would have to drastically change its own practices, particularly considering that the environmental impact of international air travel undertaken for IUCN operations far outstripped that of the new building. So, faced with having to alter its own habits, IUCN essentially had to acknowledge that a performative architecture is only as good as the ways of its occupants.

Balancing Architectures

In view of the near-obsessive preoccupation with environmental performance, one would assume that the premium placed on energy and material flows would have a determining effect on the physicality of the architecture. But this was only partly the case. On the one hand, the building did have to accommodate a slew of engineering feats, integrate them in a discreet way, while also providing an array of spatial qualities, sequences, and ambiences that would remain unencumbered by the technological armature required to make the extension measurably sustainable. On the other hand, the architects began exploring a logic for the architecture independent of its operative systems by trying to identify advantages and disadvantages of the heterogeneous mix of technical and tectonic components. With the diverse collection of technologies in play, not to mention all of the materials assessed, it was becoming clear for the design team that this would be no 'pure' architecture, certainly not by exacting Swiss standards.

On the contrary, the mechanical engineering systems were actually impure and messy, born of bricolage rather than devised from some immaculate formula. So why should the design of the building shy away from this hybrid compilation achieved via the accumulation of discrete parts? This very question would be decisive in the design of an architectural assembly that, while serving present purposes, could be adaptive to other needs, incomplete rather than being 'finished,' and open to new uses if necessary – and all that within a given envelope for a low, fat box.

For this task, the notion of an "other ordering" introduced by Alison and Peter Smithson in the 1960s seemed quite apt for bringing together disparate elements and allowing them to coexist in an amalgamated whole: the volume of the conference "think tank" floating above a sea of photovoltaic panels; fire escape balconies winding their way around the extension; courtyards intermittently perforating the mass of the building and at times reaching down to the depth of the garage; internal atria allowing for the clutter from everyday activities; and a hidden bridge crossing over to the planted

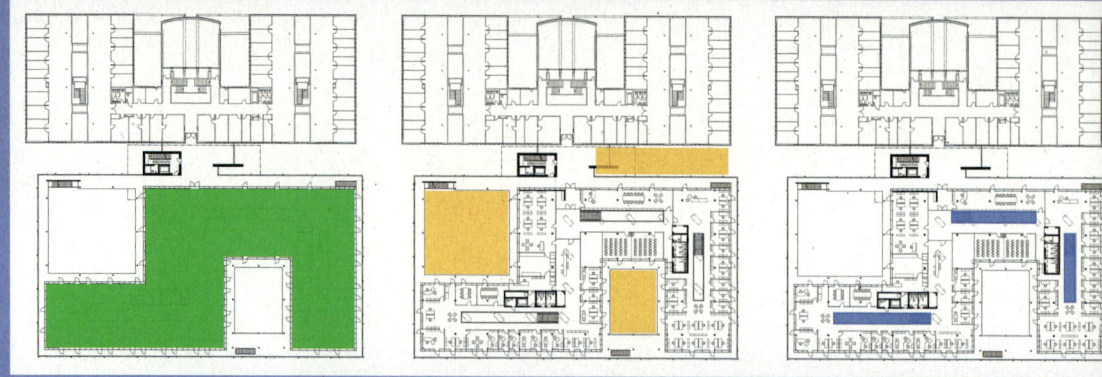

Components of the mat-building: main volume (green); courtyards (orange); atria (blue); cores (red); fire escape balconies (purple)

Perspective and interior photograph of the "think tank" looking toward Lake Geneva and the Alps beyond

"Think tank" hovering above the photovoltaic installation (Alain Bucher)

Reference image used during discussions about the horizontal, mat-like format of the project (Candilis, Josic, and Woods, Free University of Berlin, 1963)

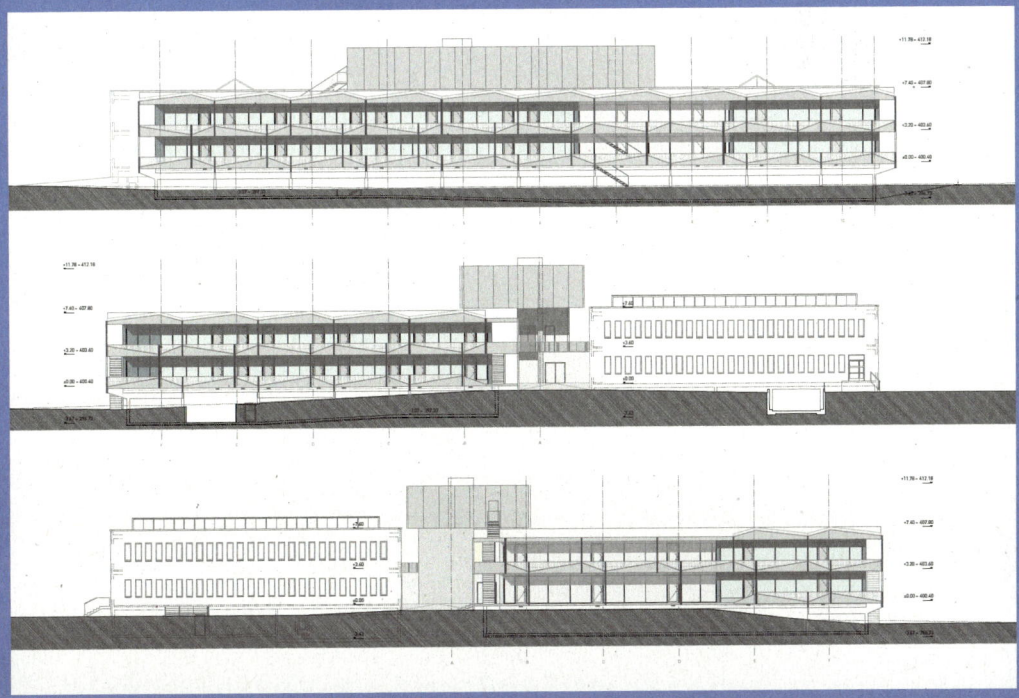

Facade drawings showing both the extension and the existing building

Exterior view of the extension (Alain Bucher, 2010)

Conglomerate of building components (Andrea Helbling, 2010)

View into the main courtyard two years after completion (Alain Bucher, 2012)

roof of the existing building, to name some of the architectural parts making up the conglomerate of the IUCN headquarters, in line with what the Smithsons would later call "conglomerate ordering."

At some point in the process, the architects merged this notion of a cumulative arrangement with the concept of a layered horizontal field not unlike that also proposed in the 1960s by Candilis, Josic, and Woods for the Free University of Berlin. This strategy would basically open up the IUCN box and extend it into the immediate surroundings, the size of the site even allowing for future extensions if needed. In place of a low, fat box, the new headquarters would be experienced as a collection of components that interact within a compressed, spatial field layered over human interactions, uses, stillness, noise, and plenty of technical equipment. In effect, the mat-building format of the new extension would yield a messy vitality over and above a purist architectural order.

The resulting spatial arrangements are comprised of somewhat simple elements whose complexity arises only from their relative position to – and interface with – each other. Whereas the components are for the most part homogeneous, the assemblages they create are patently heterogeneous and follow a conjunctive logic of things placed in relations undergoing continuous variation. Not only an apt description of the new headquarters building itself, this idea of a messy conglomerate that still coalesces into a cohesive body could just as well describe the environments with which IUCN as a global institution engages as a matter of collective concern.

And this international union committed to the conservation of nature would seem to understand that human environment-making, be it a building, a suburb, a landscape, or urbanized territory, is part and parcel of the environmental dynamics in which it takes place. In so many words, the construction of our habitat – sustainable or not – enmeshes technologies and natures to the extent that they have become mutually constitutive of the world we inhabit. If this is the case, then the lessons learned from the IUCN experiment would suggest that the issue with which we must all contend is not technology versus a nature understood as something beyond the technical realm, but rather how technology as something integral to the production of the environment can be retooled to sustain the collective habitats produced.

Housing Technology

Margarete von Lupin

Housing Technology
Essay on the B35 Prototype
Margarete von Lupin, 2012

Interested in the role of dialogue as method, author Margarete von Lupin engaged in periodic conversations with the architects over the course of several years to discuss the evolving role of technology in architecture. During some of these exchanges, the residential building on Bolleystrasse 35 in Zurich (or B35) was discussed from different vantage points, some even surprising to the architects themselves. Though not trained as an architect, she wondered what relationships could be established, if not constructed, between architecture and technology that were not already part and parcel of disciplinary discourse. Of course, there is the dictum of 'the house as a machine for living in' from long ago. There are those champions of technological expression who turn buildings inside out by exposing their technical systems on the facade. There are also those who suppress any sign of a building's installations for the sake of spatial purity – "hide the goddamn mechanical systems" in the inimitable words of Mies van der Rohe. But are there no other ways to frame the architecture-technology interface beyond either/or positions?

Insofar as Hansjürg Leibundgut, in the dual role of client and engineer, considered B35 to be an experiment in testing zero-emission technologies, von Lupin's question was pertinent for the architects, who were concerned that their project might be nothing more than a shell or housing for the latest in green technology. But to consider architecture as a 'technology' in the fullest sense of the term – as the 'thinking about making' or the 'science of practice' – would already leverage another way of approaching the age-old issue of how architecture and technology relate. This in mind, B35 would be not only a laboratory for engineering trial and error, but also a study in constructing a dialogue between the architecture of the building and the technical apparatus of its operating systems.

The design of B35 is meant to articulate this dialogue, whereby architecture neither is subservient to technical achievements, which in this case serve the worthy cause of reducing greenhouse gas emissions, nor celebrates its dependence on the technologies that make it a case study in environment-conscious design. Even so, the building was designed according to other more discipline-related criteria that had nothing to do with technology as such – the history of the neighborhood, its urban context, the nature of the parcel, qualities of habitation, spatial sequences, materiality, views, light, color, and so on. Perhaps it is these different agendas that give the building its variegated composures, all deserving of attention.

The following essay by Margarete von Lupin was written not long after the completion of B35 and was based on discussions with the client/engineer as well as the architects. Her essay was constructed as a counter-narrative to all of those reports exalting the project's technological breakthroughs.

> Since sustainability has been declared an imperative of human action, a matter of collective survival, as it were, architects have had to contend with how to translate this imperative into design practice. In the case of the B35 residential building, the ambition to implement a zero-emission prototype via new or tweaked state-of-the-art technologies gained public attention as a heated political debate on best practices in sustainable construction.

Perhaps unfairly, the architecture here took a back seat to the ideologically charged discussions that ensued. Sustainability, it would seem, was at root a technological issue alone. And it would remain so in publication after publication featuring the B35 project in terms of the latest in technological innovations meant to advance the cause of building sustainably. In the same way, the partisan lobbying for or against this or that science, standard, or technical solution, in effect, would sideline the pressing contemporary urban and architectural questions raised by the proposed design.

Though discussions focused primarily on the B35 prototype, the commissioned project actually consisted of two apartment buildings to be built for separate clients on a steeply sloped parcel on Bolleystrasse 33 and 35 in Zurich. Sitting side by side, the five-story structures could not be more different from each other on all counts, although both aimed in their own way to be sustainable. One is white, the other black. One has condominium units, the other rental apartments. One is parallel to the street, the other perpendicular. One is a part-skeletal structure with hung bands of prefabricated concrete facade elements; the other a monolithic concrete structure punctuated by various window types, some with glowing green glass reflecting

Architecture journal *Hochparterre* featuring the technical installations of B35 (August 2011)

Bolleystrasse 35 apartment building in Zurich (Stephan Rappo, 2011)

146

the surroundings. One complies with Swiss Minergie codes for minimum energy use through maximum insulation, the other surpasses these codes by reducing CO_2 emissions for building operations without the need for excessive insulating materials. One utilizes available construction technologies, the other grew into a research experiment in testing technologies in novel combinations, while also developing new ones to optimize a building's environmental performance. And though conceived as an ensemble, one building went virtually unnoticed, the other was unexpectedly subjected to the glare of publicity due to its technological innovations.

B33 situated parallel and B35 perpendicular to the street

Site model showing the two volumes in their context

Neighborhood of freestanding buildings, many dating back to the late 19th century

Still, before the pioneering spirit of the client/engineer for the B35 prototype was put to the test in rounds of negotiations among the architects, university colleagues, members of the press, and municipal authorities, the design team had other concerns altogether. While environmentally minded, the team was not originally preoccupied with technology per se, but rather with the location of the project as part of the city as well as the specific history of the neighborhood in which it was to be built.

The parcel is located in what is now an affluent Zurich neighborhood of freestanding multistory apartment buildings, many of which date back to the early industrial period of the late 19th century. Key here for the urban design authorities of the city of Zurich was that this particular urban structure had to be maintained regardless of what was designed. This meant that at least two buildings had to be implemented on the site, as opposed to the more economically and ecologically sound solution of building one larger structure spanning the entire length of the plot.

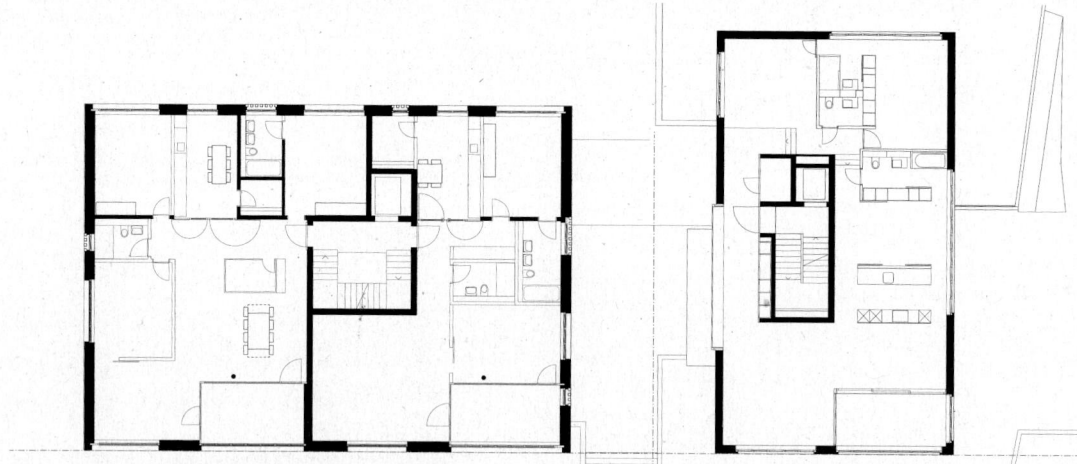

Plans of upper level; B33 (left) and B35 (right)

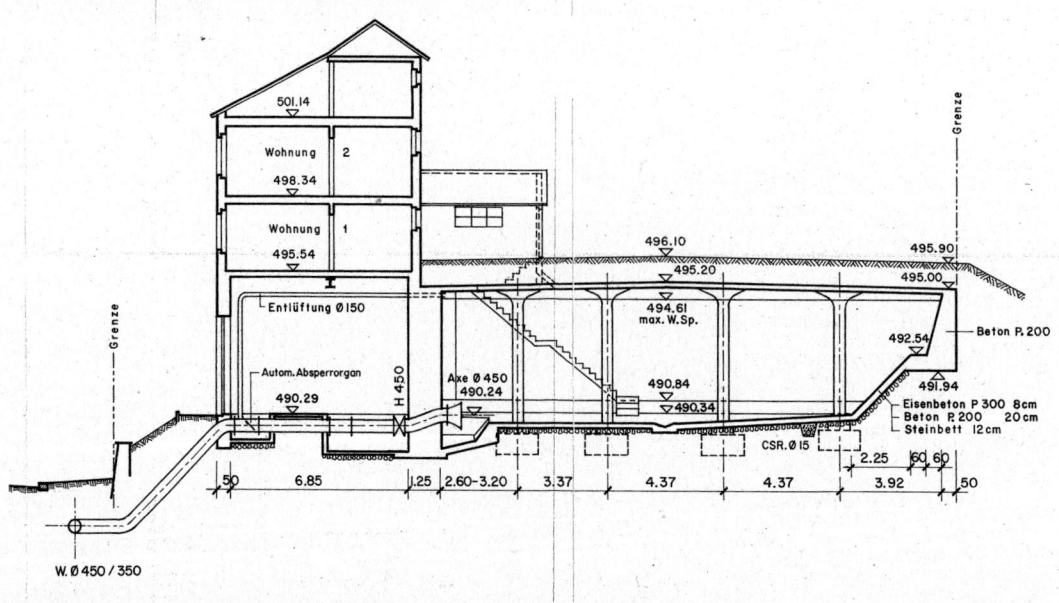

Section through the former water reservoir from the early 1920s (drawing, 1975)

So early on in the process, at least for city officials, sustaining the cultural identity of the neighborhood took precedence over any other design consideration.

Interior view of existing water reservoir (Reinhard Zimmermann, 2007)

Adaptive reuse of water reservoir as communal space (Reinhard Zimmerman, 2011)

The site was already occupied by a subterranean water reservoir from the 1920s running the full length of the parcel. This bunker-like structure was supported by 40 large mushroom-shaped columns (following the patented 'beamless slab' principle developed by Swiss engineer Robert Maillart in the early 20th century) and capped at one end with a house for the caretaker. In the 1990s, the reservoir was decommissioned and the city of Zurich decided to sell the property, the intention being to densify the neighborhood. It was at this point that municipal authorities initiated a discussion about the scale of a new building on the site, which led to the measure of subdividing it into two smaller parcels. The main design issue for the clients and architects was how much of the reservoir could be retained, considering both its historical value and the amount of energy embedded in its material stock. The client for one of the parcels opted for demolition to maximize sellable floor area in the condominium building (B33). The other client wanted to preserve and restore the space as a reactivated artifact from the past and make it a collectively shared feature of the apartment building (B35). Due to budget constraints and conflicting requirements from the two different owners, ultimately only a quarter of the reservoir's original volume of 6,500m³ could be saved and integrated into the new B35 residential building as an exemplary case of adaptive reuse. Already at this preliminary stage, the project would begin to take form in a give-and-take between ecological and economic considerations.

Street view of Bolleystrasse 33 and 35 (Reinhard Zimmerman, 2011)

That said, the volumes of both residential buildings were basically predetermined, not only by the size and slope of the parcel, but also by the rather strict building codes stipulating the number of floors, maximum height, and setbacks from the property lines. Any design proposition would have to fit within this straightjacket of preset dimensions. Environmental issues aside, both buildings would also have to comply with the requirement for a new garage that, by law, has to provide so many parking spaces per unit, all of which would somehow be situated next to, below, or around the remaining part of the reservoir. As is so often the case, the proviso of a parking garage, however questionable it might be in our time, defined all design moves thereafter. Insofar as appeals to the city to reduce the number of specified parking spaces went unheeded, it was decided that one garage would be shared by the two addresses to minimize its impact on the site.

Just as determinant for the design were the stringent energy codes that set a high standard for the thermal performance of the building's envelope, including the allowable percentage of openings per square meter of usable area. And this goes irrespective of the type of resource used for heating and cooling,

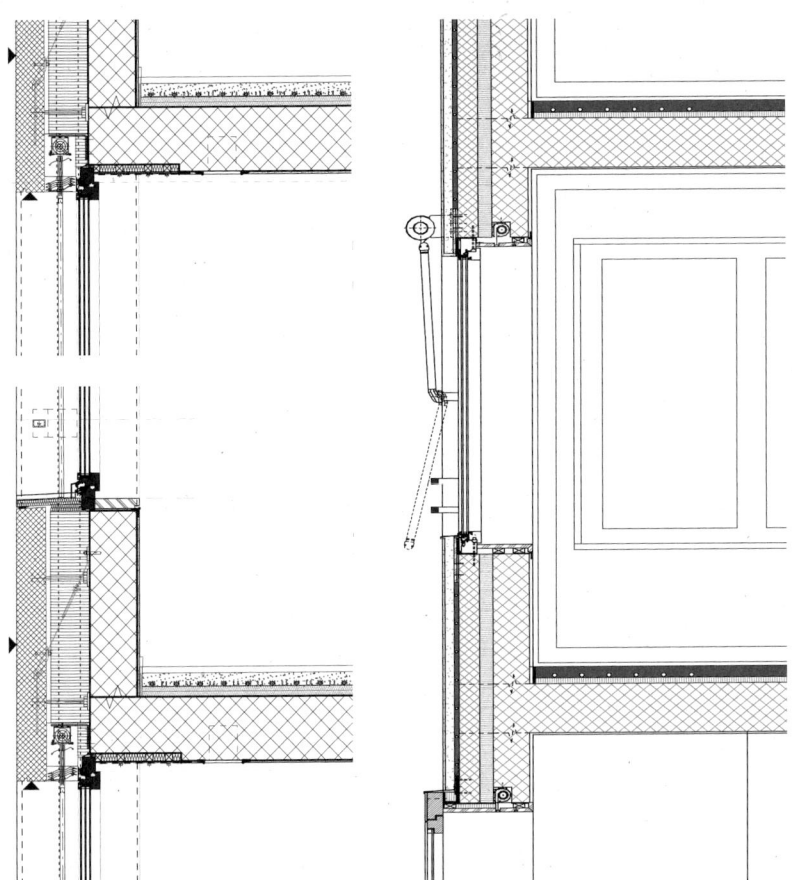

Facade construction details; B33 (left) and B35 (right)

B35 facade detail with reflective thermal M-glass (Reinhard Zimmermann)

that is, whether renewable or not. The B33 condominium building would be designed straightforwardly in accordance with the Minergie standard, inasmuch as the client was not open to anything out of the ordinary in this regard. Yet the B35 apartment

Housing Technology

building was another story. The client and engineer for the project – Hansjürg Leibundgut, mechanical engineering professor at ETH Zurich – was eager to make it a case study in zero-emission architecture, a bid that would require substantial deviations from Swiss energy codes. But this was easier said than done. For it would take much bargaining with building authorities before they reluctantly agreed to grant an exception and thus allow the experiment to proceed.

From this point on, B35 would evolve less as just another energy-efficient building and more as a platform for investigating technologies required to further optimize building operations. A number of components were developed in vitro (in a research laboratory), ranging from geothermal heat exchangers, heat pumps, and hybrid solar collectors to ventilation airboxes, digitally steered electricity, and dedicated software for coordinating all systems. These were then tested in vivo (on the construction site) with the aim of showcasing exemplary technical applications that could be commercially utilized throughout the industry. In so many words, B35 was fast becoming an energy-optimizing machine in which one could live and, as such, would reframe architecture as a carrier of technology.

For the architects and the client/engineer alike, the question was raised as to what degree the architecture should express the building's technical armature. Should back-of-house services become the front-of-house face of B35? Or rather, could the architectural and the technical meet in more subtle ways and

Technical installations for optimizing building operations (Stephan Rappo, 2011)

thus make the building their interface? Taking into account, however, that some of the proposed technologies were still in development (in vitro, so to speak) and that others would no doubt soon replace them, the architects opted for a reduced spatial solution which would make the building as flexible in its use as it is adaptable to technological change.

B35 facade detail with airbox vent and terrace balustrade above (Reinhard Zimmermann)

B33 facade detail with prefabricated concrete panels (Reinhard Zimmermann)

In essence, B35 consists of a core and an envelope, with the space in between conceived as an open loft that can be subdivided on each floor as needed. The circulation core, for example, sits as a freestanding element in space and is outfitted with more shafts than normally required in view of accommodating future technical installations. Similarly, all internal partitions are lightweight, non-load-bearing walls that can be easily removed if necessary. Each floor incorporates a loggia that, as a buffer between inside and outside, can function as both a winter garden and a balcony for warmer seasons.

As for the envelope, the rough concrete enclosure is integral to the structural system. Constructed as a monolithic element, it requires little insulating material due to the sophisticated renewable energy concept of the building that draws on the thermal storage capacity of the earth as well as solar radiation captured by collectors mounted on the shed roof. Components such as sun-shading screens, handrails, downpipes, or external air vents are attached to the facade without fuss so that they can be easily replaced, thereby giving the building a forthright appearance, one that is composed but does not proclaim how high-tech it really is.

As it stands now, B35 would seem to have two lives that, although in dialogue with each other, play out according to parallel itineraries. The 'architectural life' of the building unfolds sporadically in its everyday use by the residents and more gradually in the long duration of its own material life span. The 'technological life' of the building systems is registered in the constant input and output of data electronically processed in response to user needs or seasonal variations of climate. In contrast to the *longue durée* of architecture, the technical systems are increasingly transient

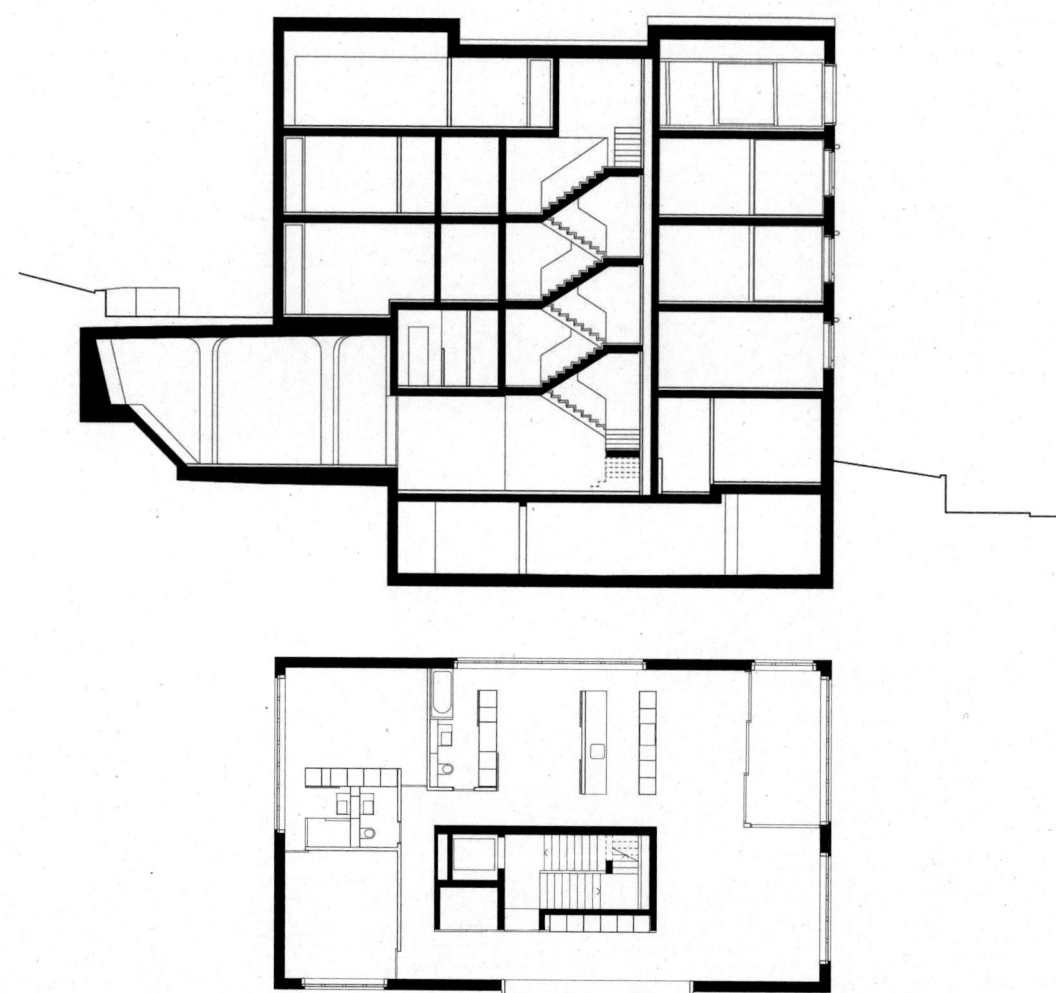

Section with existing reservoir and upper-floor plan with freestanding core

Space between core and envelope, including winter garden (Reinhard Zimmermann)

on account of ever-faster cycles of innovation and obsolescence. Given these out-of-sync lives between the 'slow technology' of architecture and the 'fast technology' of its operating systems, one is left to wonder whether debates on best practices in sustainable construction will settle on long- or short-lived solutions.

B35 Prototype

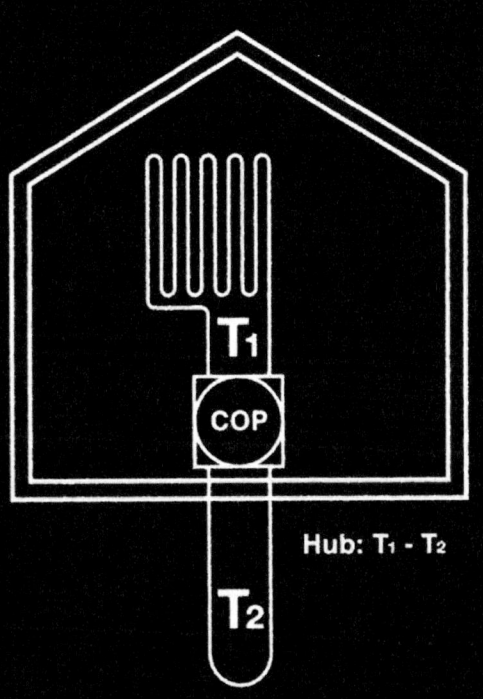

Apartment Building

Discourses

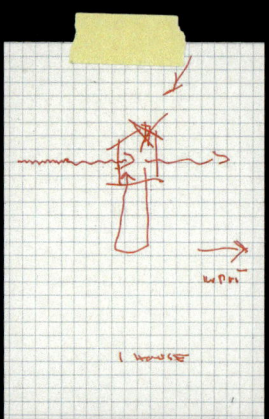

engineer vs. bricoleur
Claude Lévi-Strauss, 1962

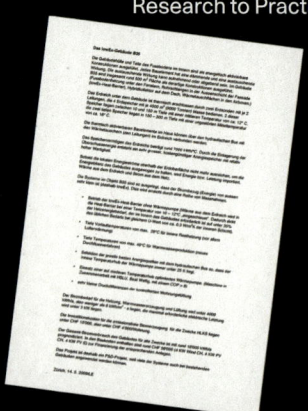

Use

circular flows

Energy

geothermal storage and replenishment

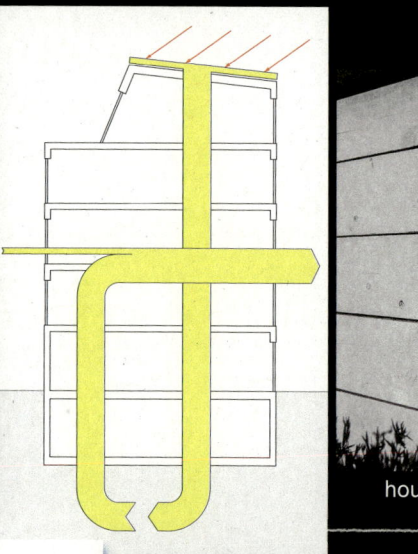

Materials

house with roots

Economy

Technology

in vitro ... in vivo ... in vitro ...

system thinking

Methodology

Policy

no labels

Hansjürg Leibundgut,
Zero Emission LowEx,
2008

zero emissions counter-
conference, 2010

158

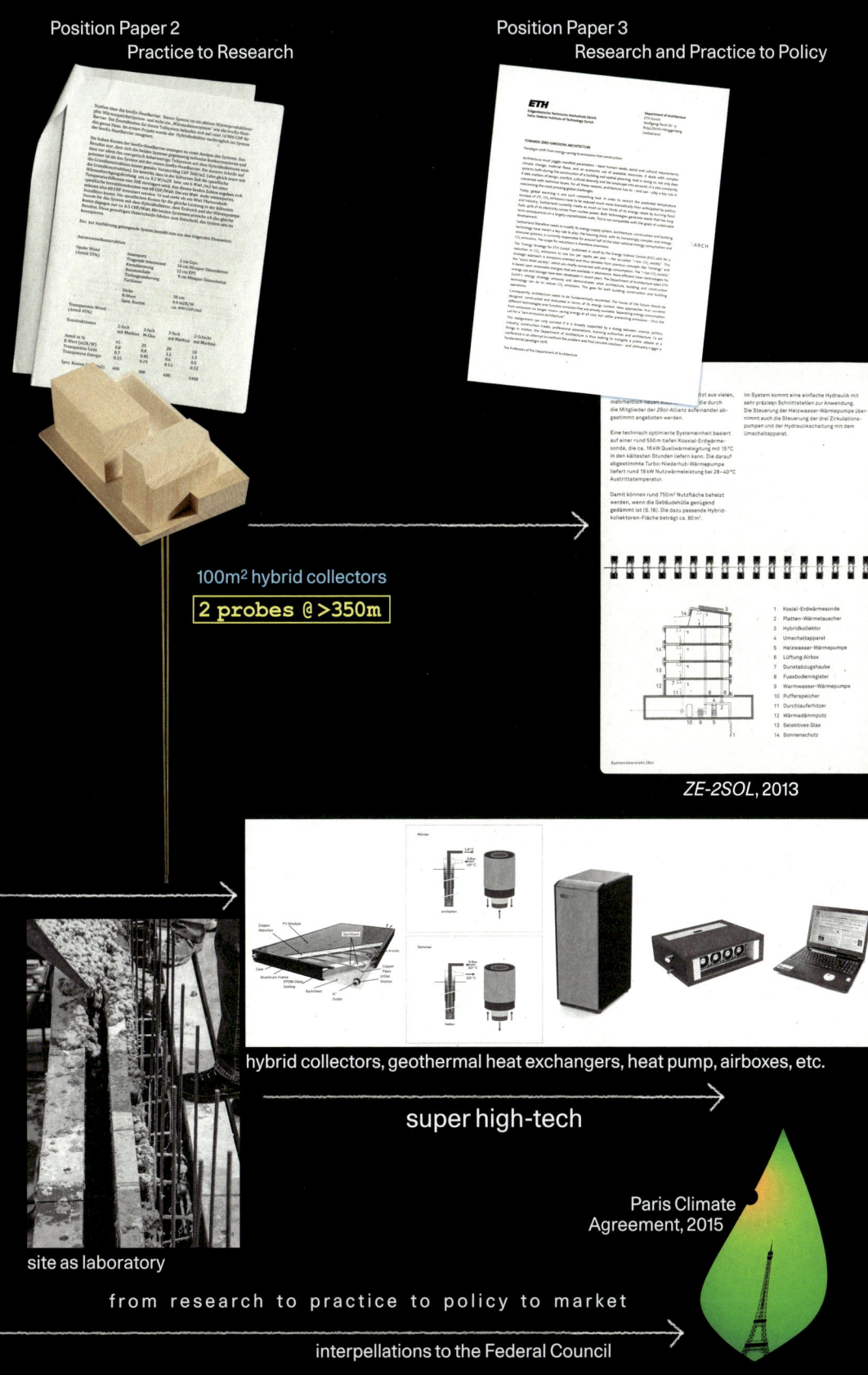

B35 Prototype

B35 Prototype
Apartment Building, Bolleystrasse 35, Zurich
2007–2012

Sometimes, a quick sketch can have far-reaching implications. Two colleagues at ETH Zurich – an engineer and an architect – were casually talking one day over lunch about the prospect of a cross-disciplinary research project on how to make cities sustainable, acknowledging that they are anything but environmentally sound. To tackle such a mammoth task would first of all need a clear direction, not to mention specific objectives, which were hurriedly jotted down on a notepad while eating.

Tentatively, the architect sketched a typical house with a pitched roof and a chimney, the arrows coming into and out of the house meant to highlight its relationship to the environment in terms of input and output. The engineer immediately crossed out the chimney, arguing against any further emissions into the atmosphere, however negligible they may seem. While talking about thermodynamic laws, heat-loss values, and tons of CO_2 released by buildings, he suggested arrows that loop through the house and its surroundings to emphasize the need for circular flows of available resources: what goes in and what goes out must be restorative and regenerative. And with that little house multiplied indefinitely, the same principle applies to cities, insofar as circular flows must be pursued at all scales. A matrix was drawn with various sizes along the x-axis (small, medium, large) and various input and output flows

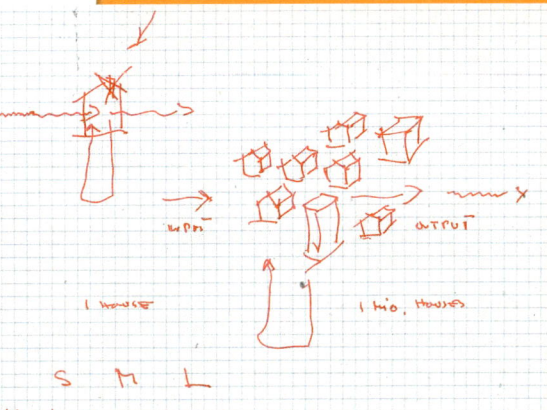

Position paper 1 by Hansjürg Leibundgut entitled "LowEx-B35 Prototype," May 14, 2009

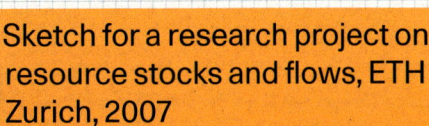

Sketch for a research project on resource stocks and flows, ETH Zurich, 2007

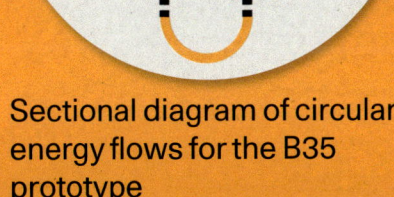

Sectional diagram of circular energy flows for the B35 prototype along the y-axis (energy, water, materials, information, capital, people) in order to identify a general framework for research that could be carried out on multiple fronts – at the architectural, urban, and territorial levels.

During a follow-up lunch discussion, Hansjürg Leibundgut, mechanical engineer and expert in fluid dynamics, brought up the idea of conducting a full-scale, real-life experiment that would demonstrate the principles of circular flows sketched earlier, in effect making a bridge from research to practice. By chance, he was just then in the process of buying a piece of land in the city of Zurich – the site of a former water reservoir – that could be opportunely used as a test site for experimenting with building technologies beneficial to the natural environment. So the little house with looping arrows sketched on a piece of paper would evolve into a zero-emission building prototype that could serve as a model for widespread use throughout the city and beyond.

Position Paper 1 – Research to Practice

As the architects were designing the house on Bolleystrasse 35 in Zurich, Leibundgut – both client and engineer for the building – attended a project meeting in early 2009 with a detailed position paper outlining what the house would have to do regarding its environmental performance. The paper – entitled "LowEx-B35 Prototype" – reads like an engineer's manifesto, positioning the work not only as cutting-edge research on particular technical components for optimizing energy stocks and flows within the building sector, but also relative to a broader discourse on mitigating its negative impact on the environment.

This was timely, considering that at the same time the European Union had issued its own position paper in preparation for the United Nations Climate Change Conference in Copenhagen to introduce binding legislation for transitioning to a low-carbon economy. That said, B35 would comply with this mandate by being a 'low exergy' building, meaning that the energy required for its operations would have the least detrimental effect on the larger ecological system of which it is a part, on which it draws, and to which the energy returns in circular loops. In short, when a system (say, a building) and its surroundings reach energy-equilibrium, exergy is zero. And if it could achieve this, only then could the project be considered a true 'prototype' in zero-emission construction.

As might be expected, this was already much to digest for the architects. But Leibundgut's position paper went on to itemize

Model with two geothermal probes reaching 380 m into the ground

Image illustrating the principle of a 'house with roots' for harvesting energy from the ground

Section through Zurich showing the depth of the geothermal probes

Diagram showing four activated geothermal storage zones of B35 (*LowEx Building Design*, 2011)

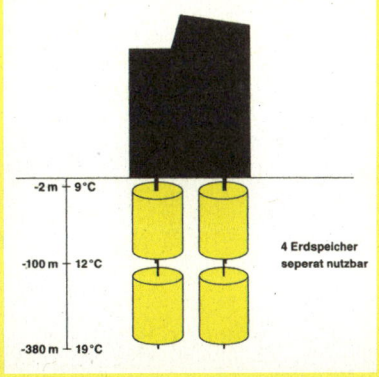

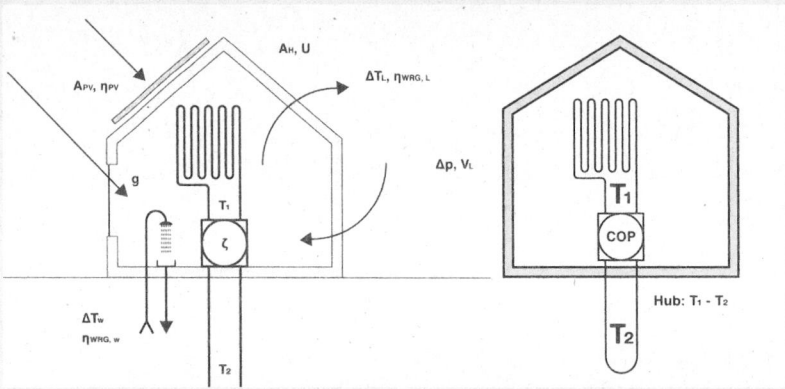

System diagrams; the heat pump with a specific coefficient of performance (COP) is situated between the geothermal reservoir below and the spaces above

Section with part of the existing water reservoir as multifunctional space

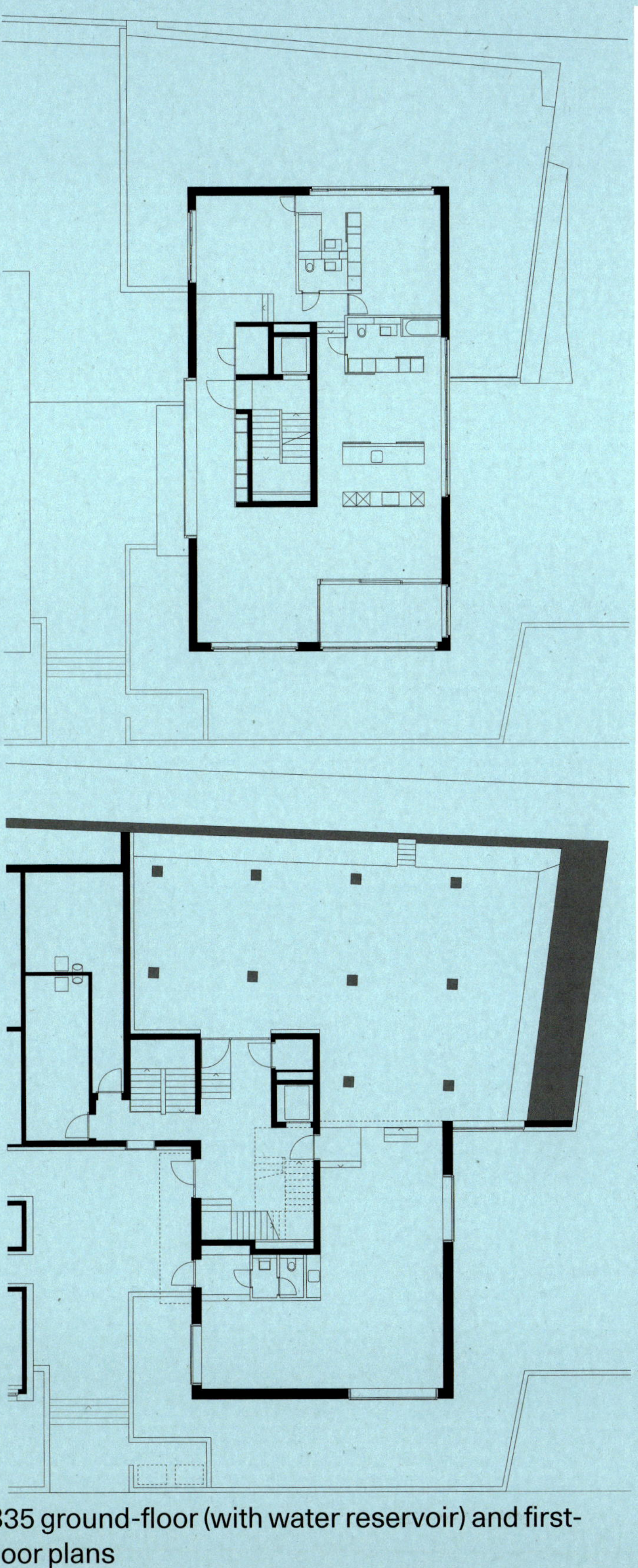

Concept model wrapped with radiant heat coils connected to geothermal storage below

B35 ground-floor (with water reservoir) and first-floor plans a number of more tangible measures to be implemented in B35. For one thing, the ground beneath the building would be used as a geothermal reservoir for cooling and heating, accessed by two energy-exchange probes made from a pair of pipes extending 100m and 380m deep that take advantage of the constant temperatures at varying levels, while activating four storage zones of 4,500m³ of earth each. Although a 'house with roots' for harvesting energy from the ground seemed clear enough as a figurative idea, the means for achieving it technically would still have to be developed. A key question was whether the building itself could function as a generator to replenish the geothermal reservoir with solar energy in the summer for use in the winter. The notion of collecting energy in one season to be used in another was again a lucid principle that would have to be developed to make it technically feasible and cost-effective.

    At this time, a discussion came up regarding how to reuse the large subterranean water reservoir on the site that had been decommissioned by the city some years earlier. It was part of a network of such structures built as a precautionary measure to supply Zurich with water in times of shortage. The engineer toyed with the idea of converting this volume into a potential hydrothermal energy bank by filling it with water and then using the mass for storing energy when needed, a solution which would eliminate the need for the geothermal reservoir in the ground. Admittedly far-fetched, the proposition was quickly discarded, but the issues of energy storage and replenishment remained front and center.

    This theme was picked up in the position paper when addressing the building's envelope. Since the water reservoir as energy reservoir had been dropped in favor of geothermal storage, the building enclosure was to be realized as a thermo-activated facade that would capture solar heat to be stored in the ground, while minimizing the amount of insulation needed. At one point there was even talk of no insulating material whatsoever. Instead, the entire facade, including the roof, would be wrapped in

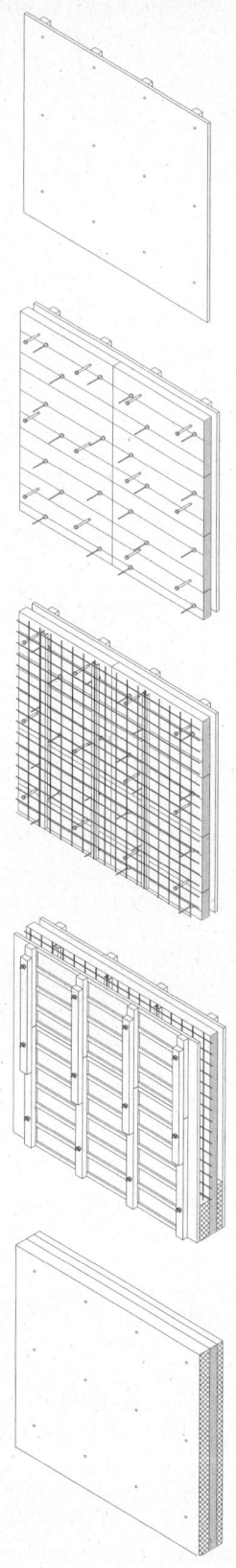

Step-by-step construction of poured-in-place wall

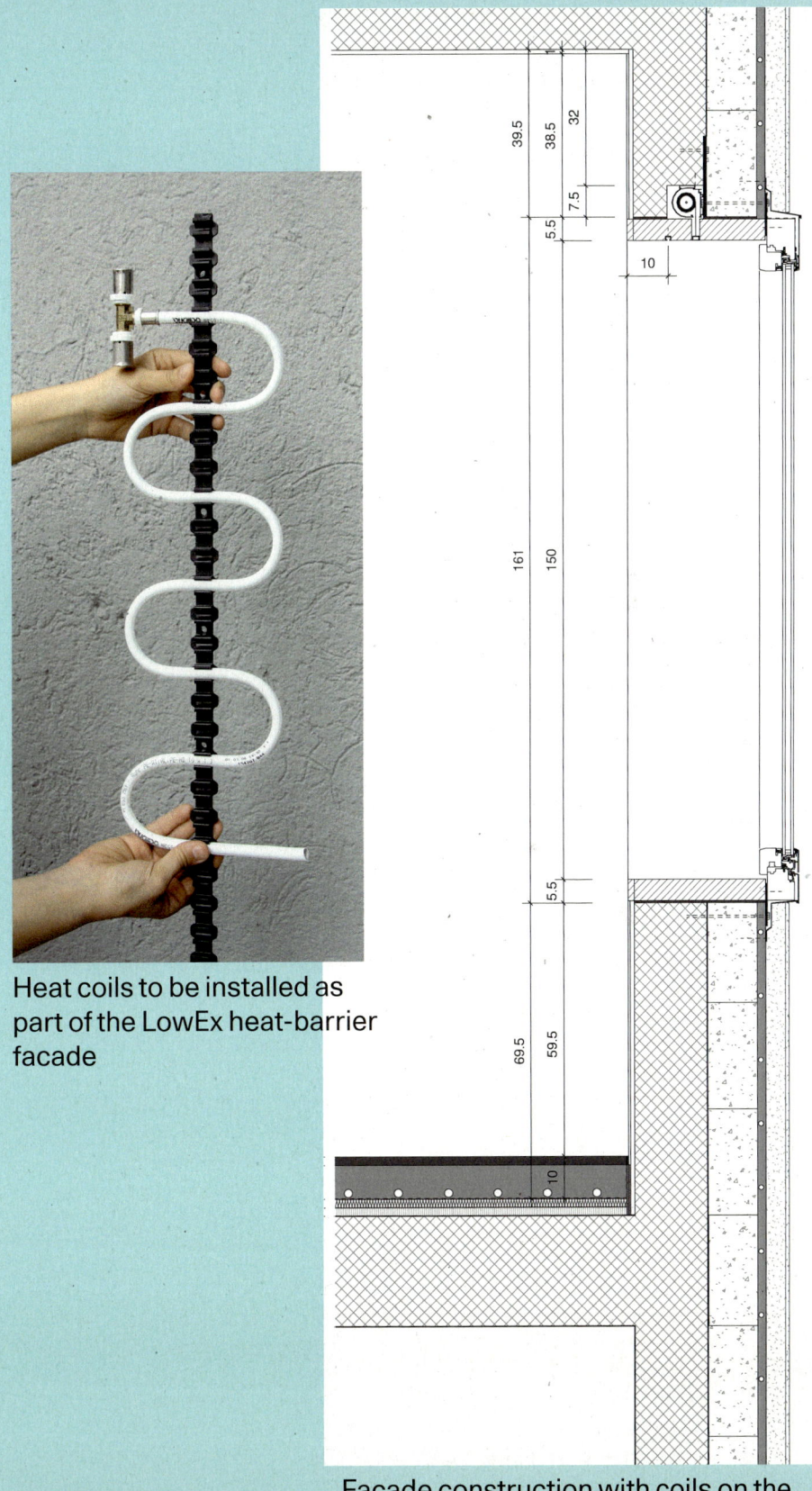

Heat coils to be installed as part of the LowEx heat-barrier facade

Facade construction with coils on the outer layer (solution rejected)

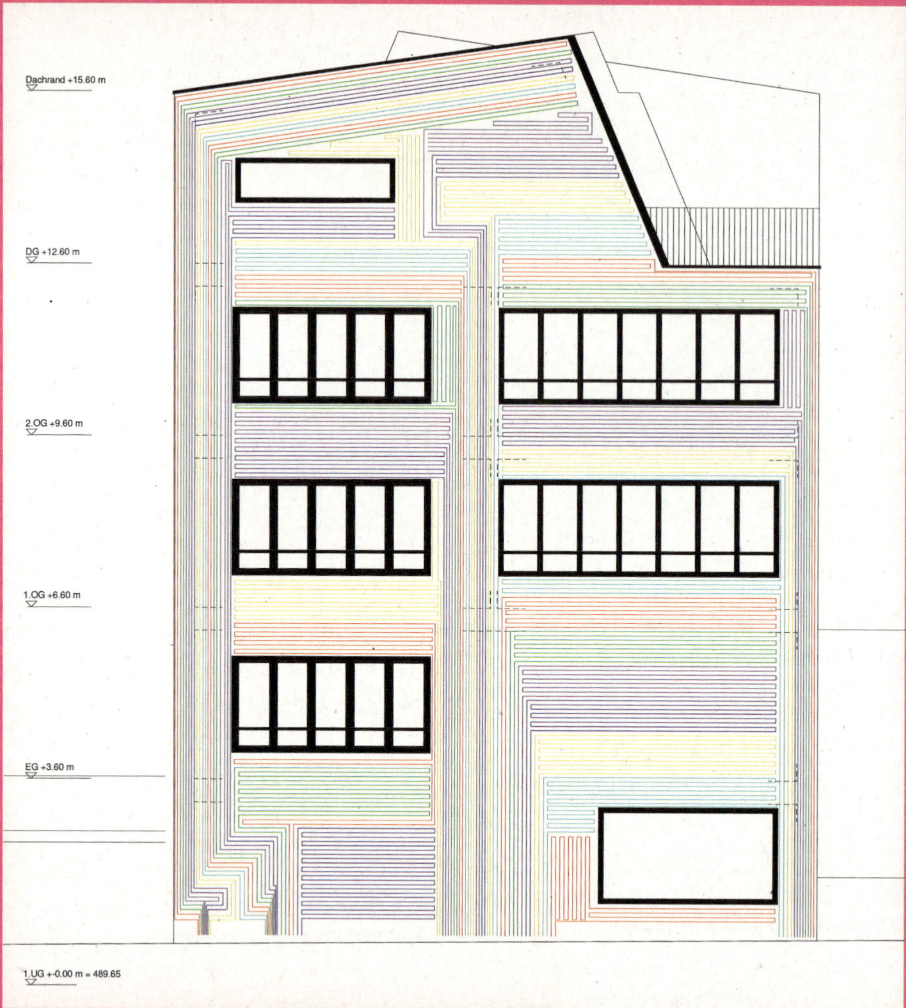

Thermo-activated facade with web of radiant heat coils for heating and cooling

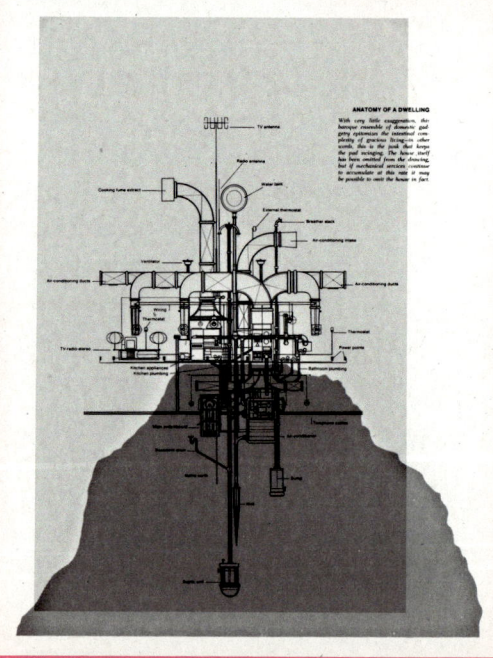

François Dallegret, *Anatomy of a Dwelling*, drawing for "A Home is Not a House" by Reyner Banham, *Art in America*, 1965

a web of coils coupled (via a photovoltaic-powered heat pump) to the geothermal reservoir to make the entire enclosure also seasonally responsive as an integral part of the overall technical machinery of B35. The argument made in the position paper was that by using emission-free sources, the issue would no longer be about 'saving' energy per se, but rather about increasing its overall quality. With this principle put into practice, energy could basically be 'wasted' because it is renewable and thus superabundant as an endless, clean, and free source of energy that is available whether used or not. But try telling that to those who have been expounding the benefits of energy savings for decades, albeit because of the habitual reliance on non-renewables, and your experiment most likely faces prompt dismissal as a mere flight of fancy.

Discussions nevertheless continued among the engineer and architects concerning the design and construction of the thermally activated enclosure that needed to be load-bearing, insulating, and outfitted with coils for either heating or cooling the facade. Developed in collaboration with a local construction company, the solution called for a seemingly monolithic wall made of insulating concrete poured in place, within which a thin layer of insulation would be encased. The first full-scale tests were disastrous because the insulation boards did not remain in place during the pouring process. Subsequently, rods would be inserted to secure these inner boards to the formwork, and with this the problem was solved. The coils, embedded in a thin layer of cement, would be attached on the outside and covered with another layer of insulating plaster painted black to increase the absorption of heat for replenishing the geothermal reservoir. Though constructed with known technologies, the multiple functions of the facade, or "LowEx Heat Barrier" as the engineer called it, made it a complex piece of machinery in its own right. As such, it would feature in an exhibition in mid-2009 showcasing ETH research on sustainable resource use that included a one-to-one detail mock-up of the B35 facade.

While all of this was taking place, Leibundgut – founding member of the Institute of Technology in Architecture at ETH Zurich – launched a research initiative on energy-optimizing building components to further develop them for implementation in practice. B35 would figure as but one prototype among many meant to advance sustainable construction techniques. In preparing a more detailed agenda for his research group, he outlined what basically amounted to a technical anatomy of a house, with a number of complex constituent parts to be coordinated in such a way as to achieve optimal synergy in their combined operation. The wish list included

On-site test of concrete wall encasing insulation boards

Wall mock-up with heat coils for an exhibition showcasing ETH Zurich research, Mainau, 2009

3D-printed model of the monolithic building envelope

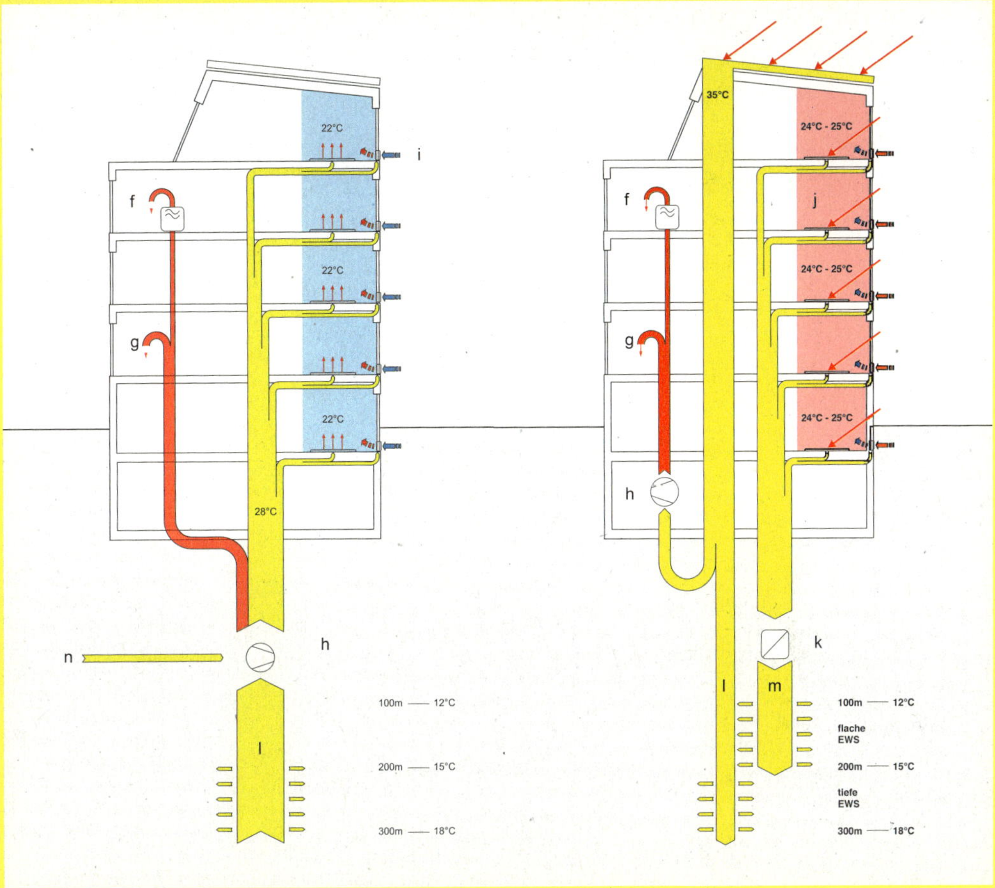

Energy flow diagrams (summer and winter)

hybrid collectors

geothermal heat exchangers

heat pump

airboxes

software

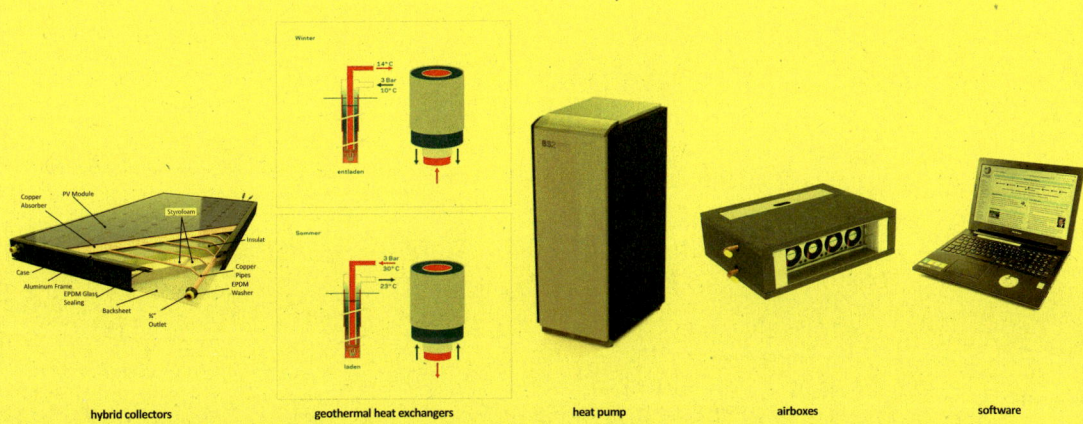

Technical components: hybrid collectors, geothermal heat exchangers, heat pump, airboxes, and software

Position paper 2 by Hansjürg Leibundgut entitled "LowEx Variation," November 14, 2009

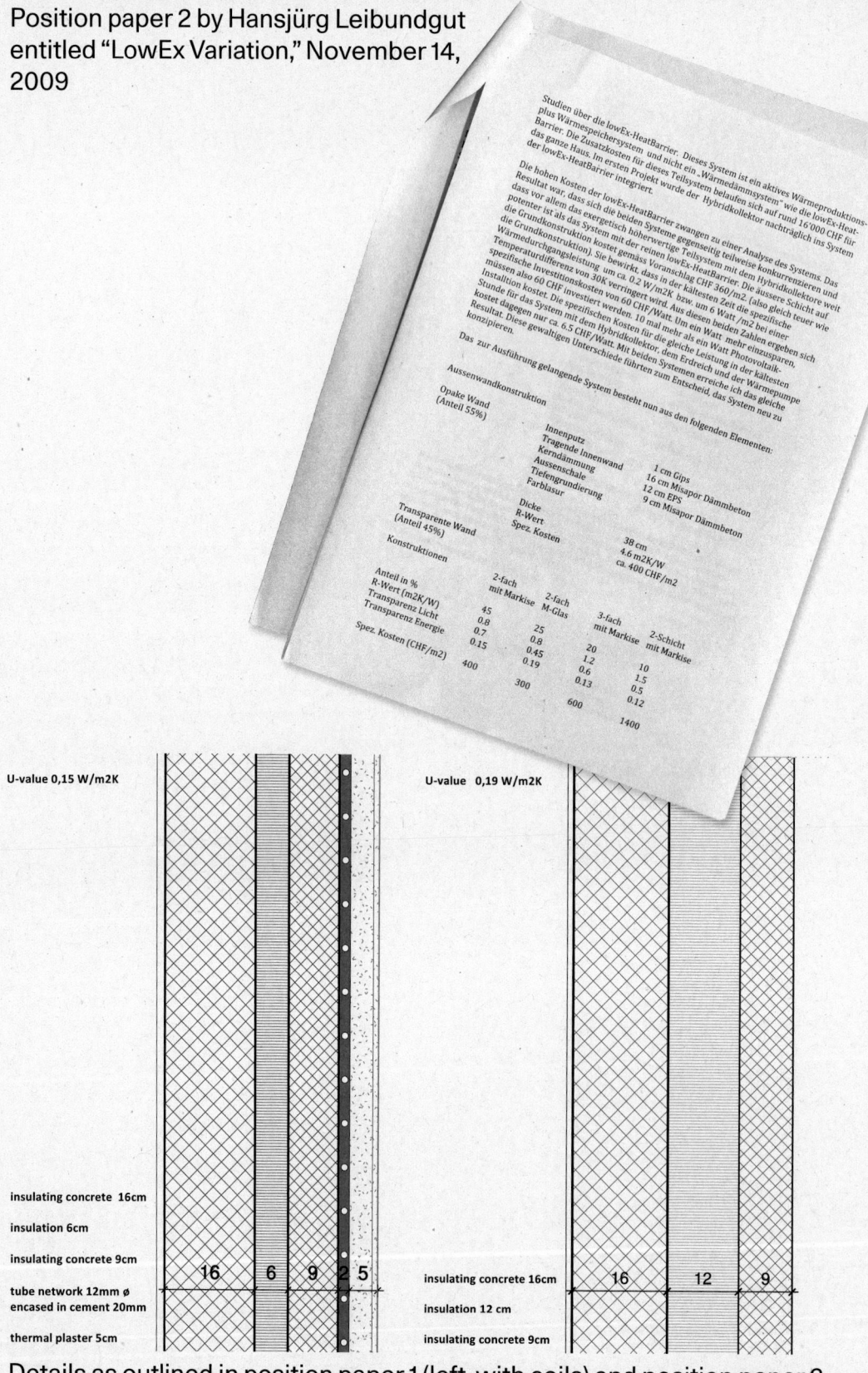

Details as outlined in position paper 1 (left, with coils) and position paper 2 (right, without coils and with more insulation)

new heat pumps with the highest coefficient of performance possible, digitally steered electricity, hybrid collectors comprised of photovoltaic and solar water panels, devices for heat recovery from sewage water, hydraulic bus systems for thermal distribution, and specially designed airboxes for decentralized ventilation, to mention only some of the innovations foreseen for the house of the future. From this list it became clear that to build sustainably, in view of current *and* yet-unanticipated needs, requires an ultra-high-tech approach to construction. The more technology, the more sustainable, so the argument went, which essentially made architecture but a carrier of the latest in green technology.

Position Paper 2 – Practice to Research

Only six months after the first position paper had been presented to the architects and with the permit approved by the city for the new apartment building on Bolleystrasse 35, the client/engineer drafted yet another position paper outlining changes to the technical and energy concept for B35. In essence, the four-page paper was a detailed justification for rejecting the earlier thermo-activated facade proposal. As innovative as it might have been as a research study, the roughly 6 km of coils that would wrap around the building and across the roof were outrageously expensive, if not ecologically questionable, due to the amount of material and energy required to produce them. But the engineer would not budge on his emission-free premise, nor would he let go of the geothermal reservoir beneath the building.

To compensate for the coils in the facade, an alternative had to be devised for replenishing the energy storage system in the ground. This led to a compound solution comprised of 50 m² of hybrid collectors mounted on the roof, 14 airboxes for ventilation installed in precise locations where the facade and floor slabs meet, and 800 m² of floor area supplied with radiant coils, all of which would be interconnected to heat or cool the building, with any excess energy removed and stored in the ground for use at a later time. The looping flows of energy moving hydraulically through the building pass through the heat pump, which serves as the heart of the overall system in regulating temperature according to need.

It goes without saying that sophisticated digital and sensory equipment are required for coordinating all of this technical gadgetry and making this or that device fulfill this or that task. And B35 has its share of software and sensors. Akin to a cybernetic organism that has enhanced abilities due to the integration of technical components that rely on feedback mechanisms, the building functions to temper the interior environment without the user's awareness of its interconnected and communicating systems. As technology-driven as B35 was becoming, there were moments when one wondered if the architecture would eventually disappear within the networks of tubes, cables, and coils connecting the geothermal reservoir below with the hybrid collectors above and everything in between, not unlike the well-known drawing Anatomy of a Dwelling by François Dallegret from the mid-1960s showing an unruly ensemble of domestic technology, but minus the house. That prospect notwithstanding, B35 would remain a project for a house, its architects opting for a non-representation of its admittedly short-lived technologies.

Since B35 was not being implemented in a laboratory but on a construction site, the changes proposed in Leibundgut's second position paper had to be incorporated on the run, that is, as the working drawings were being produced. So it was literally back to the drawing board, and that facade section with the coils and nearly no insulation was modified according to the engineer's new specifications scrupulously spelled out layer by layer, material by material, and performance value by performance value. While the facade was still a 'monolithic' wall of insulating concrete poured in place, the main difference was that there were no more coils and thus the thickness of the insulating boards had to be doubled (from 6cm to 12cm). But black it would remain, not only for aesthetic reasons but due to the simple fact that the color had already been approved by the city. Even with this alternative facade construction, which the engineer referred to simply as a "LowEx Variation," the rather heretical notion of building to 'waste' energy still stood, though in an environmentally minded way.

Radiant coils installed on top of floor slabs and on the roof of the water reservoir

Although the B35 prototype was becoming more refined as an interface of a building's technical operations and ecological systems, the research objectives did not always align with the realities on

Construction photograph showing airboxes and ductwork (blue) before being encased in the floor slab

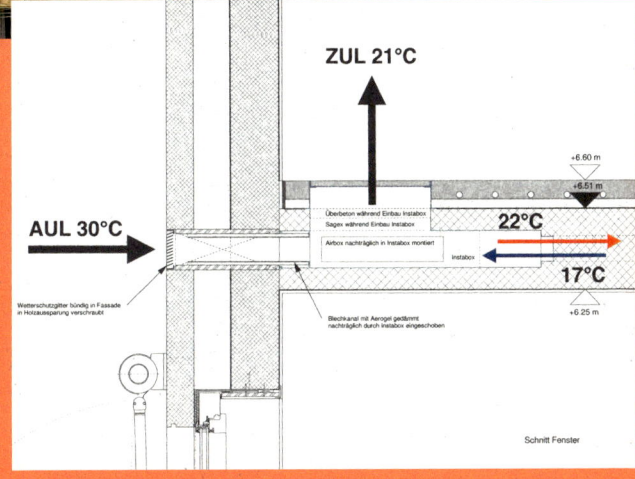

Section through airbox; summer scenario with an outdoor temperature of 30°C and indoor temperature of 21°C

Hybrid collectors comprised of photovoltaic and solar water panels

Installation of M-glass, heat-barrier window

TOWARDS ZERO-EMISSIONS ARCHITECTURE

Paradigm shift from energy-saving to emissions-free construction

Architecture must juggle manifold parameters – basic human needs, social and cultural requirements, climate change, material flows, and an economic use of available resources. It deals with complex systems both during the construction of a building and spatial planning. And in doing so, not only does it take matters of design, comfort, cultural diversity and the landscape into account; it is also constantly concerned with technical issues. For all these reasons, architecture has to – and can – play a key role in overcoming the most pressing global challenges.

Today, global warming is one such compelling task. In order to restrict the predicted temperature increase of 2°C, CO_2 emissions have to be reduced much more dramatically than anticipated by politics and industry. Switzerland currently meets as much as two thirds of its energy needs by burning fossil fuels. 40% of its electricity comes from nuclear power. Both technologies generate waste that has long-term consequences on a largely unpredictable scale. This is not compatible with the goals of sustainable development.

Switzerland therefore needs to modify its energy supply system. Architecture, construction and building technology have herein a key role to play: the housing stock, with its increasingly complex and energy-intensive systems, is currently responsible for around half of the total national energy consumption and CO_2 emissions. The scope for reductions is therefore enormous.

The "Energy Strategy for ETH Zurich" published in 2008 by the Energy Science Centre (ESC) calls for a reduction in CO_2 emissions to one ton per capita per year – the so-called "1-ton CO_2 society". This strategic approach is emissions-oriented and thus deviates from previous concepts like "minergy" and the "2000-Watt society", which are chiefly concerned with energy consumption. The "1-ton CO_2 society" is based upon renewable energies that are available in abundance. More efficient clean technologies for energy use and storage have been developed in recent years. The Department of Architecture takes ETH Zurich's energy strategy seriously and demonstrates what architecture, building and construction technology can do to reduce CO_2 emissions. This goes for both building construction and building operations.

Consequently, architecture needs to be fundamentally reoriented. The house of the future should be designed, constructed and evaluated in terms of its energy context. New approaches that combine different technologies and function emission-free are already available. Separating energy consumption from emissions no longer means saving energy at all cost, but rather preventing emissions – thus the call for a "zero emissions architecture".

This realignment can only succeed if it is broadly supported by a dialog between science, politics, industry, construction trades, professional associations, licensing authorities and architecture. To set things in motion, the Department of Architecture is thus looking to instigate a public debate at a conference in an attempt to confront the problem and find concrete solutions – and ultimately trigger a fundamental paradigm shift.

The Professors of the Department of Architecture

Faculty position paper entitled "Towards Zero-Emissions Architecture," April 21, 2010

Symposium on zero-emission architecture, ETH Zurich, November 19, 2010

the construction site. This meant going back to the laboratory, as it were, for further work on some of the components. The fans in the airboxes, for instance, were too loud for a residential building and so the motors required modification. There was also more development needed to increase the heat pump's coefficient of performance in order to surpass industry standards. The hybrid collectors on the roof would require adjustments as would the connections from the underground energy-exchange probes to the hydraulic bus distributors in the basement. Substantial work was also needed to make the various software packages compatible. Because each component had its own software and every company had its own system, the packages did not speak the same language and, even worse, were not communicating with each other at all. The digital brain of B35, in other words, was being hampered by computer babble even before the residents moved in.

The inevitable misalignments between research and practice were taken by the engineer more as an opportunity for further experimentation than cause for alarm. Even in error, he found something new, something important, something to build on. Back at the Institute of Technology in Architecture, mechanical engineers, software programmers, and specialists in building physics and dynamic building simulation pooled their expertise to push the envelope of system standards, while working to resolve any setbacks in component performance along the way. In the process, a series of industry start-ups were launched for manufacturing the requisite machines and constituent parts for projects like B35. In this sense, the B35 prototype constituted a threshold project situated between a laboratory for R&D and a test site for construction practice. While it is a place of residence with a fixed address, the project importantly became a platform for researching future trajectories of sustainable technologies that proceeded as much by the methodical reasoning of a scientist and systems thinker as by the trial-and-error tinkering of a bricoleur. It is little wonder that Leibundgut's collaborators at the institute referred to him fondly as "Daniel Düsentrieb" (the mad scientist Gyro Gearloose from the Donald Duck cartoon series).

Position Paper 3 – Research and Practice to Policy

While the architects were trying to incorporate the numerous system changes into the project as stipulated by the engineer, they were invited to participate in another exhibition, again with the B35 prototype featured as an example of best practice. The show, entitled *Building for the 2000-Watt Society*, was organized by the Building Department of the City of Zurich in late 2009 and was to be opened by a conference on architecture's contribution to reducing energy consumption to the benchmark of 2000 watts per person – amounting to a two-thirds reduction of the average used in Switzerland at the time. Considering the efforts taken to optimize the building's environmental performance, B35 seemed to be well-suited for this purpose, notwithstanding its claim that renewable energy could be 'wasted.'

But there were conflicting issues in play between the agenda to save energy by reducing consumption (2000 watts) and the agenda to reduce emissions by using renewable energy (LowEx), boiling down to a difference between quantitative and qualitative measures. B35 would nevertheless appear in the exhibition, but the architects and the engineer were officially uninvited to the conference just a few months prior to the event because the organizers were concerned that this very clash might cast doubt on the city's energy policy. This was perhaps understandable on account of Leibundgut's growing reputation as a renegade engineer or "energy Mephisto" as some would call him.

Having been barred from the conference, the two colleagues met again for lunch to discuss how best to deal with this slap in the face from city officials, while proactively addressing the delicate issue of energy politics. Strategies were quickly sketched out as were the main action points for initiating an overdue change in policymaking. It was decided that a position paper on behalf of the architecture faculty of ETH Zurich would be drafted, laying out new terms for reducing emissions in the building sector. This paper would serve as the basis for a symposium on zero-emission construction meant to further the cause through public debate. And if all of this went well, then perhaps more binding talks with governmental agencies would ensue. In the meantime, however, there were still pressing issues to be resolved with B35, the house on Bolleystrasse for which construction had just begun.

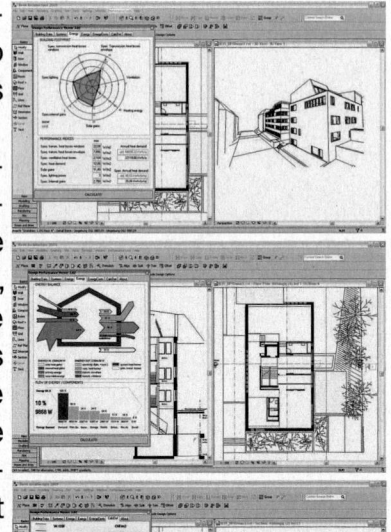

Digital model simulating energy-performance ratios and correlated costs, ETH Zurich, 2012

The faculty position paper – aimed at bridging academic research, building practice, and policymaking – would have to go through rounds of internal debate before being ratified and made public in 2010. There had been an earlier report from 2008 signed by all departments outlining the "Energy Strategy for ETH Zurich," which had already called for a reduction of CO_2 emissions to one ton per capita per year. That document promoted what is called the "one-ton-CO_2 society" and thereby deviated from both Swiss Minergie standards for low energy use and the 2000-watt society principle adopted by the city. Even then, the position of ETH Zurich as a publicly funded institution was at odds with that of public policy.

When the later position paper – entitled "Towards Zero-Emissions Architecture" – was ratified unanimously by the architecture faculty in April 2010, it expanded the argument in calling for a paradigm shift from energy-savings to emission-free construction, which was especially urgent, it was argued, to keep the global average temperature increase to well below 2 degrees Celsius. The paper thus anticipated the targets of the 2015 Paris Agreement some years later that pursued efforts to limit this increase to 1.5 degrees Celsius to further mitigate the impact on climate change. Acknowledging that the building stock in Switzerland accounts for nearly half of the energy consumed and CO_2 released into the atmosphere there, the 2010 faculty position paper underlined the drastic need to change the nation's energy supply system that in turn would require a change in how buildings are built and operated. The main goals of low emissions, low exergy, low material flows, low embedded energy, and low cost even exceeded some of the objectives of the B35 research, not to mention those of the building itself. Academic research, especially in this case, was exposed as being political to the core.

With the paper ratified, a televised press conference was held to announce the coming symposium on zero-emission architecture in November 2010, with the B35 prototype shown to substantiate the faculty's position. The symposium itself was considered successful by architects in articulating the necessary measures for aligning science, politics, industry, construction trades, professional associations, certification authorities, and architectural practice in order to make the proposed paradigm shift in energy policy palatable for policymakers. Yet the press reframed the symposium as an affront not only to Minergie and the 2000-watt society, but to the building industry as well. Keep in mind that trade lobbies here are strong, inasmuch as manufacturers stand to make a hefty profit from the surplus of materials required to meet such stringent standards – more

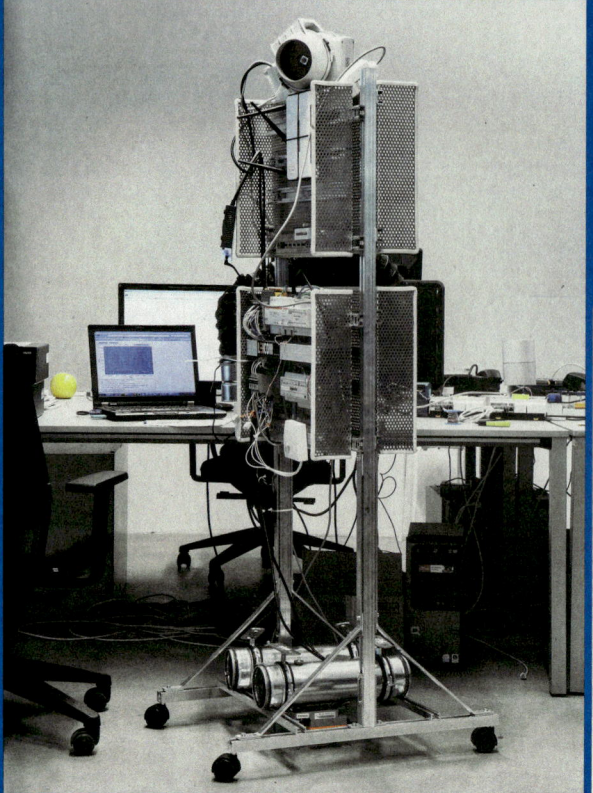

Laboratory of the software development start-up Mivune, Zurich (Stephan Rappo, 2011)

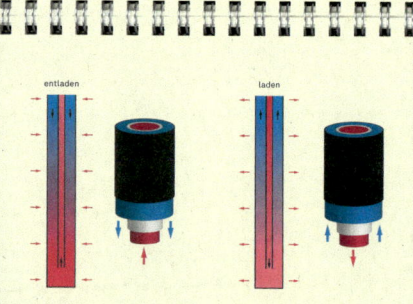

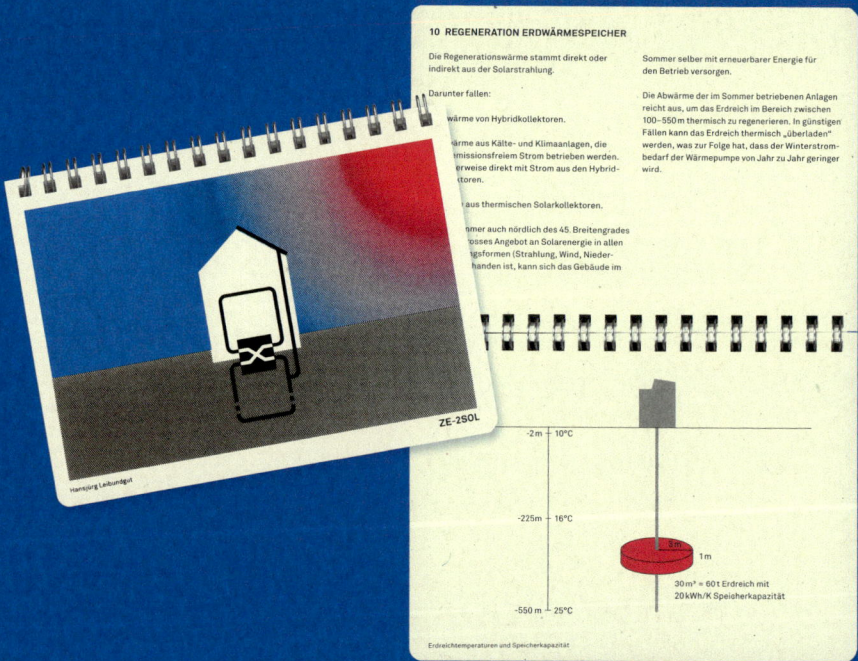

Pamphlet *ZE-2SOL* by Hansjürg Leibundgut on emission-free construction, 2013

insulation, more thermal glass, more complex facade assemblies, and so on. Somewhat flippantly, one newspaper even portrayed the event as a funeral for these venerable standards due to the all-black attire of architects in the audience. In any case, there was a predictable division among those in favor of a course change and those advocates of status quo energy policy, and B35 had become the battleground where these differences would collide.

Just a month later, the debate moved to the national level. Members of the Swiss Parliament submitted several pointed questions, or "interpellations," to the Federal Council requesting clarification on how to handle the political fallout of the faculty position paper from ETH Zurich. "Why is the Department of Architecture undermining federal energy politics?" "Is zero-emissions a legitimate paradigm shift or an economically detrimental sham?" And for heaven's sake, "Why attack Swiss industry?" Such was the gravity of the matter at hand, and these questions would make their way back to the engineer and architect who, in using B35 to prompt deliberation on sustainable ways to build, had set this whole process in motion.

In trying to navigate the highly politicized terrain of energy policy in a country already known for its environment-conscious practices, the two colleagues – with the support of other faculty members and the board of ETH Zurich – engaged in discussions with city officials responsible for the 2000-watt society initiative, members of the Minergie association, and politicians on both sides of the divide to identify common ground. It would take much mediation to eventually agree that the overriding goals of more conscientious energy use and reduced emissions were essentially oriented toward the same ends. The unresolved issue was how to get there.

Whereas the construction of B35 was completed in mid-2011, the research involved in that project would continue amidst even more heated debates on the future of energy use, the future of standards and certification labels, and the future of technology in the building sector. The definition of the 2000-watt society, for example, was revised to include the issue of emissions in its agenda (addressing not only their quantity but also their quality); Minergie likewise expanded its qualification standards for buildings with low emissions; and Leibundgut continued to work at the nexus of science and politics. Along with publishing his book *LowEx Building Design* and pamphlet *ZE-2SOL* on zero emissions as well as exploring the potential of solar energy to cool buildings in tropical climates, he went on to launch the REDEM (Reduction of

Emissions) initiative at the cantonal level of Zurich, which – though ultimately rejected by the cantonal parliament – aimed to set even more demanding energy standards for both new and refurbished buildings.

Even though the prototype on Bolleystrasse 35 had stirred up heated debates at the time as an example of the way forward in sustainable construction, while also prompting much-needed policy revisions, subsequent research would begin to highlight the blind spots not only of the project's underlying premises, but of the overall debate as well. By expanding the focus on energy and emissions to include the entire production and supply chain of materials and products, for instance, more recent work has brought the sustainability agenda to bear on upstream and downstream practices, that is, on practices operating long before and after building operations are even an issue. And with this sort of reorientation now drawing the attention of more architects, engineers, and policymakers to the bigger stakes of building sustainably, one wonders how those B35-like experiments still to come might serve to reposition research, practice, and policy once again.

Ceçi n'est pas un musée

Guggenheim Helsinki

	Use Circuits	Material Circuits

Discourses

René Magritte, *La Trahison des images* (*Ceçi n'est pas une pipe*), 1929

Use

the commons

Energy

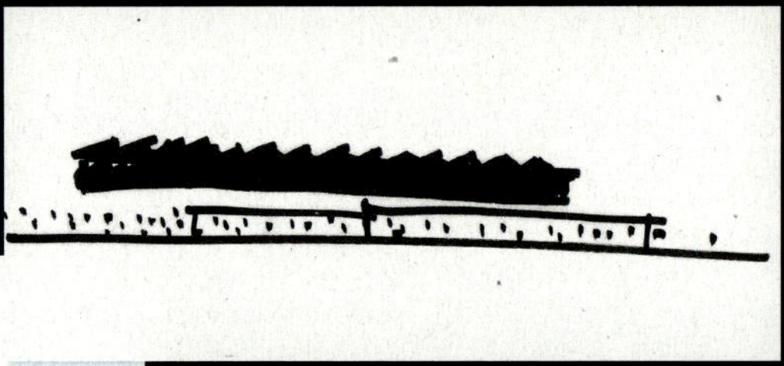

reuse existing building

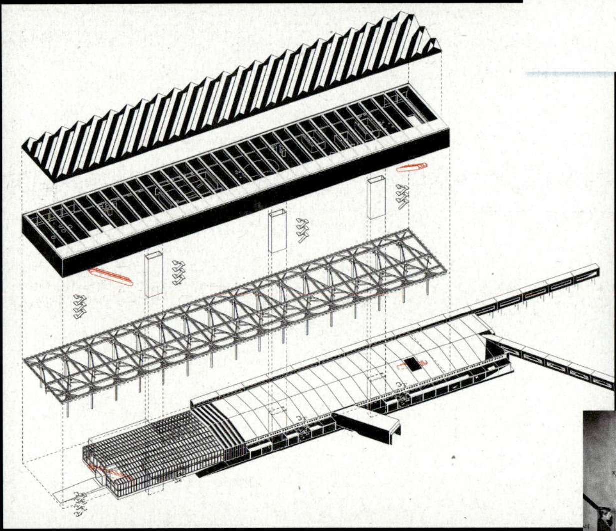

Materials

mine the city
full-zero concept

Economy

detective wall in the TV series *Life*, 2007

Technology

Methodology

fake competition     competing competitions

Policy

2011

186

| Energy Circuits | Aesthetic Circuits | Money Circuits |

Michael Sorkin et al., *The Helsinki Effect*, 2016

Guggenheim Abu Dhabi

3,000 m² hybrid collectors
8 probes @ >350m

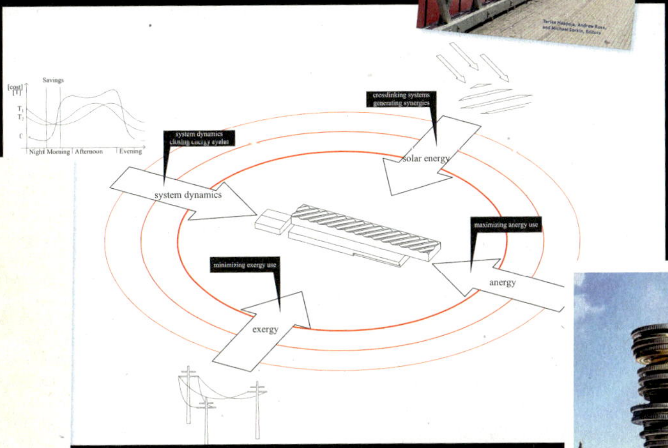

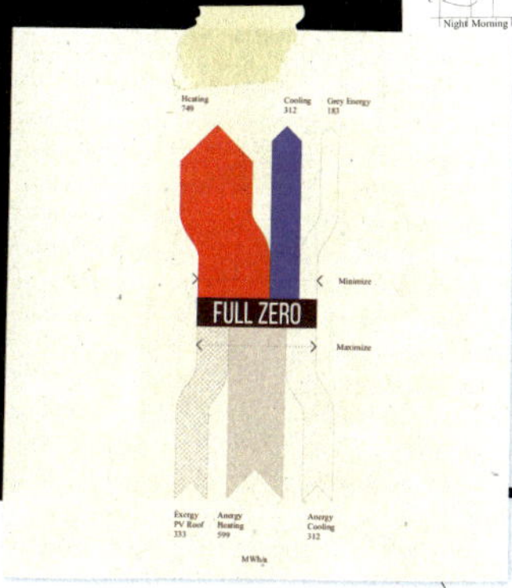

district grids

Kaarin Taipale, *Guggenheimin varjossa*, 2012

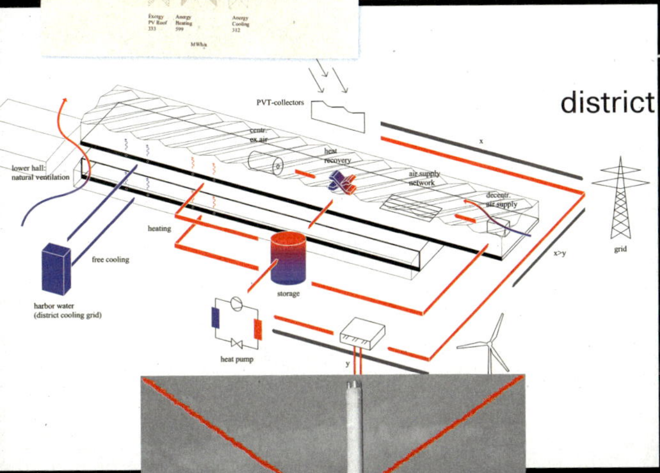

15.0 kg CO$_2$-eq./m²/a — 2020
7.5 kg CO$_2$-eq./m²/a — 2045
0.0 kg CO$_2$-eq./m²/a — 2070

no coal

heim sinki **NOW**

Makasiiniranta quality and concept competition

developer competition — 2022

Ceci n'est pas un musée

Ceçi n'est pas un musée
Guggenheim Helsinki
2014–2015

United under the rallying call "Occupy Guggenheim," activists gathered in the Fifth Avenue flagship museum in March 2014 to raise awareness about unfair labor practices and unsustainable resource excesses associated with the new Abu Dhabi branch then under construction. Fake dollar bills featuring Frank Gehry's exuberant design were thrown from the spiral ramp of the New York Guggenheim. For a moment, the central rotunda was filled with what appeared to be confetti in protest of the disparity between "ultra-luxury art" and "ultra-low wages" paid to immigrant workers throughout the Gulf region, not to mention the exorbitant use of material and energy required to sustain iconic form. Projections on the outside of the museum made the action inside an impromptu public event for passersby in an effort to prompt collective concern.

    This act of defiance was only one of several such prominent actions undertaken by Global Ultra Luxury Faction (GULF), all of which essentially appropriated the cultural capital of Guggenheim to criticize the institution's indifference to its own exploitative modes of operation as exemplified in Abu Dhabi.

    On a mock-up of Guggenheim's corporate website, GULF also issued a fake press release at the same time announcing an open "Sustainable Design Competition for the Abu Dhabi Branch" that, if actually carried out, would replace Gehry's scheme with a

Intervention in the New York Guggenheim rotunda criticizing the museum's exploitative practices, 2014 (GULF)

Fake dollar bill protesting unsustainable and unfair labor practices in Abu Dhabi, 2014 (Noah Fischer, Collective Occupy Museums)

Projections by Global Ultra Luxury Faction (GULF) on the New York Guggenheim Museum, 2014/2016

socially and environmentally conscious proposal. Though only a spoof, this architecture competition was staged to spotlight the exclusivity of high culture for the 1%, asking hypothetically: "What would constitute a museum that is informed by the principles of sustainability, accountability, and social justice?"

Aware of the sway that competitions have on architects, GULF hijacked the medium of the design competition to advance a well-intentioned cause bearing not only on cultural patrons like Guggenheim, but also on design practices that uncritically cater to such clients. Architecture was thereby implicated for its role in upholding the status quo of 'ultra-design' at the service of the privileged few. It would not be long before GULF would join forces with other like-minded activists to launch yet another competition, this time for real and in response to Guggenheim's official competition for a new satellite museum in Helsinki, one meant to set the record straight once and for all in response to past critiques and thus save the reputation of the Guggenheim brand.

Competing Competitions

Design competitions are notorious as a means to solicit ideas from architects for little or no compensation. The call for entries for this or that project in any given setting usually serves to raise the profile of a venue as well as the value of the property to be developed, including that of its immediate surroundings. While investors are always eager to get a bang for their buck, countless architects – their corps of engineers and landscape architects included – more often than not find themselves shamelessly exploited when exploring design solutions to the challenge at hand in the hope of winning a prized commission. Unfair terms and conditions notwithstanding, designers will no doubt continue to submit their best laid plans essentially for free, willingly submitting to the game of give-and-take that comes with any competition bid.

The status quo of architecture competitions is troubling enough in and of itself. Yet add a high-profile player like Guggenheim to the mix as a patron keen on expanding its transnational reach with a new game-changing museum, and the stakes are raised considerably for all parties involved, be they in favor of the venture or not. This was certainly the case when two open competitions for promoting the arts in Helsinki were announced concurrently in mid-2014, one for a new Guggenheim in the heart of the city, the other calling for public alternatives to the Guggenheim model of culture-led development. The desire to capitalize on a global success story by

The Helsinki Effect, Terike Haapoja, Andrew Ross, and Michael Sorkin, eds.; a publication on the counter-competition, 2016 (cover art: Klas Eriksson, *Forza Rosa Fluff;* photograph by Annika von Hausswolff, 2015)

bringing the "Bilbao Effect" to Finland was countered by what would be called the "Helsinki Effect" to promote projects rooted in local values and driven by local initiative. The competing competitions seemed to advocate similar goals in trying to stimulate ideas about possible paths for Helsinki's revival. The decisive issue, however, was whether development would proceed locally from within the host context or globally via a model from outside.

The prospect of a new Guggenheim rising on prime property along Helsinki's South Harbor was controversial from the outset, to say the least, setting off a flow of claims and counterclaims regarding the city's future development, debates about the role of architecture as cultural agent of change, and discourses about sustainable practices of urban renewal.

Those supporting the official project included the city's mayor, local business elites, centrist political parties, and, of course, the Solomon R. Guggenheim Foundation, all of whom campaigned for launching an international design competition that would eventually be made public under the heading Helsinki Now.

Opposition to the venture came by way of a coalition of local and international activists, including Checkpoint Helsinki and the New York–based nonprofit organizations GULF and Terreform, who, in alliance with leftist politicians of the Social Democratic Party, launched The Next Helsinki competition in protest of the one officially underway.

In an effort to rid itself of the Abu Dhabi stigma, Guggenheim opted for an open competition rather than directly commissioning a star architect for another blockbuster project. The scale of the proposed museum in Helsinki was significantly reduced in comparison to other affiliated branches to minimize costs – half the size of Bilbao and a third of the one in Abu Dhabi. Just as important were the strict standards for ensuring a minimal ecological footprint, both during construction and throughout the building's operational life cycle. Above all, there would be no iconic form! With these stipulations, the brief for the Guggenheim Helsinki Design Competition read like a mission statement from an institution in the process of redressing its self-image by appearing to be more modest in its ambition, more attentive to public needs, and more aware of the project's environmental impact.

The counter-competition, though similar in content and aspiration to Guggenheim's bid, was nevertheless positioned in resistance to the global franchise playbook of Bilbao Effect architecture. Organizers of The Next Helsinki competition projected all the ills correlated with such practices onto the official brief, going so far as to suggest that Guggenheim's about-face reforms did nothing more than pay lip service to a noble cause for the sake of more profit. The core issue here was whether the proposed project would be done with or without Guggenheim, and whether a public-funded initiative drawing on local resources would not be more beneficial for promoting the arts than a public-private partnership with a global player running the show.

Despite all efforts to distinguish the two design programs, most entries for both competitions fell into the trap of producing form for form's sake, with proposed schemes playing into the scenario of a gentrified harbor district. All in all, the competing competitions, while differing on the issue of how the project would be financed, seemed to converge on the matter of how architecture might spearhead cultural-led development, regardless of the claims and counterclaims from either side.

Entry GH-1128435973

Among the 1,700 projects submitted for Guggenheim Helsinki, entry GH-1128435973 could just as well have been submitted to the alternative competition. It fulfilled the requirements of the official brief, while managing to incorporate the critique of a franchise museum into the design strategy, thereby complying with the anti-Guggenheim stance of The Next Helsinki mandate as well. In essence, the entry had a dual agenda, proposing a museum that at the same time

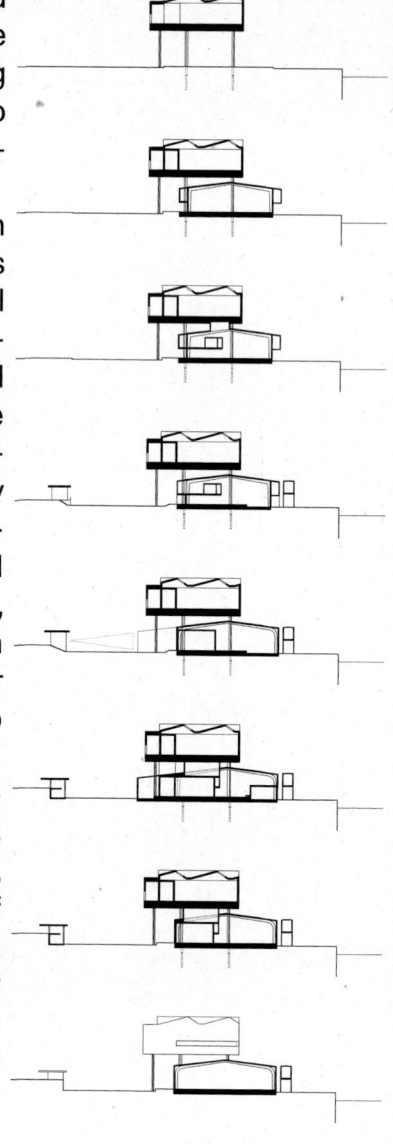

Sectional sequence through ferry terminal and exhibition hall

is *not* a museum in any ordinary sense, as its title suggested: Ceçi n'est pas un musée – a nod to André Malraux's use of the phrase alluding to René Magritte's famous painting *Ceçi n'est pas une pipe*. In the end, this ambiguity caught the jury's attention in that the project was awarded second place among the shortlisted finalists.

In the initial competition phase, the designers opted for an approach that would incite debate among disparate team members. For this role-playing game, pitting protagonists against antagonists, a large bulletin board was assembled on a wall in the atelier, not unlike those used by detectives to solve a case. Different positions – even contradictory ones – were mapped out concerning what a contemporary museum could be or not be. Was it possible to no longer do as museums do?

During the six short weeks available for crafting a viable response to this very question, strategies were in constant flux as multiple voices weighed in on the design process. Spatial diagrams were arranged and rearranged on the wall alongside theoretical references, site information, functional requirements, energy performance, aesthetic considerations, and the like. The interconnected lines of thought and cross-references offered clues about possible design solutions.

Having advanced to the second phase, the team could expand upon the early rounds of strategizing by way of on-site discussions with a range of stakeholders from both sides of the Guggenheim face-off. These included activists from Checkpoint Helsinki opposed to the official competition, local politicians for and against the project, and museum curators from Guggenheim and competing local institutions. In dialogue with experts from other disciplines, the project was developed in more detail along five thematic circuits pertaining to (a) fluctuations of use of the building over time; (b) material streams throughout the building's life cycle; (c) energy flows through and beyond the building; (d) short- and long-term transformation of the building's aesthetic; and (e) shifting channels of monetary resources in view of the politics of culture-led development. In response to these interrelated circuits, emphasis was placed on how to maximize the building's overall performance through minimal architectural means.

(a) Use Circuits

Considering the self-imposed challenge of designing a museum that is not a museum, the team envisioned a two-in-one facility, with one volume hovering above the other. Set into an ambiguous

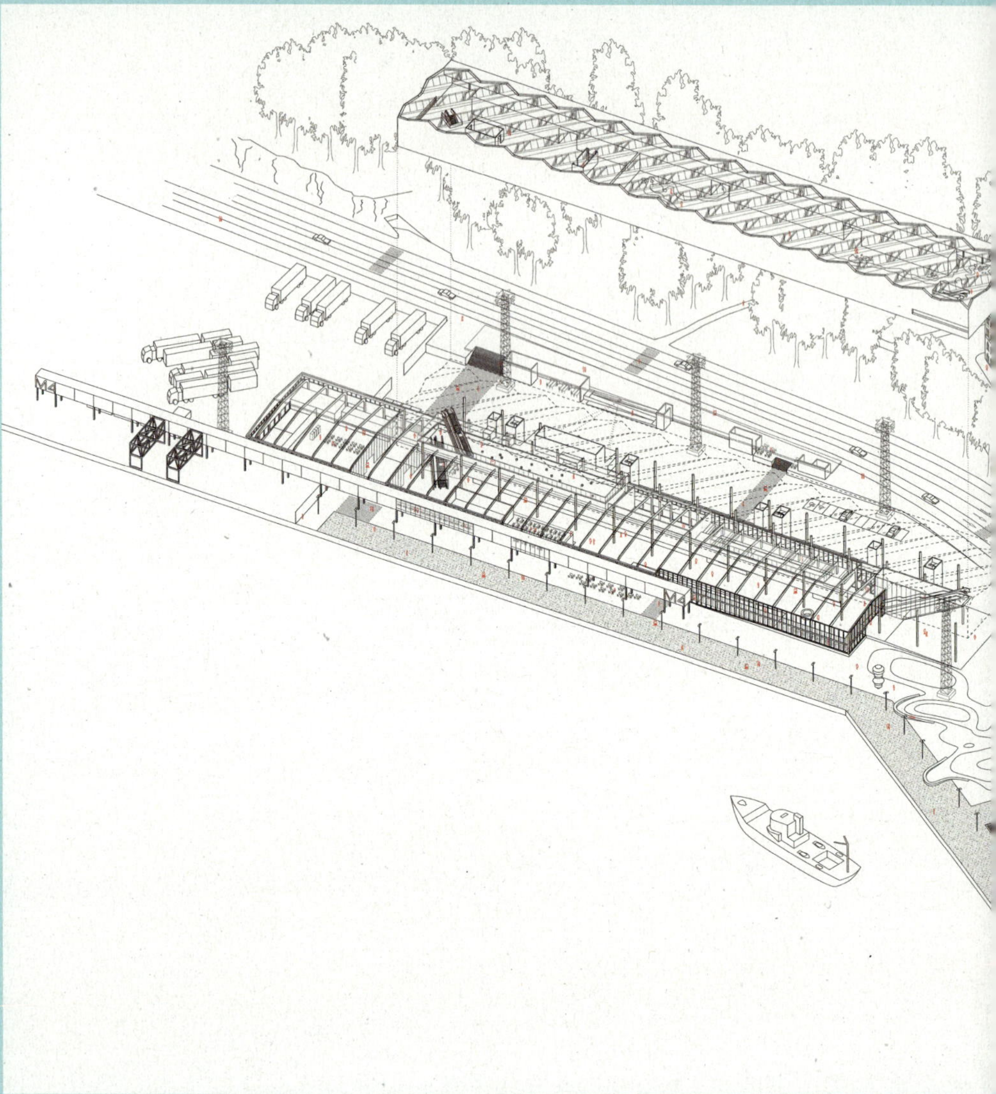

Exploded axonometric drawing; lower part for public activities and upper part for exhibitions

Phase one competition boards of entry GH-1128435973 Ceçi n'est pas un musée

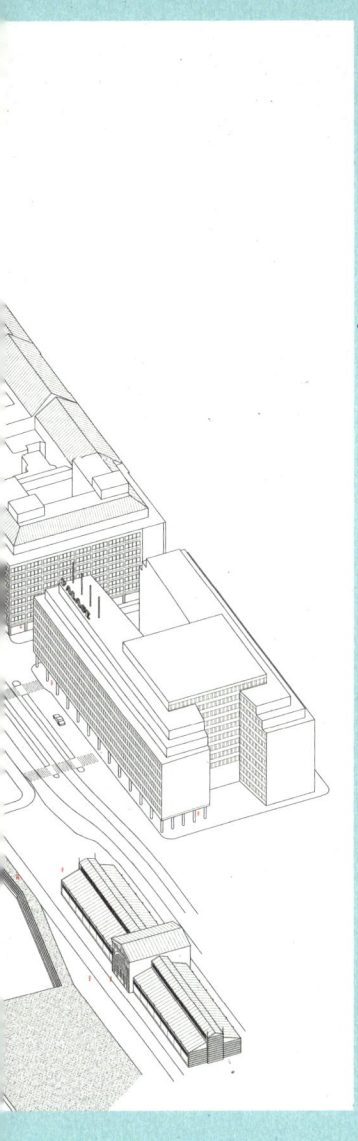
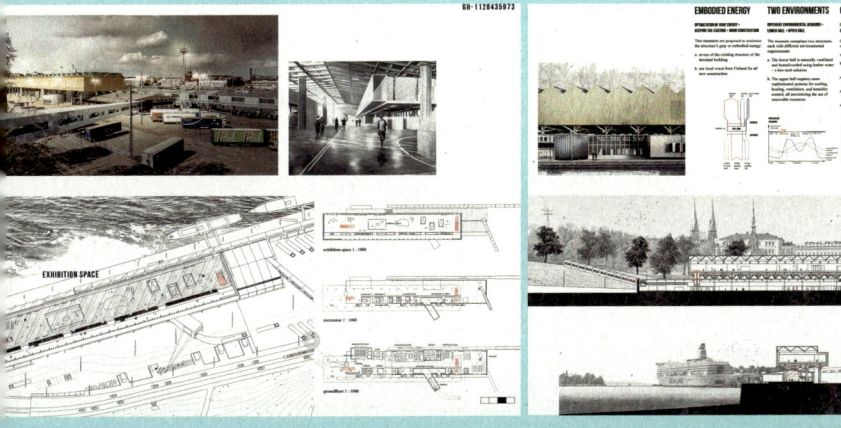

Pinboard used during the initial competition phase, 2014

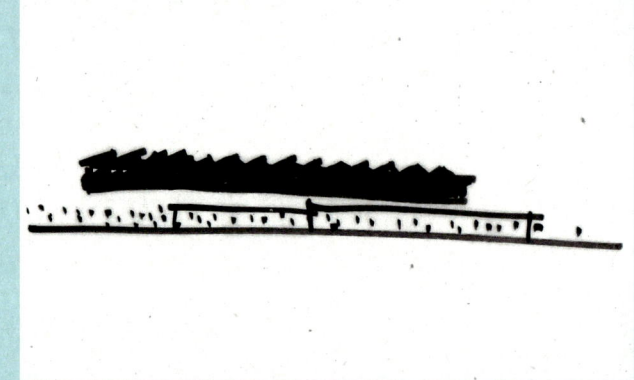

Sectional strategy of the design proposal

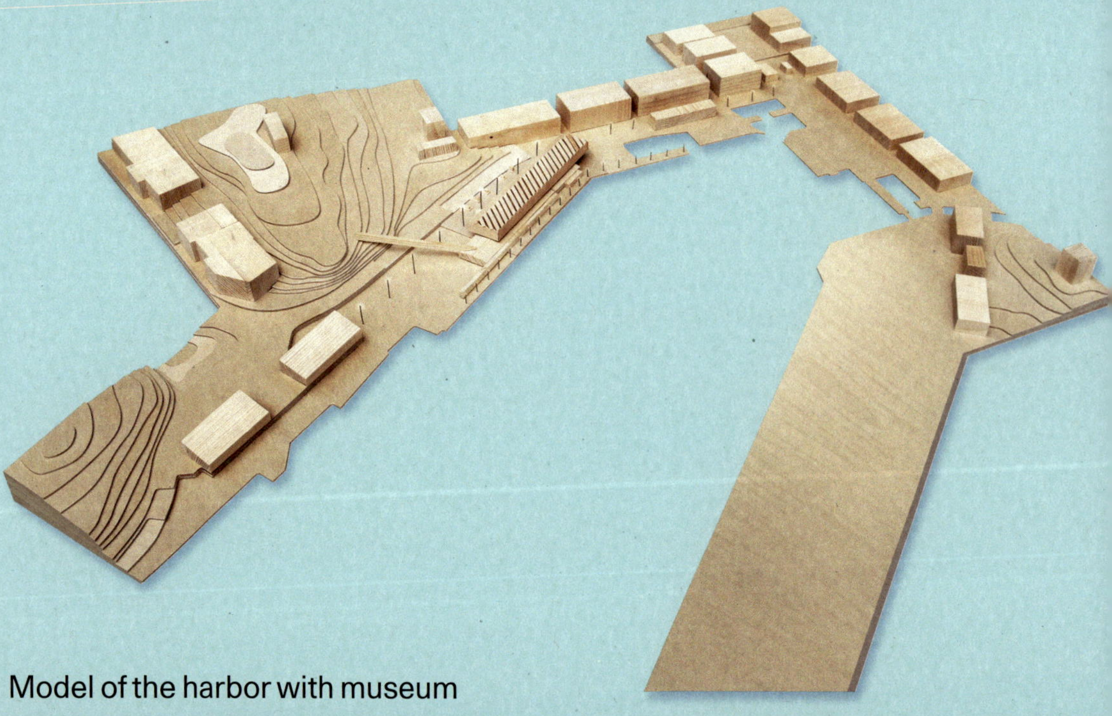

Model of the harbor with museum

Still from the TV series *Life* showing a detective wall with evidence assembled, 2007 (Ravich-Shariat Productions)

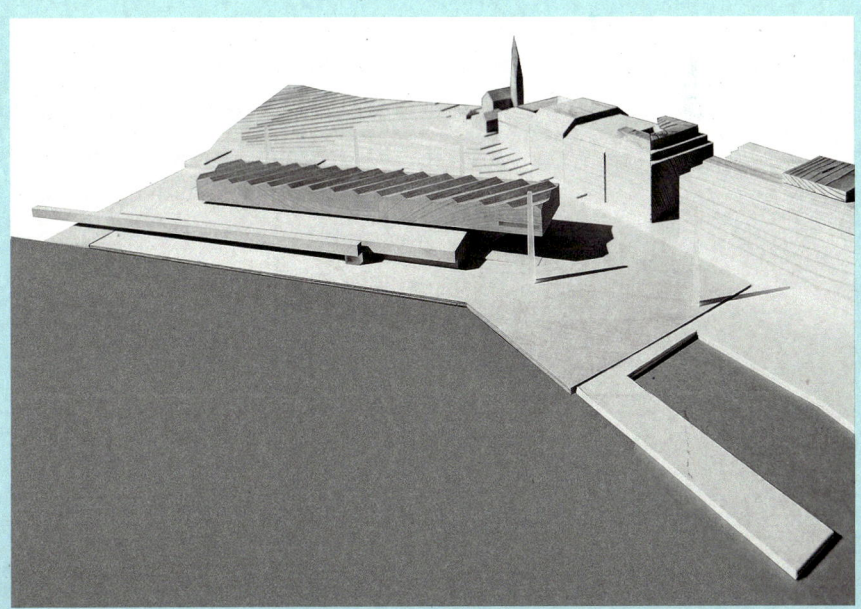

Proposed scheme between port facility and boardwalk

Ceçi n'est pas un musée

dialogue, the volumes share the same site, yet each has its own distinct qualities: one old, the other new; one open, the other insular; one informal, the other formal. The twin parts, though contradictory in their properties, are nonetheless mutually reinforcing in their interrelated uses. So what began as a two-in-one scheme, in effect evolved into an x-in-one facility that is at once determined and indeterminate.

The lower part opens directly onto the tarmac of the South Harbor. It was decided early on to keep the existing ferry terminal and maintain its original function as a hub for arriving and departing passengers, and thus its role as the city's port of entry. Additionally, it was expanded to become a collective threshold accessible to all free of charge, offering a communal domain of open-ended uses. Part workshop, part community center, part gathering place, this space – essentially informal in character – extends the pedestrian boardwalk into the building for public events within the city. Given this embedded potential in what already exists, a relatively neutral scheme was devised to facilitate the proliferation of unplanned uses and social exchange.

Above the flurry of activities on the harbor level, the upper volume serves as the museum proper for housing art. Although more formal, this space nevertheless has the utilitarian bluntness of a warehouse, with skylights, rough finishes, and straightforward installations. Removed from everyday life below, this hall on stilts offers a place of refuge and upholds the notion of the museum as an 'other space.' Flexibility is the rule, inasmuch as this column-free container can house numerous shows simultaneously as easily as it can accommodate one large exhibition. The volume does not rely on internal complexity, but rather settles for a discreet form to do the job. Here, art determines the way it is experienced instead of the building determining how it is shown.

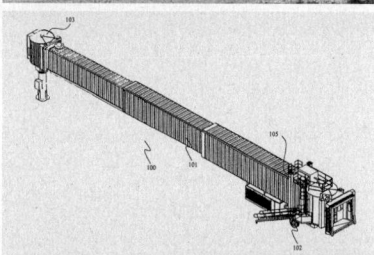

All things considered, such design moves could have been made *with* or *without* Guggenheim. Bearing in mind, however, that the announcement of yet another Guggenheim venture was ambivalently

Array of references of industrial harbor architecture informing the design proposal

received in Helsinki from the very beginning, the team even speculated about the facility changing hands over time, with Guggenheim being only a provisional tenant. This made sense in light of the recent history of failed franchises around the globe, be it in Rio, Guadalajara, New York, Vilnius, or Taichung. Even the small branches of the brand in Soho, Las Vegas, and Berlin proved to be short-lived. So why assume that Guggenheim would settle down in Helsinki? And for that matter, why design a museum for a particular patron at all? Given the prospect that the building may well outlive the client, the scheme was intentionally unspecific by design and could accommodate even unanticipated uses, to say nothing of ever-changing needs of ever-changing clients. As maxim and method, Ceçi n'est pas un musée seems to have been on the right track all along.

(b) Material Circuits

In view of the stipulations in the competition brief that the museum had to be sustainable, one would think that the choice of materials, their source, their embedded energy, and how they are assembled and then disassembled for reuse would have been a central issue in any submitted proposal. In hindsight, however, this proved not to be the case, with most entries having chosen the purely formal route. But for any project to have been truly sustainable, it would have to have gone beyond the rather obvious call for wood as *the* solution, as if this measure alone would make any project environmentally sound.

Whereas entry GH-1128435973 did indeed make use of Finnish timber where it made sense, other more pressing matters were addressed as well, not least of which being how to utilize the available material stock of the existing Makasiini Terminal on site to reduce the gray energy footprint of the proposal. Consequently, the terminal was incorporated into the design, very much in the spirit of the axiom "Never demolish, never remove, or replace, always add, transform, and re-use!" The decision to keep the building not only made environmental sense, but it also backed up the idea of maintaining the terminal's original function as part of the museum's expanded program.

The notion of mining the city's existing buildings made sense considering the recent history of building reuse for cultural purposes as part of a broader approach to urban revitalization in Helsinki. A case in point is the large conversion project of the Cable Factory that successfully transformed an industrial facility into a new hub for the arts. A similar reclamation initiative involved the renovation of the

Sectional model through the Makasiini Terminal and exhibition space

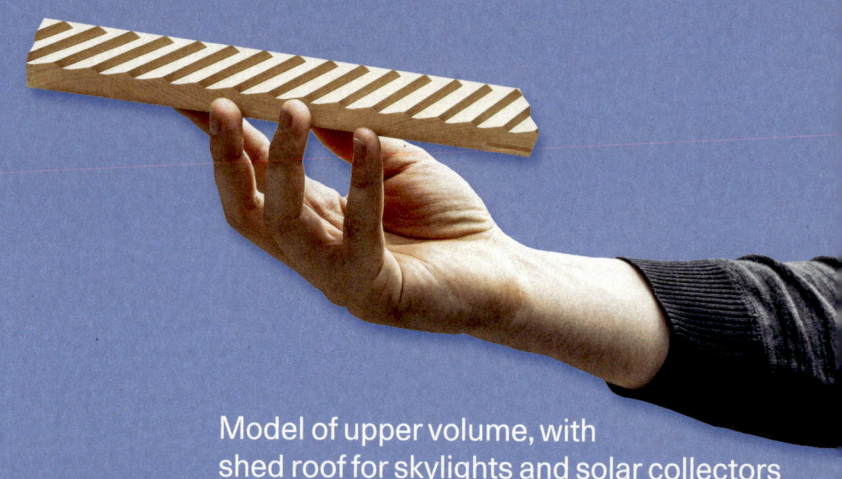

Model of upper volume, with shed roof for skylights and solar collectors

Piecemeal facade assembly of the existing ferry terminal

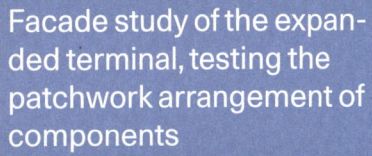

Facade study of the expanded terminal, testing the patchwork arrangement of components

Study exploring the relationship of facade materials

defunct Suvilahti Power Plant as the center of a new cultural district. And the same goes for the remodeling of the Tennis Palace for the Helsinki Art Museum, or HAM, which is now home to the country's largest art collection. All such precedents attest to the viability of repurposing the city's building stock, which made the proposal to keep the Makasiini Terminal in Helsinki's South Harbor all the more justified.

The idea of mining the city's building stock was also applied to the materials used for the terminal extension. The existing terminal itself was already a bricolage of construction components, so it only seemed reasonable to follow the same logic for the lower volume. Building elements from local demolition sites would essentially be recommissioned as part of the new facade assembly for the terminal, thereby making the ground level spaces a veritable depository of reused materials, while resituating the Guggenheim brand within a discourse on circular material circuits – a first for this cultural benefactor of the arts.

(c) Energy Circuits

In collaboration with the next generation of mechanical engineers and energy reseachers from the office Keoto (as in Kyoto Protocol), a pathbreaking concept was developed that aimed at making the architecture produce more energy than it embodies and consumes in time. To achieve this, what first had to be accounted for was (α) the building's embodied or gray energy, (β) the building's operational energy, and (γ) the building's energy production capacity over time. With a wry sense of humor, the engineers and architects used the formula (α) + (β) = (γ) to calculate that it would take only 50 years for the building to generate enough energy to cancel out that embedded in its construction, plus that needed for its operations during that time. From this it follows that the longer the building lasts, the smaller its ecological footprint, considering that throughout this period the building would eventually reduce its own energy 'debt' to near zero.

ZERO: Countdown to Tomorrow, 1950s–60s, Valerie Hillings, with contributions by Daniel Birnbaum, Edouard Derom, Johan Pas, Dirk Pörschmann, and Margriet Schavemaker (New York: Guggenheim Museum Publications, 2014)

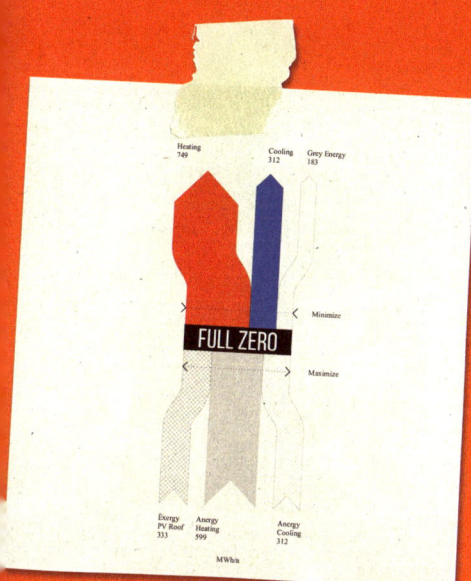

Energy flows of the proposal's full-zero concept (Keoto)

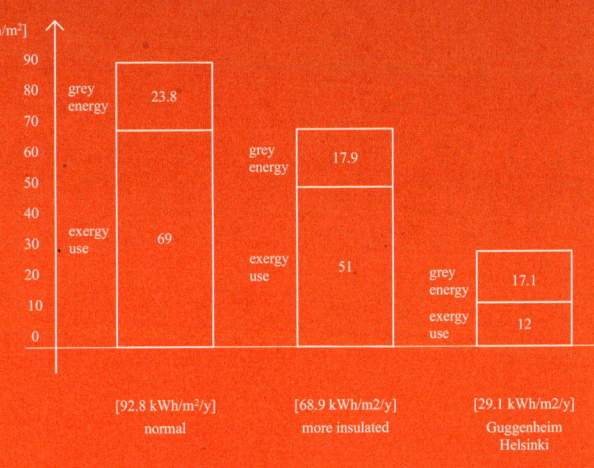

Comparative diagram showing gray energy and exergy use in kWh/m² per annum

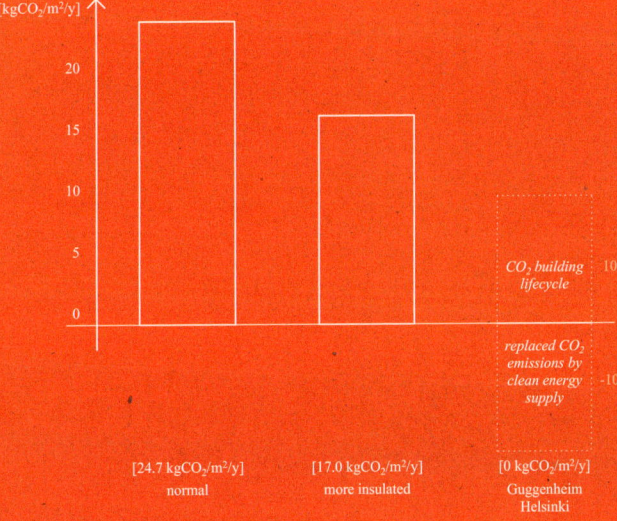

Comparative diagram showing CO_2 emissions in kg CO_2/m² per annum

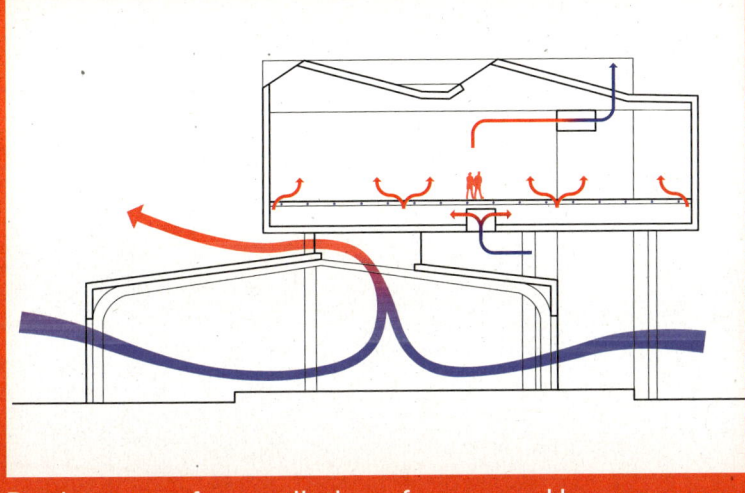

Dual strategy for ventilation of upper and lower spaces

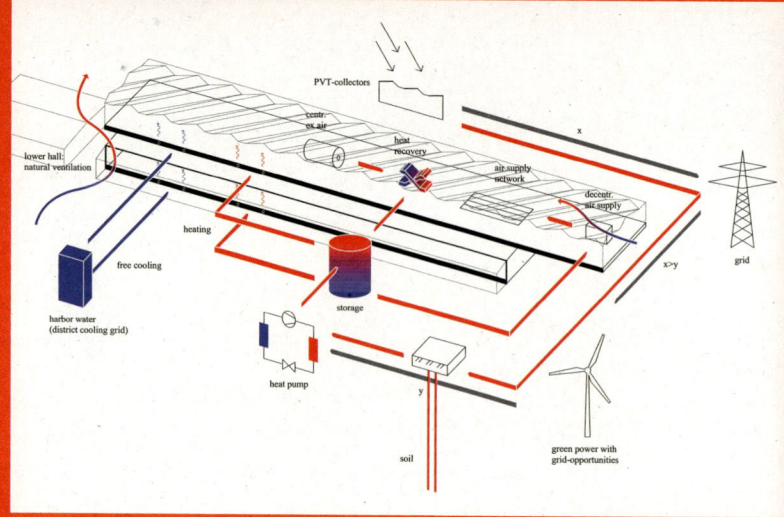

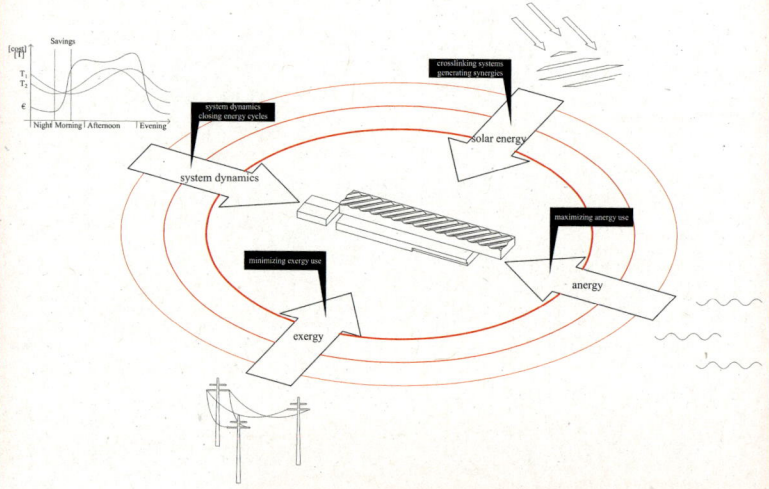

Integration of the building in the network of municipal grids

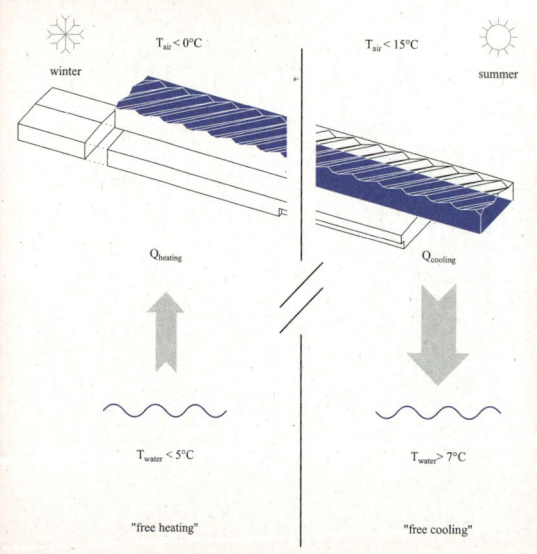

Use of harbor water for cooling and heating in summer and winter

But this was only one zero on the table. The engineers had proposed a 'full-zero concept,' which also aimed to minimize greenhouse gas emissions over the building's life cycle, if not eliminate them altogether via a near-zero carbon architecture. Based on the materials used, the energy-generating capacity of the hybrid collectors on the roof, and the use of harbor water for heating and cooling, among other measures, the building itself would be a repository of low-carbon components as well as a generator of renewable energy, constituting a double-0 or '00-museum,' as it were.

Additionally, the building made use of the storage capacity of several existing municipal grids, thus embedding the facility in a larger citywide energy network.

As for the electrical grid, photovoltaic panels (integrated in the hybrid collectors on the shed roof) would feed excess energy into this network, using it as a sink for later use, when necessary, which had become a standard practice by that time.

Keeping in mind that Helsinki's district cooling grid capitalizes on the abundance of water in the harbor as a super-energy reservoir, the proposed building would take advantage of this emission-free solution for its own needs as well.

An entirely different approach, however, was sought with regards to Helsinki's heating grid, which surprisingly still relies on imported coal and natural gas from Russia. Instead of drawing from this CO_2-intensive system, the proposed museum would feed its emission-free energy surplus into this grid.

In sum, these measures were meant to make the Guggenheim Helsinki function as an integral node in the overall municipal energy system to reduce the city's dependence on fossil fuels over time and improve the environmental impact of its thermal network. By integrating the building into the greater infrastructural context, at times taking, at times giving, it becomes part of a greater public works project. Moreover, such measures promised to make the proposed Guggenheim an ecological landmark, not in terms of its form per se, but due to its environmental performance.

(d) Aesthetic Circuits

In addition to the more technical aspects of the design, aesthetic considerations were debated with equal intensity. The competition site is located at the threshold between two fundamentally different parts of the city, one strictly industrial and serving harbor operations, the other a gentrified district along the boardwalk full of leisurely amenities. From the side of pro-growth business elites and politicians, nothing could be better than a new icon landing in the harbor that would set off a wave of upscale development throughout the revitalized waterfront district – a 'dreamville' if there ever was one. Then again, the design team, having sided with pro-harbor advocates, was adamant about maintaining the industrial function of the site and underscoring the proposed building's role as a transitional space between disparate urban contexts, as if to insert a hyphen between them. To this end, an inventory was made of the attendant machinery of everyday harbor architecture that could be combined with the civic services of a museum.

The tarmac itself was treated as the connective element of both realms, being developed as the choreographic underlay for all ground-level activities – port operations, maintenance, and museum deliveries included. Along with the customary graphics of arrows and dashed lines for directing flows of traffic, subtle depressions in the surface were to create pockets where rainwater or melting snow could collect, generating shallow puddles of water and thin ice slicks distributed so as to direct the movement of visitors. On top of these more intentional design moves come the haphazard traces of everyday use combined with general wear and tear, all adding yet another veneer to the harbor's blacktop.

In collaboration with Berlin-based artist Karin Sander, studies were made for how the facades could respond over time to various environmental conditions, particularly those that come with the harsh climate of Helsinki. Inspired by her so-called *Gebrauchsbilder* (use- or patina-paintings), which result from circumstantial processes on site that leave their traces on a canvas left in a particular location, the museum facades would likewise directly index the dynamics of the surroundings, their appearance always subject to change in reaction to rain, snow, and sun. The outer envelope of the upper volume, for instance, was to be constructed of a doubled screen of expanded metal mesh mounted in front of a water- and wind-resistant, brass-coated foil that reflects light. The overlap of these layers, plus any accumulated snow, ice, dew, dirt, and gull droppings, would produce an erratic moiré effect not unlike the shimmering polar lights of the aurora borealis common in the region. The haptic quality of surface in this case would essentially be produced by happenstance and the inclemency of the elements. Even the building's aging process would be registered as part of the open effect of its ever-changing aesthetic expression.

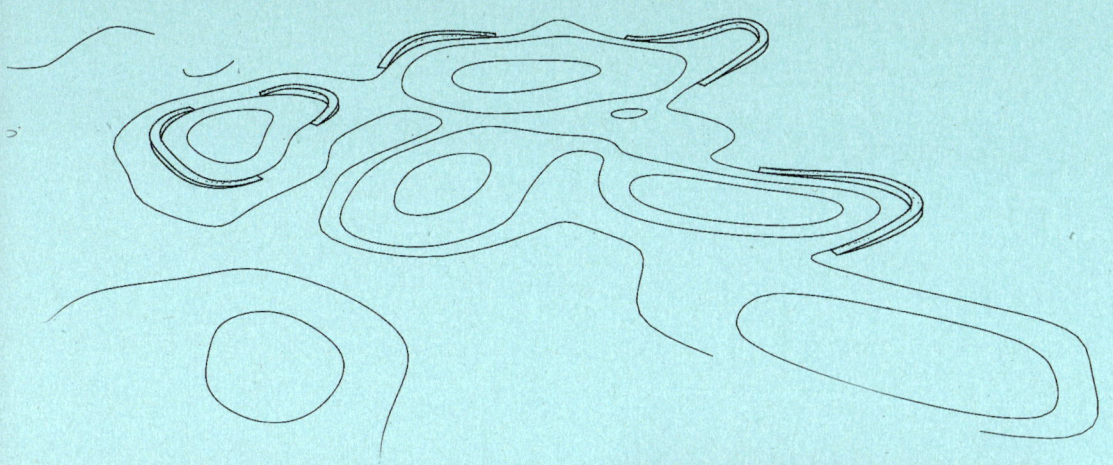

Tarmac surface sculpted to collect snow and rain as part of the harbor level landscape

Reference image for the tarmac level showing construction stencils for the MoMA roof garden, 2004

Modulated landscape topography

207

Karin Sander, *Gebrauchsbild 168, Einen Winter im Garten, 2013–14*, produced by leaving a canvas on the ground for a year (courtesy Karin Sander)

Image of snow collecting on a metal mesh used as reference for the facade

Material study of the double-layered screen of expanded metal mesh mounted in front of brass-coated foils

Facade study of upper volume with moiré pattern

(e) Money Circuits

Looking back on the Guggenheim Helsinki episode that would have brought a new branch museum to the Finnish capital in an effort to raise its cultural profile, it becomes clear that the story had little to do with architecture in the end, save for its role as a pawn in the heady game of global finance and the politics of culture-led development. Though competition finalists did everything possible to reduce the construction and operational costs of their respective submissions, any savings on this design front were negligible compared to the speculative sums associated with the entire venture over and above the cost of a new museum.

At issue for promoters of the Guggenheim Helsinki were the enticing – yet unrealistic – projections for incoming revenue to the city brought in by hordes of tourists and visitors, estimated at a lofty $60 million per year. There was also all the lucrative real estate development in the harbor district that a brand-name venue would purportedly set in motion. Given, however, that this grand plan was to be financed with a mixture of public and private money (the former footing the bulk of the $180 million bill), it would be Finnish taxpayers at the end of the day who would bear most of the burden. As Social Democrats argued: "Everything was to be financed by the city – the land, the construction, the upkeep of the building, the salaries, the license fee, everything." Furthermore, money from public coffers would finance not only the museum but also the infrastructural upgrades associated with development-led revitalization – and that in a welfare state undergoing austerity measures to recover from an economic downturn.

As questionable as such spending might have been, it was believed among conservative circles that a 'world-class' museum was key to catalyzing urban regeneration in Helsinki, enchanted as they were by the 'Cinderella' story of Bilbao. In keeping with this dream, Helsinki would be crowned as a capital of culture and design. It would thus enter the global intercity competition to attract mobile capital that pits city against city and sends financiers scrambling to find new private investment spaces for corporate capital to circulate, extract, and accumulate. As it would seem, the vehicle of choice these days to reinvigorate urban economies is the museum, which itself has become the art-washed embodiment of financialization at large.

Under these circumstances, it hardly comes as a surprise that the City Council of Helsinki eventually rejected the controversial Guggenheim project in late 2016, bringing a long and expensive

Proposed building in its urban context viewed from across the harbor

Parking lot on the site of what would have been the location of the Guggenheim Helsinki

process to a full stop nearly two years after the official competition and the counter-competition were announced. One is left to wonder if the project would have had another fate if Guggenheim had not been part of the equation. Moreover, it remains anyone's guess if a museum was indeed the appropriate program for a design competition in this context, let alone for stimulating the economy in a city that already has an abundance of art venues that are sustainable in and of themselves as local institutions. For the time being, however, and in spite of all the debates that both competitions prompted about promoting the arts, about reinvigorating civic space, and about foregrounding environmental sustainability, the only thing to show for that effort is a lackluster parking lot at the harbor silently claiming "Il n'y a pas de musée."

In mid-2021, however, the City of Helsinki announced yet another competition, this time for the large-scale redevelopment of the entire waterfront district, including, of all things, a new architecture and design museum. The caveat in this latest call for bids is that the work is to be carried out by operators in the construction and real estate industry, or consortia thereof. If this particular venture does indeed deliver on its promise, then the prime piece of property on which Guggenheim once wanted to build will be transferred from the coffers of the city to the portfolio of investors and developers, with the private sector announced as the ultimate winner of the competition.

Experiments in Timber Prefab

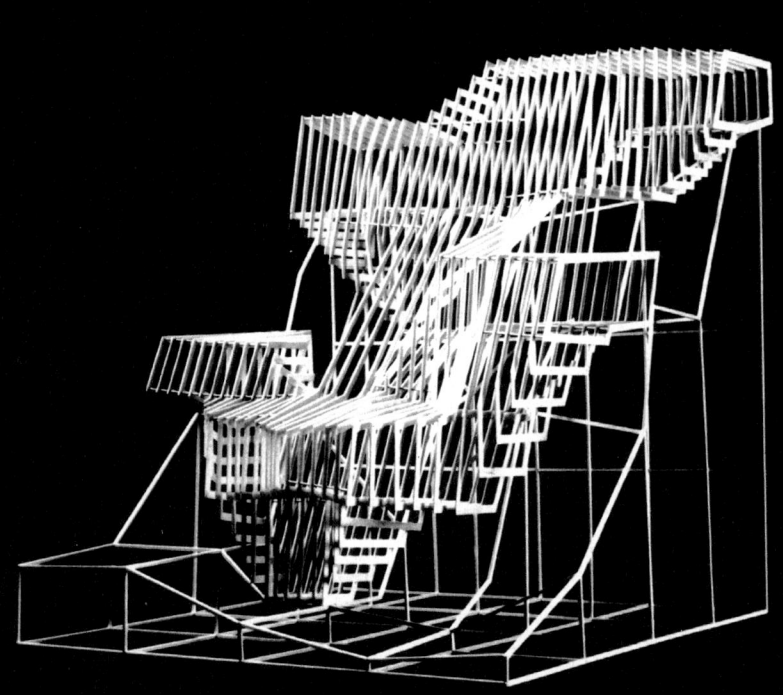

A Genealogy of Projects

reduce ... reduce embodied energy

$1m^3$ wood stores 1 metric tonne of CO_2

collective housing
Shinkenchiku, 1992–1993

single family house
Haus Trüb, 1996–1997

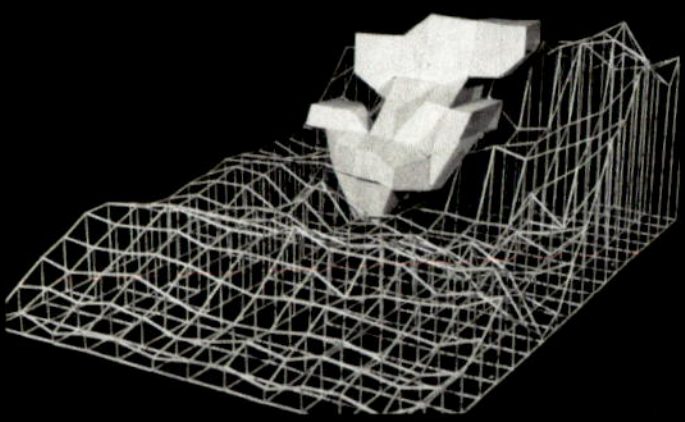

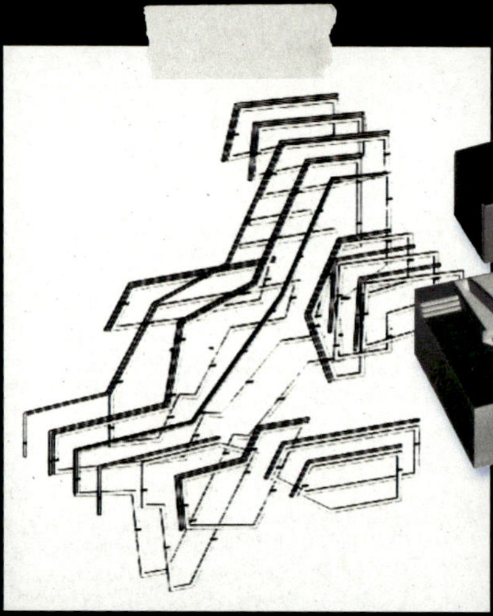

Hochparterre on timber architecture, Jan./Feb.1999

envisioning computer-aided manufacturing

realizing computer-aided manufacturing

forest maintenance, Oberallmeindkorporation Schwyz (OAK), 2018

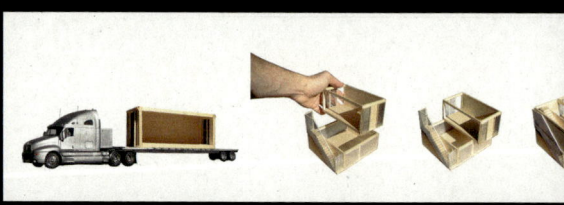

minimize transport

Swiss Forestry Law, 1876

Timber + Prefab   Timber + Prefab + Energy Flows

reduce time on site
increase time in the shop

reduce greenhouse gas emissions

restaurant addition
Hotel Hof Weissbad, 2003–2004 →

primary school
Steinmürli, 2015–2017 →

apartment buildings
Russenweg, 2016–2022 →

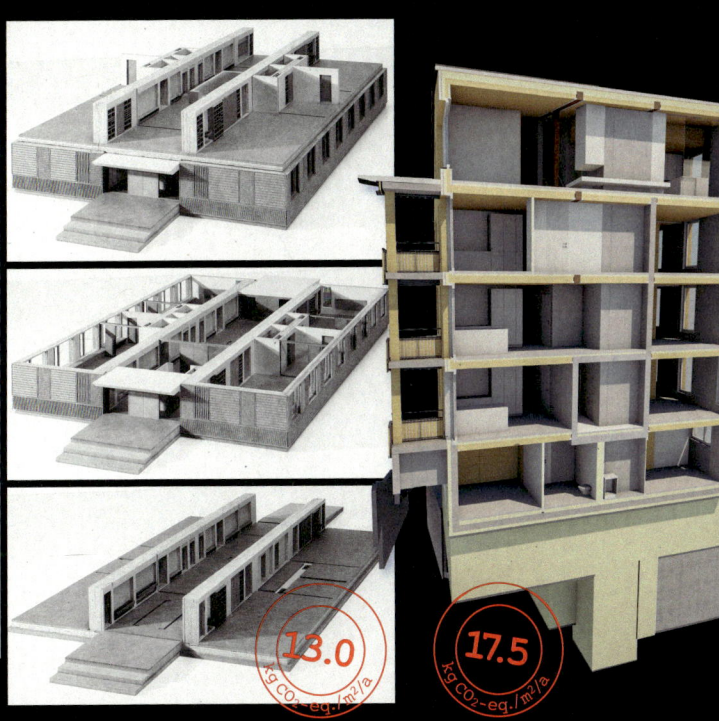

13.0 kg CO_2-eq./m²/a

17.5 kg CO_2-eq./m²/a

no PV panels
3 probes @ 160m

480 m² PV panels
11 probes @ 220m

Minergie-P-Eco

2000-watt society

manage supply chains ...
from forest to saw mill to carpenter shop to construction site to ...

1 metric ton CO_2 per person per annum

Experiments in Timber Prefab

Experiments in Timber Prefab
A Genealogy of Projects
ca. 1992–2022

Surveying a succession of projects over a span of some 30 years offers insights into a number of shifts in how architecture is thought about and how it is made. Sure, each project is distinct in its approach and appearance, yet there are common threads linking them in a broader genealogy that reflects the evolution of a body of design work relative to the evolution of environmental awareness in design practice. Whereas all of the projects respond to specific functional requirements, they equally stand as experiments bearing on larger issues concerning architecture's role in mitigating the negative effects of building construction on the environment.

Take a design experiment from the early 1990s as a case in point in exploring other agendas for architecture. The entry for a 1993 competition sponsored by the journals *Shinkenchiku* and *The Japan Architect* responded to the call for innovative ideas in residential design by proposing a scheme for collective housing. Since the architects were eager to push the limits of conventional construction, they sought Arup's engineering expertise to expand the discourse on architectural performance in view of potential technological breakthroughs at the time. In what amounted to a *pas de trois*, the design process was choreographed around three correlated issues of materiality, manufacturing, and energy flows, which, in hindsight, would play an increasingly decisive role in later projects.

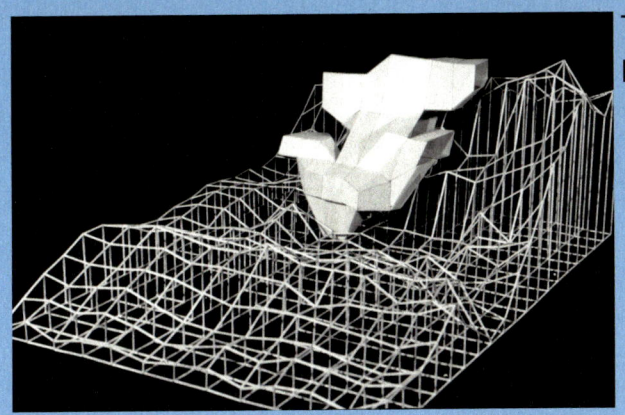

Timber structure of housing project, Los Angeles, 1992

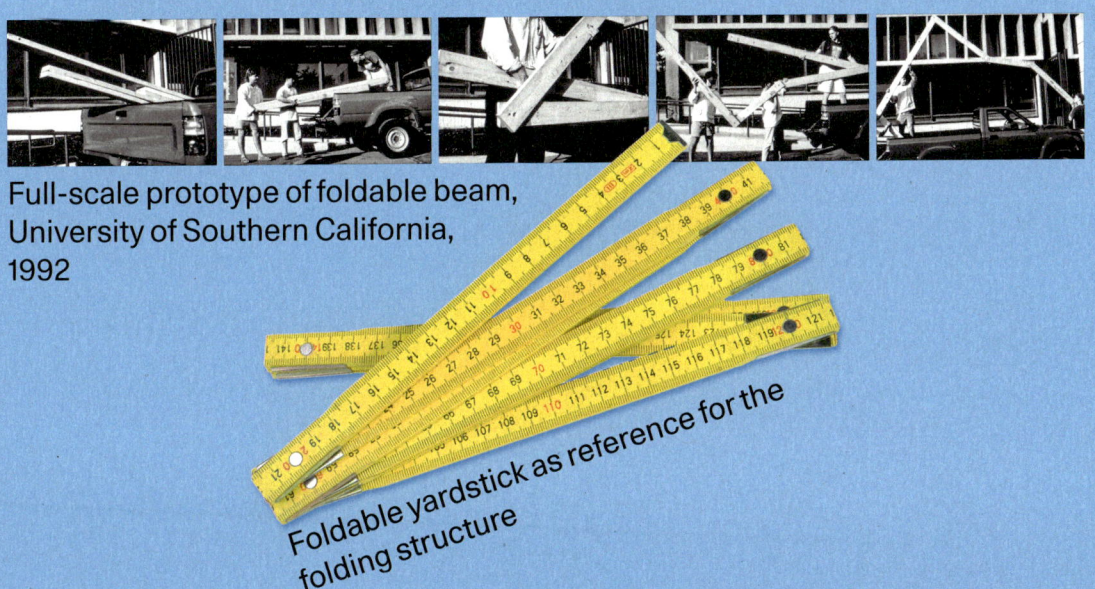

Full-scale prototype of foldable beam, University of Southern California, 1992

Foldable yardstick as reference for the folding structure

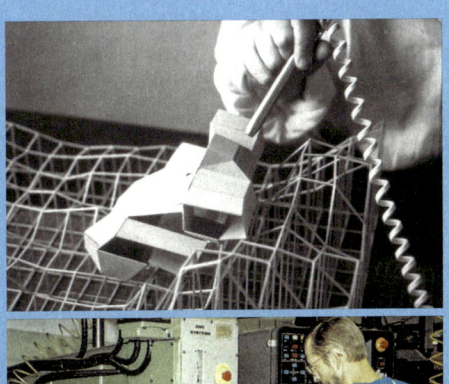

Staged CAAD-CAM scan of model and suggested data transfer from atelier to milling machine

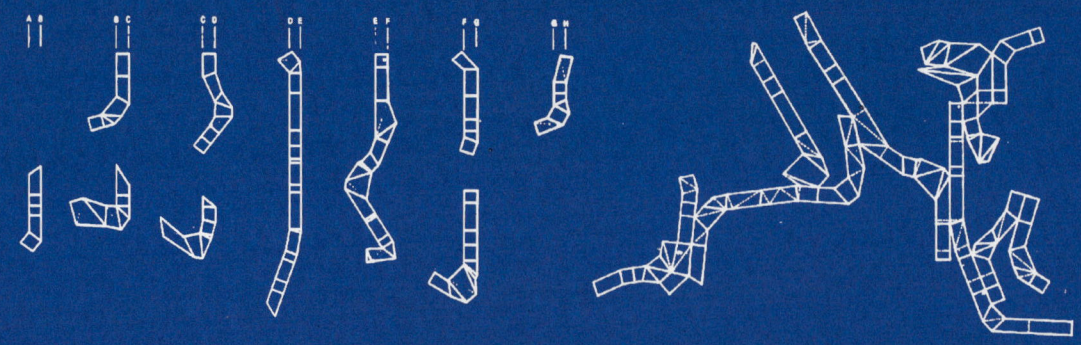

Unfolded envelope of facade panels

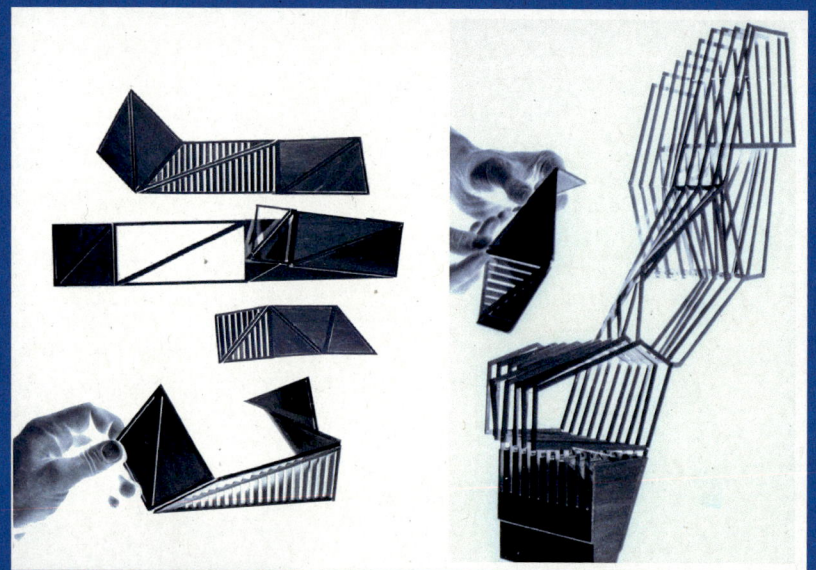

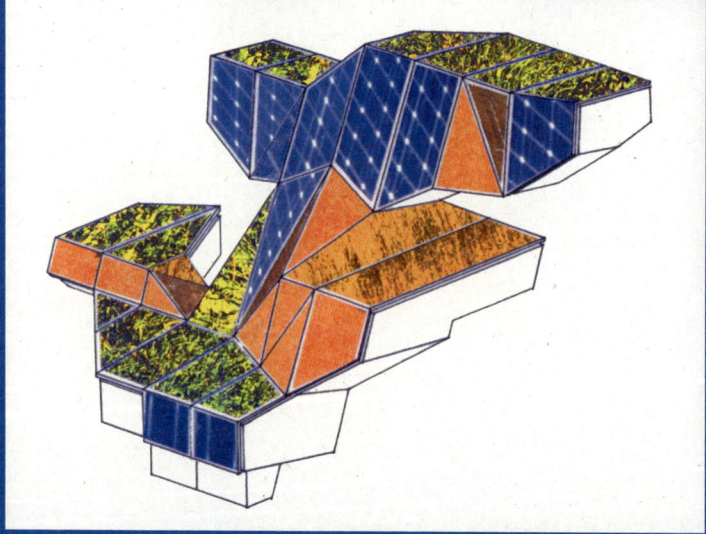

Secondary layer of photovoltaic panels applied onto building volume

Sectional tomography of the *Shinkenchiku* project

As for the question concerning materials, the architects – working at the time in Los Angeles and intrigued by what could be done with conventional balloon framing used for housing construction in the United States – investigated alternative options for assembling timber frameworks with mass-produced elements, ranging from 2 × 4 to 2 × 12 profiles (measured in inches). Was it possible to use standard lumber cut to different lengths and fastened together with pivot joints to produce folding beams? Much like a yardstick found on any building site, such a system would certainly facilitate transport and assembly, while producing a novel, pliable form that is adaptable to any terrain. The same principle could be applied to the architectural skin, which, when folded and fastened into place, would tie the structural members together.

With regard to fabrication, the architects began to speculate about computer-aided manufacturing even before it was commonly available in practice. The real issue here was how to achieve a higher level of precision in making a complex form via a more precise exchange of information between design in the atelier, production in the factory, and on-site assembly. In an ideal scenario, a scale model of the project could be digitally scanned, and the data sent to the manufacturer, who could cut the timber pieces before folding them as prefab elements ready for transport. But this dream remained literally on the drawing board until computation would take hold and establish new standards across the board.

With respect to the issue of energy flows, the project used renewable resources where possible, drawing primarily on those of the sun and the thermal mass of the earth. One idea was that photovoltaic panels could be integrated as a second facade layer to take advantage of the abundance of California sunshine for producing electricity. Other surfaces would serve either as sun-shading elements to avoid overheating or as planters to insulate the interior and retain rainwater. Another idea was to somehow tap into the energy stored in the ground for the purposes of heating and cooling the building. Admittedly sketchy due to the architects' lack of knowledge of how this might be realized, this design intuition would later come to fruition by way of geothermal earth probes coupled with heat pumps that, through rounds of trial and error, would become more refined from project to project as an ecologically minded means of tapping into and channeling clean energy flows.

The *Shinkenchiku* experiment, while naïve at times, was carried out in the spirit of pushing the envelope of architecture beyond its standard repertoire of materials and methods, albeit tweaked to other more sustainable ends. As such, these early explorations in timber construction, prefabrication, and the use of renewable energy would lay the groundwork for a series of subsequent projects that would become experiments in their own right in trying to realize what had been only intuited via a pliable form cascading down a slope somewhere in Los Angeles. Yet what could not have been known then was that as the parameters became more complex, especially those concerning a building's environmental responsiveness, the form itself would become less and less pronounced.

Timber

The scene shifted to Switzerland in the mid-1990s, where another opportunity arose to further test the potential of timber construction, this time in a single-family house in the community of Horgen on the outskirts of Zurich. Insofar as the question of materiality usually takes a back seat early on in the design process to other issues such as responding to the site or to programmatic requirements, the choice of wood for the house – rather than masonry as was customary at the time – was decisive from the outset.

Still fascinated with the possibilities of using wood as an alternative resource, the architects turned to none other than Hermann Blumer, the pioneer in timber technology who had advised them in their work on the Esslingen Triangle a few years earlier and had caught them off guard by proposing a building made completely out of wood, basement included. Even though this rather audacious idea was not pursued in Esslingen, Blumer was seen as the go-to expert for the new house. Initially trained as a carpenter and having later studied engineering, he would go on to expand his father's woodworking shop in the remote region of Appenzell into the leading Swiss timber construction company of Blumer-Lehmann as it is known today. Although his university studies focused on concrete and steel due primarily to the fact that wood was viewed as an

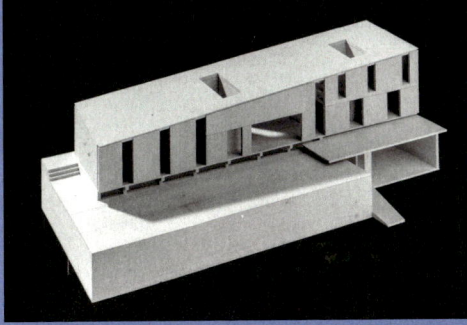
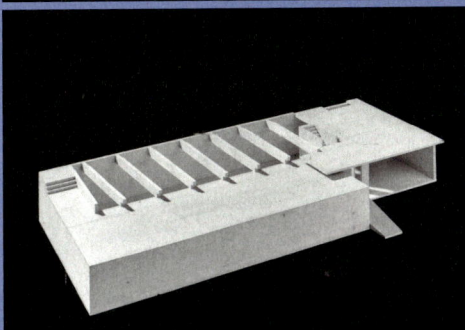

Two-part structure of the Horgen house; concrete below and prefab timber above, 1996

Assembly process of prefab timber panels, including black waterproofing membrane

Benedikt Loderer, "An American House," *Hochparterre*, issue "Timber-Architecture," January/February 1999

inferior construction material, even outdated considering its traditional use throughout the small Alpine country, he was one of the first to explore contemporary applications of timber using state-of-the-art technology. And so, it made sense to bring him on board for a project meant to do just that.

The design for the house consists of a relatively straightforward composition of two volumes, one made of concrete and anchored into the sloped site, the other made of wood sitting on top. But the simplicity of the design was offset by the complexity of the wider discourse about the role of wood as a construction material vis-à-vis its long-term availability as a natural resource. Blumer's broader vision aimed at nothing short of rematerializing the entire building sector by using renewable local materials. His objective was to initiate a far-reaching 'material turn' throughout the industry, and this at a time when sustainability as an urgent cause was still in its infancy.

On the face of it, an abundance of wood would seem to be guaranteed in a country with plenty of forests. Yet this was not always the case. As Blumer was quick to point out, there had been rampant deforestation across Switzerland in the 19th century, due in no small part to the use of wood as fuel for heating buildings, to a surge of its use in vernacular construction, and to an increasing demand for more agricultural land. Not only did this lead to dwindling supplies of a precious resource, but it also led to topsoil erosion, mudslides, and floods. In response, a groundbreaking national law for safeguarding forests was ratified in 1876 aiming to bring about a shift from exploitation to restoration. This in turn would result in a proto-circular material economy that today, among other benefits of managing resources and mitigating CO_2 emissions, would hypothetically yield more than enough wood for the construction industry. In view of the present-day popularity of wood in Switzerland, however, domestic supply can only meet about 40% of the demand (if not even less), despite the steady increase of the country's forests in the last decades.

For the architects, this was already quite a bit to account for. But for Blumer, this particular history had even more profound ramifications for architecture, if not for the environment at large. Being an expert in both concrete and timber engineering, he pointed out that the difference between the two materials with respect to their embodied energy and greenhouse gas emissions is significant. A 24 cm concrete slab, for example, has an embodied energy value of 760 MJ/m^2, while the requisite concrete processing emits 76 kg/m^2 of greenhouse gases. By comparison, a 30 cm timber slab comprised of hollow box beams has an embodied energy value of 550 MJ/m² and emits in its processing only 33 kg/m² of greenhouse gases. Said simply, wood requires less energy and releases less CO_2 in its production. So went the argument. Of course, one would expect such a stark contrast in material values from an expert campaigning for a major material turn. In the interim since that early discussion with Blumer, the touted advantages of wood over concrete have been cited again and again to become a familiar refrain among timber advocates, one that understandably irritates those in favor of concrete. But experience would show that much care must go into such broad – and biased – comparisons, as became more than apparent in later projects.

Coming back to the house project, the montage of the prefabricated timber panels for the upper volume was completed in only a few days, whereas the lower concrete volume required significantly more time for its construction in situ. So there seemed to be an advantage to building in wood, considering the amount of time saved for on-site assembly. And perhaps because the main volume of the house was built so quickly and made of wood, the local press eventually labeled it as an "American House," implying that it had been banged together in no time. But this is never the case in Switzerland. As a matter of fact, production of the wood elements back in the Appenzell workshop took its own share of time and planning due to the level of precision for which the country is known. Blumer-Lehmann explored novel methods of production by combining traditional craftsmanship with the latest in computer-aided manufacturing, thus making their craft an experiment in and of itself. As fate would have it, the architects – having envisioned this possibility for the earlier *Shinkenchiku* project – only became aware of this late in the process and would have to wait for yet another project to take full advantage of such a breakthrough in fabrication processes.

Timber + Prefab

Some years later, another project in Switzerland for a restaurant addition to an existing hotel provided an opportune chance to test computer-aided manufacturing more thoroughly in the making of prefabricated timber elements. Since the project was in Appenzell, there was no question regarding who the go-to fabricator would be. Blumer-Lehmann was contacted early on, and they – being pioneers in the field – expressed interest in using this occasion as an experiment to further advance wood technologies.

It is said that innovation excels through limitation. In the case of the restaurant addition, the primary design constraint was that construction would have to be limited to a period of six weeks because it would take place during the hotel's off-season. Prefabrication thus made sense in order to comply with the tight schedule. While the building phase was exceptionally short, the planning phase of the project was notably longer than normal (totaling more than a year) in order to meticulously choreograph the construction sequence on and off site. Here, design comprised the design of processes.

What was distinct about the approach was that it did not follow in the post-war tradition of heavy prefabrication, say, of bulky and bland concrete panels produced en masse in large factories. Instead, the prefab wood elements would be fabricated in the smaller workshops of local craftspeople who were gradually integrating digital technologies into their traditional craft. This setup hinted at another understanding of industrialization, this time pursued at a smaller scale and finer level of detail that would yield a more malleable, lightweight architecture at the nexus of tradition and contemporary technology.

As much as possible would be produced in the shop. And because the building would be assembled in parts within a short timeframe, the larger the members, the faster and more efficient the assembly. Computer-integrated manufacturing would accelerate the fabrication of the pieces due to a direct transfer of data from the architect's office to machines in the woodshop. The primary structure was digitally cut, and analogue techniques were used to build the modules. Whereas the architects were interested in exploring formal variation among the elements, the craftspeople insisted on reducing variances, favoring instead as much repetition of similar parts as possible. The more identical the elements, the more efficient the manual work, not to mention the end montage.

To assure a high degree of coordination between the various trades involved, the entire structure was initially erected indoors in a local factory hall

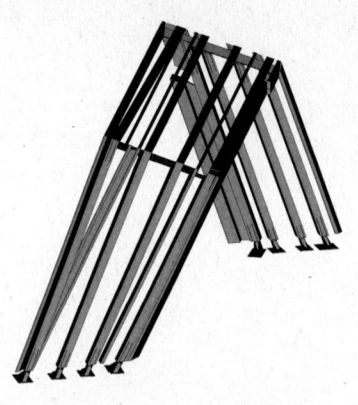
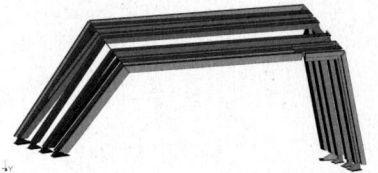

CAAD drawings of the primary modules by timber fabricator Blumer-Lehmann

Preassembly test of the modules in the Blumer-Lehmann workshop, 2004

Prefabricated modules being loaded for transport

Installation of the prefab modules on site

as a test run of the final assembly, with sequences being rehearsed and progressively improved before on-site construction began. By integrating as many trades as possible in the workshop, the large modules could be preassembled as montage-ready components comprised of structural elements, thermal insulation, electrical wiring, ductwork, and enclosure. Though unlimited in its possibilities, the size of these units was ultimately determined by transportation constraints, in particular by nothing more than the height of a highway overpass along the route from factory to site.

The restaurant in its finished state consists of a total of 11 modules interlocked with one another to form a single structural entity. The gaps between the modules are glazed, creating a repetitive rhythm of open and closed bays. For all of the building's qualities, the form nevertheless proved to be overly complex and the details excessively complicated relative to the ease of fabrication. What is more, Blumer highlighted the significant amount of material used for such a small building, in this case 110 metric tons of wood and 6 metric tons of steel. While opening up new avenues for production and construction, this experiment in timber fabrication provided hard-learned lessons about form-making that would eventually steer the architects toward a more reduced architecture, whose complexity lies less in its formal expression than in its overall performance.

Timber + Prefab + Energy Flows

A building's enhanced environmental performance is all fine and good. But with increasingly demanding design standards, the level of complexity grows exponentially. This became all the more apparent with two later projects in Switzerland – one a new primary school, the other a cluster of apartment buildings – that, in their own way, had to comply with evolving requirements for material and energy use. While both structures would further test the advantages of prefab timber using either locally sourced or EU-certified wood, they would also incorporate technologies aimed at reducing the CO_2 footprint of the energy needed for their operation. In so doing, these later experiments would turn the respective architecture proposals into complex machines made of wood.

The Steinmürli school project is a pared-down, two-story classroom pavilion added to an existing campus to accommodate the growing number of children in a neighborhood of Zurich. Considering, however, that this number will most likely decrease in the near future, the new addition would have to be easily disassembled and potentially reassembled in another part of the city. So once

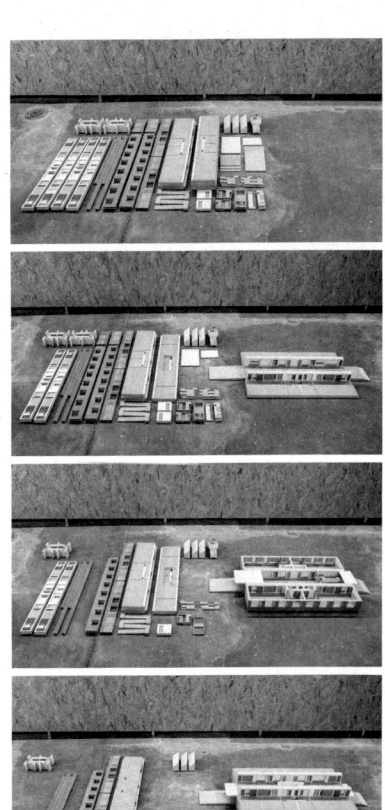

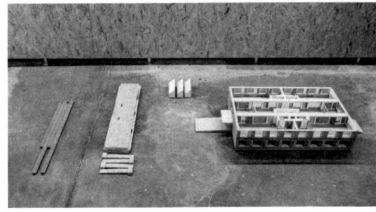

Model showing the assembly and disassembly sequence for the school building, 2017

again, prefabricated timber was a logical choice, not only with regard to material use and reuse, but also in terms of the low embodied energy of the wooden structure. The particular material choice had direct implications for the design, with the school addition being conceived as a puzzle, and each piece – elevator shaft included – carefully crafted to fit into a larger assembly. A large-scale model was built to illustrate the kit-of-parts logic and step-by-step construction process, becoming even a Humpty Dumpty–like didactic game of how to put a building together and take it apart again when shown to school children. The number of parts was reduced to what was needed. There is no core, no technical room, no basement. Most important, there is no glue for fastening the elements, which again is crucial for later disassembly. The overall result is a deceptively simple volume whose complexity lies in the intricate design and detailing of its parts.

In addition to reducing overall energy use in the building sector, the Swiss environmental performance guidelines summed up under the Minergie-P-Eco label encourage the use of renewable energy to lower greenhouse gas emissions for both building construction and operations. Inasmuch as these guidelines are now a mandate for all new school projects in the Canton of Zurich, the design of the small school pavilion explored ways to reduce the embodied energy of the structure as well as that needed for its daily use and maintenance. In keeping with earlier projects, a lean-tech approach would determine the design of the mechanical systems, with as little technology as possible being integrated into thick, space-defining walls.

The new building is heated by way of the campus-wide heating grid already in place, which utilizes residual wood chips as fuel. Though still popular throughout the country as an alternative energy resource to gas or oil, even wood-based heating systems raise questions concerning their own environmental impact in terms of carbon emissions. This potential contradiction notwithstanding and considering that the district system was available, it made sense to use it to reduce the building's CO_2 footprint as opposed to using other non-renewable energy sources for heating. When it came to cooling the classrooms of the school pavilion, the design team opted for three geothermal probes (160m deep) connected via a heat pump to coils integrated in the subfloors, which are made of gypsum-based layers to facilitate subsequent dismantling.

In view of the low thermal storage capacity of wood, not to mention its flammability, high rate of water absorption, and poor acoustic performance in terms of sound transmission, extra material had to be added to compensate for these deficiencies, making the floor slabs a composite construct of more than ten individual layers, which to some degree offset the CO_2 benefits of using wood in the first place. That compromise aside and despite such excessive requirements regarding timber construction that led to overly thick sections and a surplus of material, care was nonetheless taken to make sure that the parts could be disassembled with ease.

In keeping with the Minergie label, the classrooms are additionally ventilated by decentralized units mounted within the timber wall elements, with CO_2 sensors constantly monitoring air quality and regulating proper air quantity. What is more, sensors throughout the building gauge the amount of daylight and automatically activate shading devices when necessary, while moderating interior temperatures. All of the building's metrics are digitally controlled. Such technical measures did indeed enhance the school's overall ecological performance by making it an environmentally responsive assembly of machinic components, each fulfilling a specific purpose. As sound as this may be in principle, the design intention to minimize technology in the end required an inordinate amount of technology to moderate the requisite energy flows in such a way as to make the building more sustainable.

This particular insight informed the design of the cluster of apartment buildings in Zurich not long thereafter, a project that proved to be even more complex when trying to make prefab timber construction work for a more challenging program and for more demanding site conditions, while simultaneously trying to reduce the number of technical systems needed to minimize the buildings' environmental impact. Such were the compound challenges at hand for what would be called the 'Russenweg' project. Comprised of 24 housing units in three five-story volumes situated on a steep slope amidst numerous other existing structures, it would constitute a sensitive exercise in ecologically minded urban densification.

Even though it had been decided from the outset to use as much wood as is feasible, it became evident that construction

Site model of the Steinmürli school (lower right) situated among other campus buildings, 2015

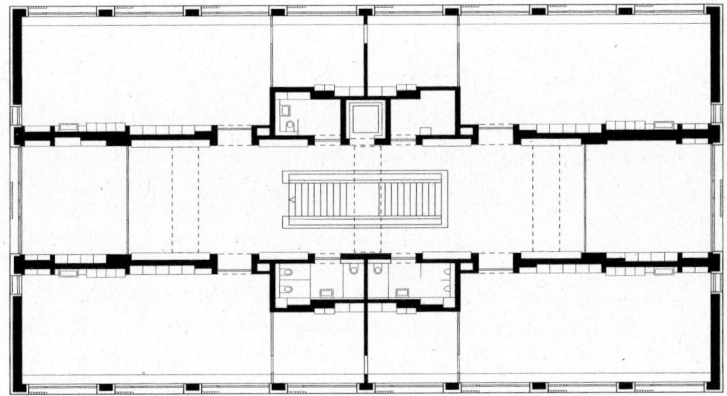

Floor plan with space-defining timber walls for storage and utilities

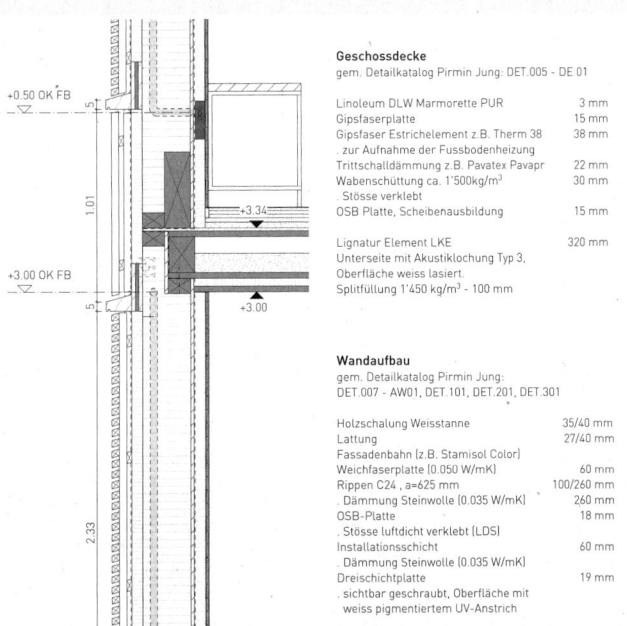

Detail showing the multiple layers of the wall and slab construction

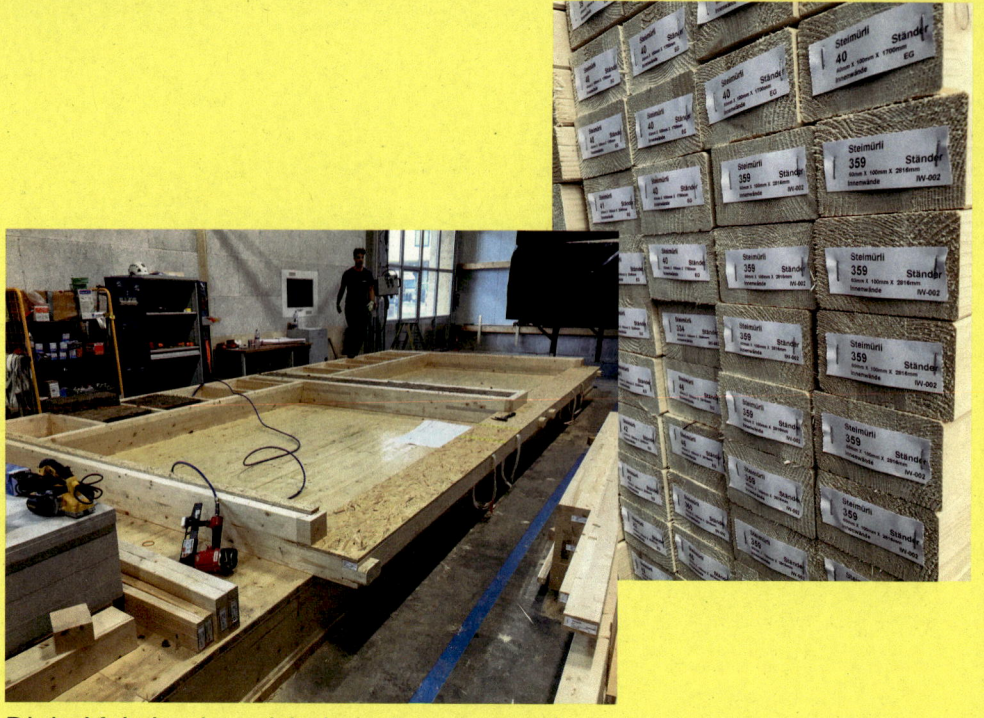

Digital fabrication of timber elements and numbering system used to identify individual members

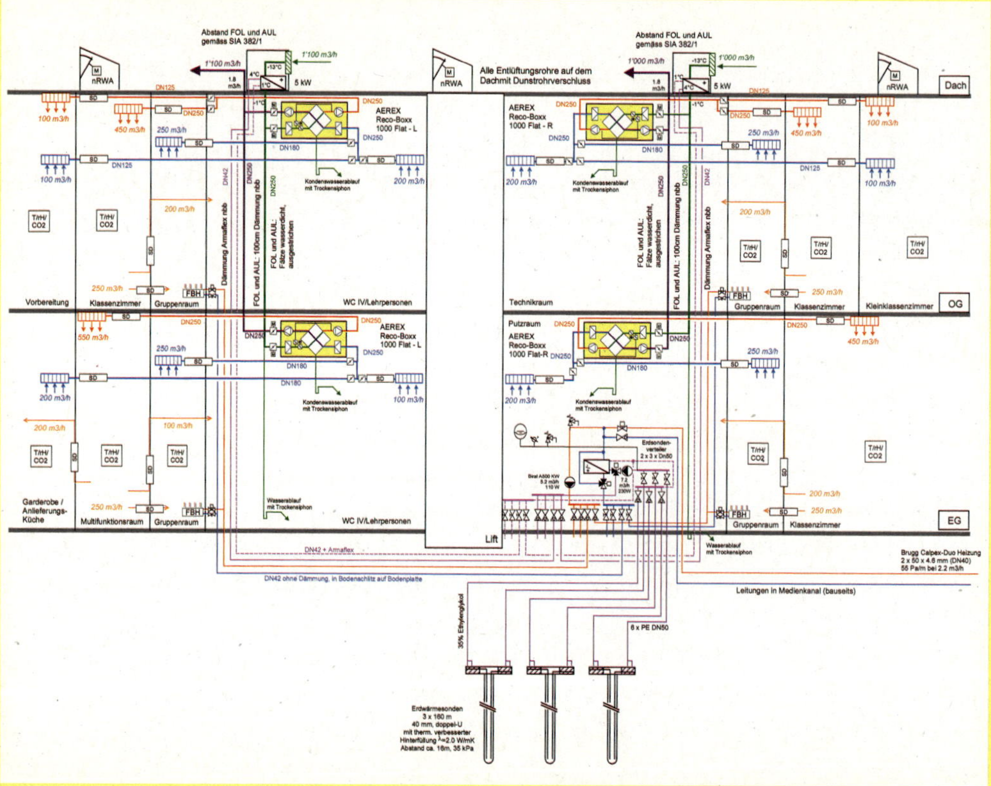

Mechanical systems, including geothermal probes (black) and ventilation units (yellow)

Timber facade of the Steinmürli school (Reinhard Zimmermann, 2017)

Interior photographs of a classroom and the stair in the school's common space (Reinhard Zimmermann, 2017)

could be optimized by way of a composite assembly of materials, with prefabricated timber used for the primary structure; concrete for party walls, circulation cores, and the base anchored into the hill; and steel beams and brackets as connecting elements throughout. Each material performs according to its specific capacity, thereby reducing the overall amount of material needed to produce a lean architectural ensemble. Incidentally, the project would have been even more lean had the city not insisted – for the sake of what it considered to be contextual appropriateness – on three instead of two buildings as originally proposed by the architects.

As with the school project before, Russenweg was also a study in harnessing renewable energy, though this time with less technology to do the job. Contrary to the school's mandated compliance with Minergie-P-Eco, the design team opted not to pursue any energy label certification for the apartment cluster. They decided instead that the Russenweg project would adhere to the alternative sustainability benchmark of the so-called 2000-watt society – a self-imposed parameter for achieving sustainability in a fuller sense via a more strategic use of less materiality and technology. Originally devised at ETH Zurich in the late 1990s, the 2000-watt standard in its initial iteration called for a drastic reduction in energy consumption per capita in industrialized societies. In time, though, the focus shifted from the *quantity* to the *quality* of energy, evolving into what could be called a "one-ton-CO_2 society" meant to cap annual greenhouse gas emissions per person by turning to renewable resources across a broad spectrum of energy demands, including those for building construction, building operations, and mobility to and from buildings.

The consulting engineer for the project drew a step-by-step diagram comparing the CO_2 values for standard housing construction with those needed to achieve the benchmark of a one-ton-CO_2 society. The first step showed the reduction accomplished by using timber as opposed to concrete construction, which lowers the structure's embodied energy.

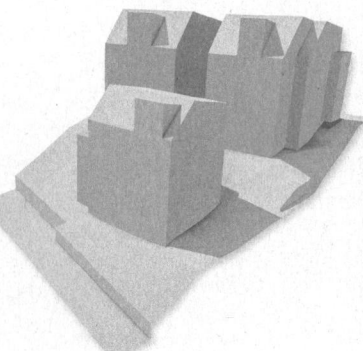

Russenweg housing cluster on sloped site, 2017

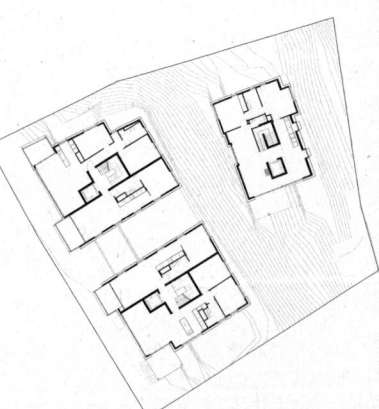

Plan of the apartment buildings

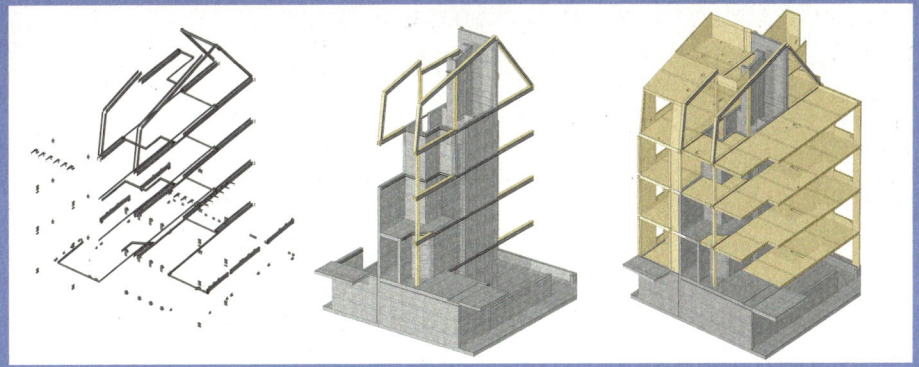

Composite material assembly of the Russenweg project: steel, concrete, and timber (left to right)

Prefab timber panel installed on site

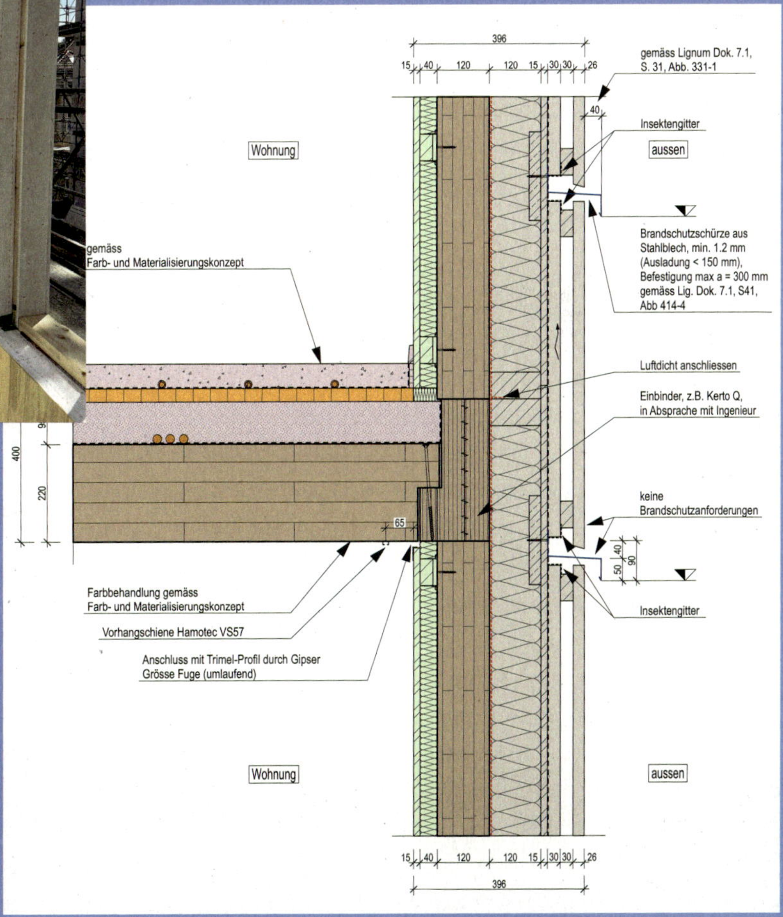

Connection detail between facade and floor, with color coding of the various layers

The second step took into consideration the use of 11 geothermal earth probes (220m deep) to reduce CO_2 emissions when cooling and heating the buildings. The third step accounted for reductions by way of photovoltaic panels on all roof surfaces to harvest solar energy. Lastly, the fourth step demonstrated that greenhouse gases could be further lowered if alternative modes of transportation were encouraged; for example, by limiting the number of parking spaces. The diagram itself, in effect, plotted out the performative DNA of the Russenweg housing project value by value, with all requisite measures to achieve these reductions ultimately being implemented. The comparative charts show – particularly with the final target bearing on mobility – that sustainable construction is not only a matter of material and technological choice, but moreover a question of how to inhabit the built environment so as to reduce our collective footprint.

A concerted effort was made to draw on lessons from previous work when trying to limit the amount of material and technology used to realize the project. When compared to the school, for instance, the number of layers in the timber slabs was nearly cut in half, even though the floor profiles of the two projects have the same thickness (40cm). In short, the same volume of material is used for Russenweg, yet with fewer layers. Likewise, technical installations for the housing cluster were greatly minimized, without compromising living standards. That said, the large number of apartments nonetheless called for extensive technical systems to satisfy the sum of demands (whether for water, electricity, heating, cooling, ventilation, or sanitation), albeit in a more environmentally conscious manner.

All in all, each experiment in this genealogy of timber prefab buildings brought with it an occasion for project-specific breakthroughs yet came with project-specific challenges as well. What was learned from the Steinmürli school and the Russenweg apartments in particular is that the drive for sustainability in the building sector seems to be impeded by the hurdle of an inherent, perhaps unsolvable paradox, at least for the time being. For both projects demonstrate that sustainability is inevitably bound to technology, and without more of it, buildings will remain essentially unsustainable. Given the increasing number of standards and codes to which buildings must comply to be deemed sustainable, even more technology will be needed, which will inevitably necessitate the use of more material. The question remains as to whether more technology and thus more material actually translate into more sustainable modes of construction, or if this ongoing conundrum only perpetuates an intractable vicious circle.

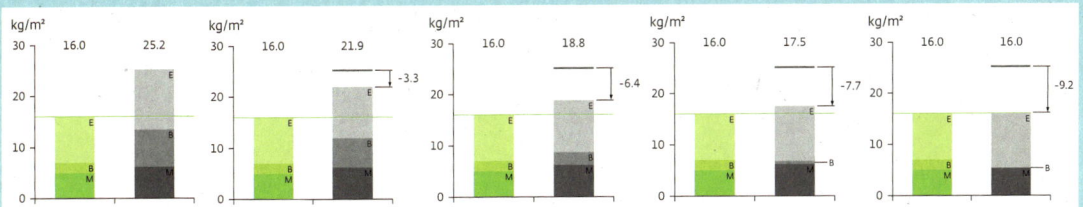

Measures to reduce greenhouse gas emissions: 2000-watt society targets (green); Russenweg project (gray) – (E) embodied energy, (B) building operations, (M) mobility (Lemon Consult, 2020)

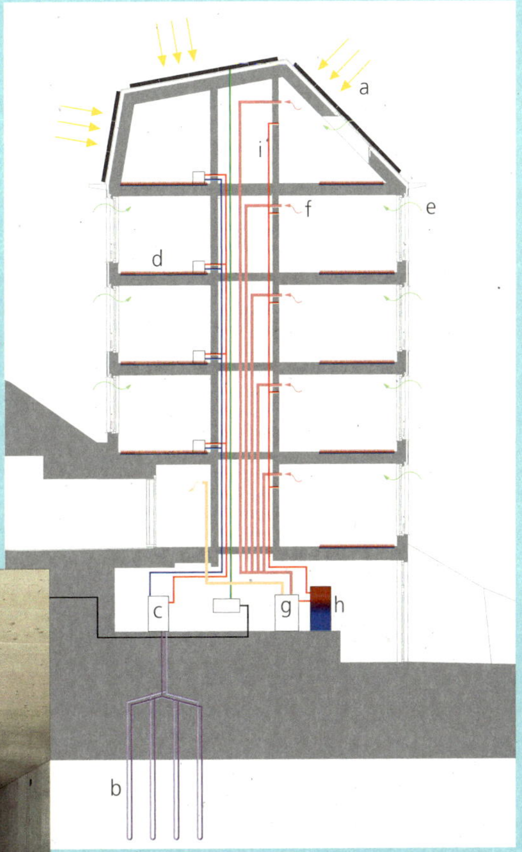

Mechanical systems: (a) photovoltaic; (b) geothermal probes; (c) heat pump; (d) floor coils; (e) air intake; (f) air exhaust; (g) ventilation unit with heat exchanger; (h) hot water tank; (i) hot water supply pipes (Lemon Consult, 2020)

Gravel layer on top of timber construction to increase the thermal mass of floor slabs

Sectional model of five-story timber structure

Russenweg housing project in different stages of construction (Reinhard Zimmermann, 2020–2022)

Clearly, the answers go beyond any particular project. Looking ahead and again drawing on some of the lessons learned concerning the three correlated issues of materiality, manufacturing, and energy flows, bold moves above and beyond architecture will have to be made to make the future of design viable.

With regard to timber construction, significantly more trees will have to be planted to increase CO_2-capture globally, while mitigating the growing imbalance between supply and demand for wood in the building sector. It goes without saying that more forests will require more careful management and maintenance to eliminate neglect and misuse, to avoid monocultures, and to better calibrate material cycles for human use. At another scale, building and safety codes, not to mention environmental performances labels, would then have to be modified to facilitate more timber construction, yet with an eye to reducing the number of performance stipulations that most often result in excessively thick profiles and additional layers.

With regard to manufacturing, the more produced in the factory or the workshop, the better. Yet care must be taken to ensure, in the case of timber construction, that local wood is used to limit transportation distances. Accordingly, the entire production and supply chain will have to be redesigned, from forest to sawmill to carpenter shop to montage on site, and ultimately to future dismantling and reuse. As to the latter, more extensive dismantling strategies will have to be devised and more opportunities for reassembly provided, though the general aim should be to make buildings that are transformable for new purposes and thus have a longer life span.

With regard to energy flows, technical infrastructure, while unavoidable for creating well-tempered habitats, must be significantly simplified, which in turn would require an adaptation of rating standards that are currently overdetermined in their demands and thus overdetermining in terms of the solutions yielded. Needless to say, technical systems must be easily replaced inasmuch as technology always fails. At a broader level, energy flows must become more integral to architectural thinking from the outset, conceptually and strategically – not an afterthought once a form is conceived – in order to achieve a more optimal balance between the passive and active use of resources. Architecture, in all these respects, could take on added value far beyond its conventional disciplinary purview to become a more adept environment-making practice adequate to the true breadth of the task.

Experiments in Harvesting Solar Energy

A Genealogy of Projects

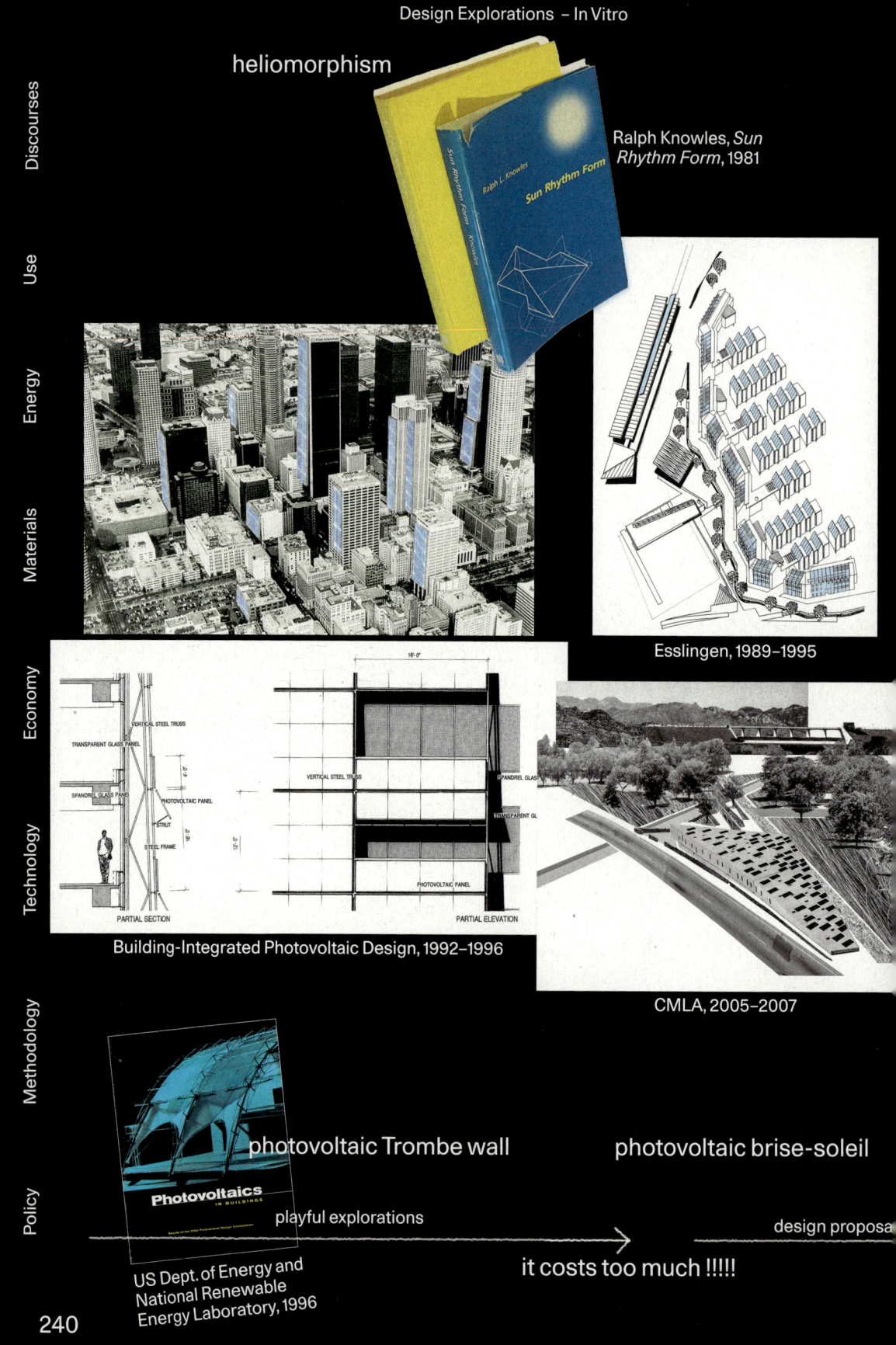

Design Explorations – In Vitro

heliomorphism

Ralph Knowles, *Sun Rhythm Form*, 1981

Discourses

Use

Energy

Materials

Esslingen, 1989–1995

Economy

Technology

Building-Integrated Photovoltaic Design, 1992–1996

CMLA, 2005–2007

Methodology

photovoltaic Trombe wall   photovoltaic brise-soleil

Policy

playful explorations →   design proposal

US Dept. of Energy and National Renewable Energy Laboratory, 1996

it costs too much !!!!!

IUCN, 2006–2011
1,400 m² PV panels

Airport, 1996–2001
8,000 m² PV panels

ZHAW, 2011–2012
2,000 m² PV panels

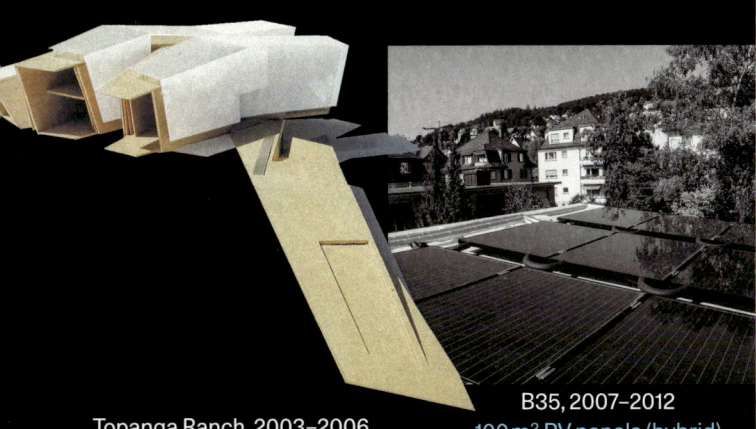

Topanga Ranch, 2003–2006
100 m² PV panels

B35, 2007–2012
100 m² PV panels (hybrid)

Riverside, 2016–2022
1,550 m² PV panels (roof and facades)

photovoltaic + warm water panels + geothermal

soft photovoltaic · hybrid collectors · vertical panels

realized → design proposals – realized

lure of nerve !!!!! → embodied energy !!!!!

Experiments in Harvesting Solar Energy

Experiments in Harvesting Solar Energy
A Genealogy of Projects
ca. 1992–2022

There was something in the air, something experimental in the drive to establish a formative relationship between environmental forces and architectural design in the late 1980s at the University of Southern California (USC). Here, two generations of faculty met head on. There were the senior professors steeped in the building science tradition of Buckminster Fuller and Konrad Wachsmann, who had explored the power of technology to engineer the future of the human environment. There was also a younger group of faculty members, who – having grown tired of the postmodern repertoire of historical citations made in the name of advancing the discipline – sought alternative ways to integrate technological thinking into design as an environment-making practice.

    Notable among the older generation was Ralph Knowles, known for his pioneering work on the solar orientation of buildings and the consequences for urban form, which had been published in *Sun Rhythm Form* in 1981. Referred to as the "Sun King" by the junior faculty, he proposed the notion of the "solar envelope" as a projective framework through which building form could be indexed to the movement of the sun – a concept that would eventually be known in academic circles as *heliomorphism*. To explore the role of natural light itself as a form generator, Knowles constructed an apparatus, the so-called Heliodon, that in time took on a somewhat mystical

Energy-generating photovoltaic installations as sun-shading canopy over the Hollywood Bowl and as sound-protection wall along the Harbor Freeway, early 1990s

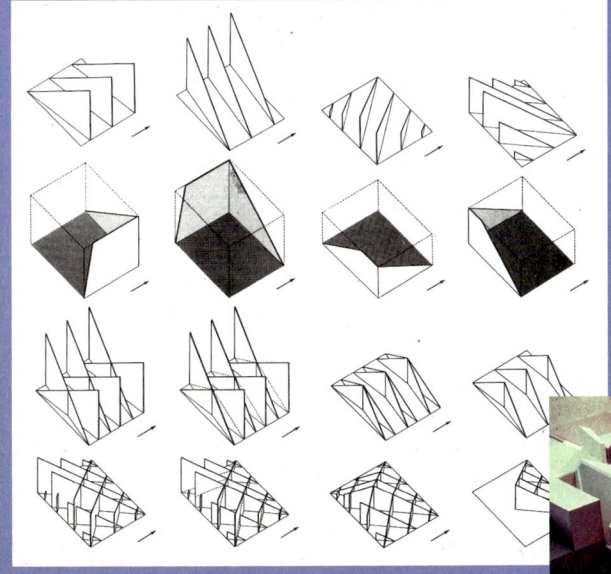

Ralph Knowles, solar envelope diagrams (*Sun Rhythm Form*, 1981)

Ralph Knowles, solar envelope massing model, Natural Forces Laboratory, USC (ca. 1990)

aura among USC students as a machine for designing with environmental parameters long before the onset of computer-aided parametric design.

Although wary of the inherent positivism in basing architecture on seemingly objective scientific premises, the younger faculty – two of whom had recently established their own office in Los Angeles – nevertheless shared Knowles's interest in bringing environmental concerns to the fore of design thinking, which provided much ground for further experimentation at the university and in practice. In rounds of debates, the issue came up regarding a more active role of design when using his machine and whether more could be done with the sun to make it an integral resource for form-making. A series of playful experiments were conducted with students that, while testing the potential of light and shadow with the Heliodon, introduced a range of other disciplinary considerations as equally important drivers of design, including ecological, contextual, functional, technical, and social matters. For some at USC, such considerations expanded the purview of design too far beyond what could be scientifically confirmed. Nonetheless, there was agreement that the sun could indeed inform form, if not be harvested both passively and actively as an infinitely abundant energy resource for human activities. It is this premise that would set off a genealogy of experiments in the practice of the young architects in the years to come, some realized and others not, exploring what they would eventually call "building-integrated photovoltaic design."

Design Explorations – In Vitro

Taking up the issues debated at the university in their atelier, the architects launched a practice-based research project exploring how architecture could establish the means for integrating environmental technologies into the urban fabric, using Los Angeles as a case study. There were two parallel agendas, one technical, the other architectural. The former concerned how to harvest solar energy for generating power to satisfy needs in different parts of the city. The latter concerned how to enhance spaces and structures of the city with this decentralized, ecologically informed urban infrastructure that, as a common utility, would offer clean and cheap energy to local communities. Clearly, a project with this ambition was not only technical and architectural, but political as well, running counter to the monopoly of big corporations that control the energy sector.

Solar-powered emergency call box, San Diego Freeway, California

Inspired by the solar-powered emergency call boxes found along any California freeway, the prototype of which dates back to the early 1960s, the architects proposed a series of site-specific interventions using photovoltaics (PV) for generating electricity, along with other functional and spatial provisions. One such intervention foresaw a linear band of photovoltaic panels mounted along a busy inner-city freeway that would serve as a sound-protection wall as well. Another proposed installation for a downtown public square combined the passive and active use of solar energy by using PV panels on the ground plane to produce electricity and heat for the surrounding buildings – a kind of augmented Trombe wall running horizontally. Another proposal involved the use of PV modules as shading devices on the south facade of high-rises; not only would the modules generate power, the void between an existing building and the new structure would be tapered to create a chimney-effect airflow, which draws air along the building's skin allowing for an even greater cooling of the interior and a marked reduction of energy needs. Still another proposal envisioned a large canopy of PV panels hung above an open-air amphitheater to provide, in addition to electricity, ample shade and a substantial surface for rainwater collection.

These speculative propositions also had a social component in that they would incorporate a citywide job-training program for the construction and maintenance of the installations. The overall goal of this project series was to investigate the large-scale architectural potential of a specific technology through multiple applications across a vast urban territory. What is more, the experiments aimed to demonstrate that architecture could perform as an ecologically responsive socio-technical infrastructure.

It is worth noting that the US Department of Energy and The National Renewable Energy Laboratory had shown interest at approximately the same time in finding ways to promote the use of alternative resources, especially considering that

URBAN SQUARE

Existing public spaces within the urban fabric may be developed as sites for integration of photovoltaic panels. The result is an open square within the densely built city center which is designed for public use as well as an environmentally conscious location for the generation of electrical power.

The urban square is built as a double layer system of photovoltaic collectors beneath a gridded network of laminated glass. Warm air between the layers is used for heating adjacent buildings. By walking above the solar energy collectors, public awareness of ecology and energy efficiency can be heightened.

Tracing the paths of shadow and light over the ground plane in the layout of the solar panels, the urban square becomes a space which is defined by the interplay of sunlight, buildings, and shadows which surround it.

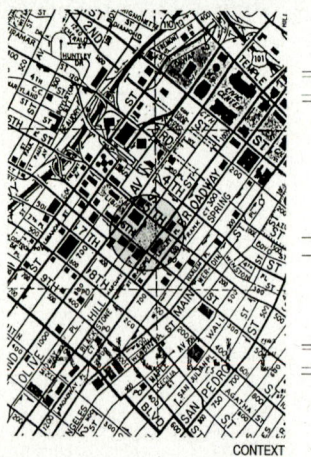
CONTEXT

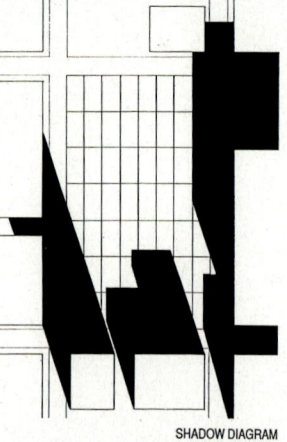
SHADOW DIAGRAM

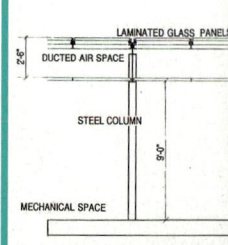

Photovoltaic panels for Pershing Square in downtown Los Angeles combining passive and active use of solar energy (early 1990s)

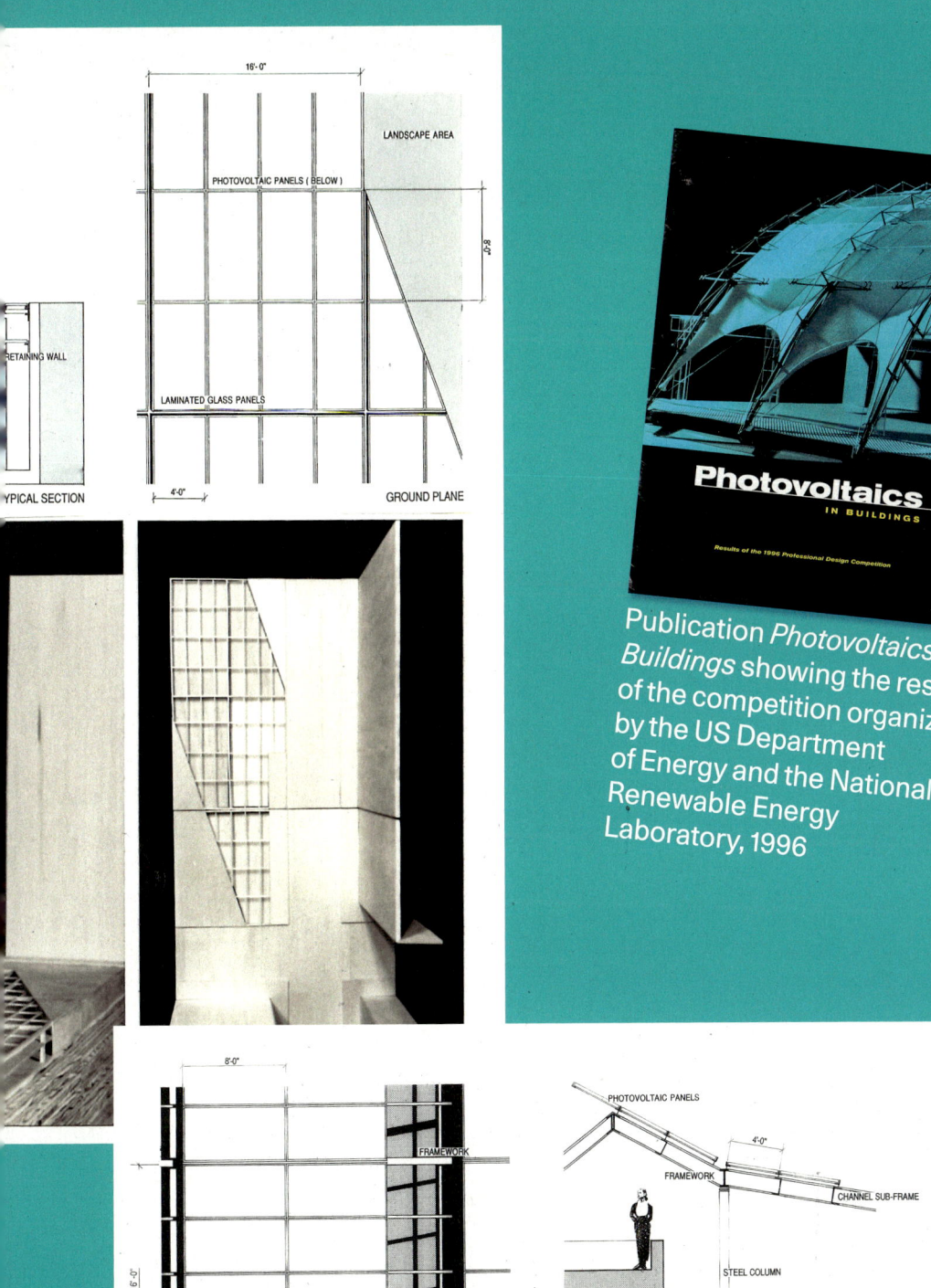

Publication *Photovoltaics in Buildings* showing the results of the competition organized by the US Department of Energy and the National Renewable Energy Laboratory, 1996

Photovoltaic-integrated shading structures for lunch shelters of the LA Unified School District (early 1990s)

247

Sketchbook pages showing initial ideas for the photo-voltaic wall running along the existing creek in Esslingen, 1989

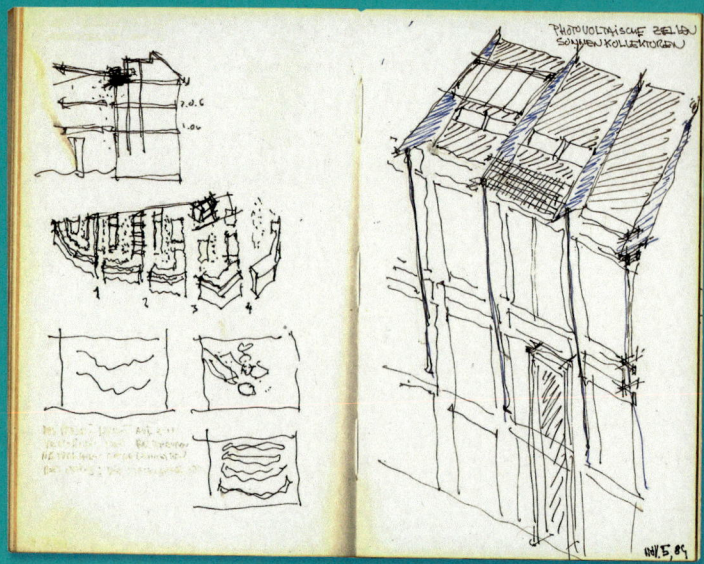

Flexible photovoltaic waterproofing membrane, Children's Museum of Los Angeles, 2005

Children's Museum of Los Angeles; different proposals for integrating PV panels, 2001 and 2005 the earlier oil crisis of the 1970s had shown just how vulnerable the country was with regard to its own energy security. To this very end, the two governmental organizations reached out to the design professions by sponsoring a national competition in the mid-1990s. The brief read like a rallying call for exploiting solar power, stating that "relatively little attention has been paid to how photovoltaics can be integrated with overall building design." The competition sought innovative approaches to this challenge that were also technically and economically feasible in order "to create a path for environmentally responsible buildings." On a more detailed note, the brief raised the question of how to conceive of photovoltaics from a design perspective, asking: "Are solar cells *scales, skins,* or *surfaces*?" This query concerned the status of photovoltaic technology vis-à-vis architecture and whether it should be woven into the fabric of a building or kept separate "like most conventional equipment today." Having already begun to explore these very issues, the architects submitted their Los Angeles case study and were awarded, much to their surprise, a merit citation not long after having received another award in Japan for their experimental housing project submitted to the *Shinkenchiku* competition in 1993. There, they had proposed a skin of photovoltaics folded around the main volume of the building to register the cascading topography of the site in the Hollywood Hills (see the chapter "Experiments in Timber Prefab").

The findings of these early experiments – conducted in vitro, so to speak – had already been put to the test in the project for the multifunctional cluster of buildings in the Swiss town of Esslingen a few years before. The competition entry from 1989 had originally envisioned a winding wall of photovoltaic panels on buildings along an existing creek, becoming something of a piece of land art at the urban scale. Various technical solutions were examined to increase the solar harvesting capacity of the scheme, including the combination of hot water and photovoltaic collectors and of PV panels and a Trombe wall construction, as well as the use of PV panels as brise-soleil. With all of these proposed solutions, it was foreseen that any surplus energy generated would be fed back and stored, as it were, in the public power grid. Just as important, no batteries would be used for energy storage. As promising as this sounded for a first big commission, none of the above solutions were implemented due to a failure of nerves on behalf of the client who, despite wanting to be progressive, cited excessive costs and lack of know-how with this technology as grounds for rejecting the idea.

This very scenario of forward-thinking propositions being rejected for whatever reason would play out in commission after commission, becoming an in-office refrain of sorts throughout the index of work – the label "PV proposed but not realized" appearing after many of the projects down the list, whether in Europe or North America.

For the Children's Museum of Los Angeles, for example, the client was expressly enthusiastic about using photovoltaic technology, among many other environmental measures, to underscore the institution's ecological posture and commitment to advancing the cause of sustainability in its own didactic programs. In an ideal case, the museum building would even feature as one of its main exhibits. Due to repeated budget shortfalls, however, the architects had to develop several schemes, each less expensive than the previous one. And in each pared-down iteration, the suggested environmental measures were deleted one by one. Although having survived rounds of budget cuts, even the flexible photovoltaic membrane on the roof that combined waterproofing with solar cells was eventually dropped – "PV proposed but not realized" for this project as well.

Despite such setbacks, the architects continued to experiment with ways to integrate environmentally sound technologies into their design propositions from the outset. The project to transform the campus of the Zurich University of Applied Sciences, for instance, offered the opportunity to not only apply technical systems to the architecture as is customary, but rather use them tectonically as space-defining elements, which seemed to make sense for a school of engineering. The PV panels were integral to the shed roof of the student ateliers as energy-generating spandrels, creating an undulating glazed and photovoltaic landscape above. Though this proposal was not realized either, further explorations of the spatial qualities of technical systems would be taken up again in later work, be it for the shed roof of the headquarters of the International Union for Conservation of Nature (IUCN) or the main exhibition space of the Guggenheim Helsinki. Important to these projects, in particular, as well as to many that would follow, was the effort to put technological concerns on par with architectural concerns as mutually informative facets of design, the intention being to overcome the late-modernist bias of treating the 'served spaces' of architecture as superior to the 'servant spaces' set aside for technical systems.

Design Explorations – In Vivo

Just after the first phase of the Esslingen project had been completed, another opportunity to use technologies for making architecture

Photovoltaic modules as space-defining elements for the shed roof of the University of Applied Sciences, Winterthur, 2011

Photovoltaic pergola running the length of the terminal for Zurich International Airport, 1999 (Christian Oberholzer)

more sustainable came by way of the competition for a new terminal building at Zurich International Airport in the mid-1990s. One of the proposed features included an array of photovoltaic louvers integrated in a cantilevered pergola running nearly the entire length of the 500 m-long structure, which contributed to a reduction of the energy needed for building operations. This was a milestone for the architects and their engineers alike, since it was the first project in their portfolio listed as "PV proposed and realized." Furthermore, it was the largest building-integrated photovoltaic installation in the country at the time, and thus, as a prominent case study in harvesting the resource of the sun, became a political tool in its own right for leveraging the use of solar energy throughout the building sector. Growing public awareness about the need for renewable energy would soon thereafter lead to state subsidies being instituted for any photovoltaic installation feeding electricity into the national grid, which promised to make architecture a truly public utility, and a decentralized one at that.

With this accomplishment, it seemed only logical to pursue further integration of photovoltaics with other technologies aimed at enhancing architecture's overall environmental performance. A case in point is the multi-family apartment project in Zurich that was being designed in the mid-2000s. The building – referred to as the "B35 prototype" – became an experiment in combining PV and hot water panels as hybrid solar collectors with geothermal probes for seasonal energy storage, which in turn were linked to a heat pump for heating and cooling. Here, the architecture was an integral part of a technical-environmental system that harnessed natural – meaning renewable – resources to temper the human-made habitat. Again, this project would become cited in larger policy debates that even reached the parliamentary level concerning appropriate codes for ensuring sustainable practices.

With the cumulative experience of these projects, the architects would grow critical of what they viewed as an intrinsic contradiction in the overall sustainability discourse; namely, that the embodied energy of all those novel technologies for making buildings more sustainable could potentially offset their ecological benefits. In other words, the amount of energy used to produce environmentally minded building systems could work against the environment. By the early 2010s, it was becoming apparent that the concern for sustainability in design practice was undergoing a fundamental shift. Up until this point, the main focus had been on a building's operational energy, both in terms of minimizing its use and in terms of reducing its emissions. Yet, with more technical systems needed to do so, what would urgently have to be accounted for as well was the embodied energy of its requisite technologies.

Underway around the same time, the headquarters for the International Union for Conservation of Nature (IUCN) proved to be a key project in that it prompted a systematic investigation of the building's energy and material performance throughout its life cycle. The large photovoltaic installation covering the entire roof of the facility was assumed to have an operation life of approximately 30 years. According to the project engineer's assessment report, roughly five years would be needed for the energy produced by the PV array to compensate for the energy embodied in its production, known as "energy-pay-back-time." The report also showed that greenhouse gas emissions during the production of PVs would likewise be offset in approximately five years in comparison to using fossil fuels, also called the "CO_2-pay-back-time." So even though photovoltaic panels are both energy- and CO_2-intensive to fabricate, the ruling assumption was (and still is) that they eventually pay off over the whole panel life.

What the IUCN assessment report did not review – though briefly mentioned, however – were the dismantling, disposal, or recycling phases of obsolete panels, any of which would require more energy and release more emissions, if not necessitate new technologies to separate compound materials. Inasmuch as PVs last for 30 years or so, they too inevitably degrade – as does any technology – and in time must be replaced. This would seem to be a critical issue in the sustainability debate with regard to the use of photovoltaics that has not yet been fully calculated into the touted benefits of solar power. No doubt, more research and development is needed to reduce the amount of material necessary for such technologies, to increase their life span, and to devise more ecological ways of recycling them. That is a given and will certainly be welcomed among next-generation researchers in the building sciences. But most important, an even more critical stance regarding the promises and perils of technology must be developed, which arguably can only come about if we question our blind faith in technological solutions alone as the harbinger of 'sustainability.'

This blind spot notwithstanding, clients of later projects have been eager to have photovoltaic technology integrated where possible, some even going so far as to request that panels be mounted on north-facing facades regardless of their lower pay-back-time, if only to add symbolic cachet to their piece of real estate. Such a tendency puts architects in a bind. On the one hand, the increased interest in sustainable architecture and 'green' technologies among

Photovoltaics combined with sunscreen creating a linear entry porch for a house in Nichols Canyon, Los Angeles, 2008 (Eric Staudenmaier)

Russenweg buildings, with photovoltaic panels at 45-, 10-, and 80-degree angles, Zurich, 2022

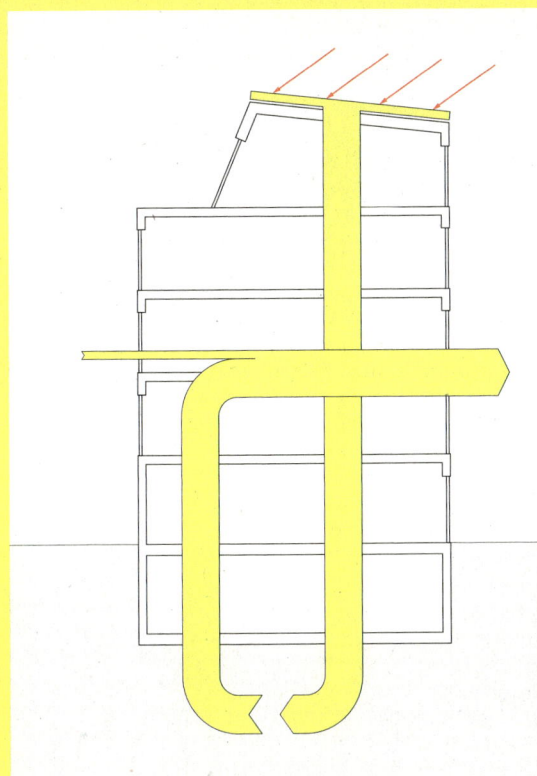

Hybrid collectors on the roof of B35, Zurich, 2012

Interaction between hybrid collectors on the roof and geothermal probes, B35, Zurich, 2007

Photovoltaics integrated into the shed roof of the IUCN building, Gland, 2009

Photovoltaic bands wrapping around all facades of the Riverside project, Solothurn, 2022 clients and the public at large must be applauded. How far we seem to have come from the days when clients were uncertain about the use of photovoltaics. For this shift in mindset puts design practice at the crux of a larger, more crucial debate about the impact of our ways of inhabiting the environment. On the other hand, 'greening' – or sustainability for the sake of appearance – would seem to debase an urgent cause bearing on the course of future development by capitalizing on the sign value of being environmentally progressive.

    For architects there has never been more at stake when saying 'yes' or 'no.' Admittedly, every effort should be made to support a client's concern about a building's impact on the larger system of which it is a part – ecologically, economically, and socially. But architects must also be willing to critically assess the bigger environmental cost of the technologies deployed in the name of sustainability by asking how 'green' green really is in the long term.

Experiments in Harvesting Solar Energy

99¢ Space

Rainer Hehl

99¢ Space
Introductory address, Architektur Galerie Berlin
Rainer Hehl, 2017

An idea can travel far and fast. This was the case for the 99¢ Space, a barn conversion for the Refugio Road Ranch in Santa Ynez, California. The invitation to present the project in an exhibition at the Architektur Galerie Berlin brought up the issue of how best to convey the project's environmental, economic, and social objectives in another cultural context. One of the early ideas was to build a full-scale mock-up of a wall section in the gallery. Since this was too costly and thus at odds with the premise of inexpensive construction, the alternative was to 'teleport' the building into an exhibition space halfway around the world via digital media. Bringing Refugio Road to Karl-Marx-Allee in one click, so to speak, would not only save money but also reduce material flows and related construction waste.

In collaboration with Los Angeles–based media artist Jenny Rodenhouse, the architects designed a site-specific installation entailing the one-to-one projection of the 99¢ Space onto the gallery wall facing the boulevard so that passersby in Berlin could see everyday life in Santa Ynez. The multi-channel video explored the potential of what Rodenhouse called "99¢ digital materiality" by producing the film with an out-of-pocket smartphone – a mass-produced, easy to use, and cheap relative to professional equipment. In keeping with the how-low-can-you-go spirit of the project, the video fit the 99¢ Space into the bounds of iPhone technology, with its accessible camera, 70 × 144 mm frames, and standard 'field of view' settings. The space on the ranch was digitally filmed and the footage subsequently disassembled, scaled, and then stitched back together from multiple points of view, reconstructed in another setting using "99¢ colors, pixels, and seams" of an everyday medium.

A Mylar curtain, like the one used for the space on the ranch, was hung along the storefront windows of the gallery opposite the large-scale video projection, bringing virtual and analogue realms face to face. Wall-mounted iPads presented episodes of the Refugio Road Ranch story, showing agricultural catalogs, material recirculation diagrams, off-grid infrastructure systems, cheap construction assemblies, stills of daily farm activities, and select pages from Karl Marx's *Das Kapital* – referring in passing to the gallery's location on Karl-Marx-Allee. As pages of a FarmTek catalog were slowly turned on one of the screens, so too were those of *Das Kapital* on an adjacent one. This not so subtle reference was meant to highlight still-relevant concepts such as 'use value,' 'means of production,' or 'commodity circulation,' while integrating them into the low-cost discourse on today's building practices.

Rainer Hehl's opening comments at the Architektur Galerie Berlin situated the 99¢ Space in a broader lineage of innovations in design thinking and making. The following is a transcript of his introductory address entitled "Doing More with Less," delivered on November 2, 2017.

> While preparing my introduction for the *99¢ Space* exhibition, I revisited some prominent examples of houses using standard prefabricated elements and soon realized how deeply anchored this idea was in the avant-garde Californian architecture that emerged after World War II. Perhaps the most famous example is Case Study House No. 8 by Charles and Ray Eames, built in the late 1940s in Los Angeles — a modular steel construction made

of carefully selected steel beams and frames from the catalog of a local steel manufacturer. Although these elements were taken from available industrial stocks and supplies, the way that they were assembled did not necessarily comply with the standard logic of prefabricated systems. It is said that collaborators from the Eames office had to weld extra fixtures and fittings in order to make the project work, turning it into an experiment in improvisation. Whereas the Eames House was designed as the architects' private residence, it soon became a landmark of mid-20th-century modern architecture, if not the prime prototype of the Case Study Movement.

Cover of *Arts & Architecture* by Ray Eames, April 1943, sold for 35¢ at the time

Initiated by John Entenza, editor of the magazine *Arts & Architecture*, the case study houses were developed as experiments in residential architecture meant to introduce new living standards to America's burgeoning middle class. This innovation in lifestyle was to be delivered by an architecture based primarily on an economy of construction and efficiency in spatial arrangement, while drawing on the aesthetics and technological possibilities of mass production. This ambition notwithstanding, the Case Study Movement in the end failed to bring about the anticipated transformation in both society and industry. The houses nonetheless constitute notable examples of how to creatively use (or misuse) the building products available on the mass market. In this respect, the 99¢ Space resonates with the Case Study

Movement in its appropriation of prefab elements for new purposes and trying to make more with less, albeit in a more ad hoc and messy way.

Recalling the Californian culture of the post-war period, there are other examples that might serve as pertinent references for the conceptual background of the exhibition as well, especially considering the environmental consciousness at the root of the 99¢ Space experiment. In the late 1960s, some 20 years after the Eames House was built, activist and author Stewart Brand published the first edition of the *Whole Earth Catalog*, a countercultural manual that featured on its cover a composite photograph of Earth from space taken by an orbiting satellite. This iconic image – and the famous *Earthrise* photograph from Apollo 8 astronauts used for the second edition cover – served as a reminder that we all share a single planet. The book was put together somewhat casually as a practical, no-frills guide for

Whole Earth Catalog, Spring 1969 (second edition), referenced by Rainer Hehl in his introductory remarks

First edition of Buckminster Fuller's book *Operating Manual for Spaceship Earth*, 1969

understanding how to live on Earth, providing a survival toolkit, as it were, full of tips ranging from conceiving of the planet as a holistic system to repairing a car or making a solar panel. Here again, the 99¢ Space resonates with this hands-on ethic of changing practices for a broader cause of bringing the built and natural environments into sync.

99¢ Space installation at the Architektur Galerie Berlin, 2017 (Jan Bitter)

As Buckminster Fuller would soon thereafter suggest in reference to his own book, Brand's publication could be read as an *Operating Manual for Spaceship Earth*, a collective habitat that already then, according to Fuller, was in a state of emergency. The challenge at hand was how to turn the situation around and bring about a sustainable state of life for all on the planet. His proposal was to envision the broadest, most inclusive worldview possible that might help us devise specific actions to be taken on the ground; in essence, bringing the big picture to bear on the minutest of measures.

    Brand's *Whole Earth Catalog* and Fuller's *Operating Manual for Spaceship Earth* reflected upon a more astute global consciousness for design practice at the onset of the environmental movement that would be attentive to the detrimental impact of human practices on Earth systems. And some three decades later, those discourses about the Anthropocene – the age of humanity as a geological force – not only revive earlier concerns but also put even more emphasis on the degree to which the planetary ecology is deteriorating as a result of human action. So the question remains of how to affect a turnaround in our ways of inhabiting the planet and what kinds of tools need to be created and deployed to sustain livelihoods for all.

Considering the range of current challenges, I have a hunch that the principles guiding the minimal interventions of the 99¢ Space and the use of renewable resources for its operations are in line with the earlier concerns of Brand and Fuller. One could argue that the project is situated between a 'macro-comprehensive' view of the world and 'micro-incisive' moves made in a particular place, between global consciousness and small-scale responsiveness to local conditions. Therefore, the references to the post-war avant-garde and the counterculture in California in the late 1960s are not meant to be nostalgic about the past, but rather are meant to foreground the ideas invested in the 99¢ Space in view of their relevance for the profession.

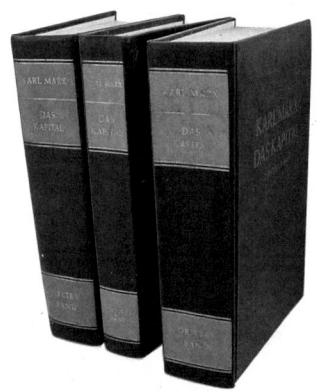

DDR standard edition of *Das Kapital*, bought at bargain rate in East Berlin prior to the fall of the Wall

As the title of the exhibition makes clear, questions of economy are central to dealing with the compound effects of collective practices. Thus, it is no surprise that Karl Marx's book *Das Kapital* features as one of the many tools presented in the exhibition. Incidentally, one of the architects bought the three volumes of *Das*

Kapital on the black market in East Berlin more than 40 years ago, prior to the fall of the Wall – volume one for 10 West German marks, volume two for 8, and volume three for only 5. Anecdote aside, it seems that the architects of the 99¢ experiment have taken cues from Marx when attempting to align economy and ecology in their work, keeping in mind that Marx viewed nature always in relation to human action. In the context of climate change and with regard to the exploits of the world market, the 99¢ Space offers a fresh take on the role of the economy in the building sector, while putting principles of sustainable construction to work in enhancing the overall environmental performance of a ranch.

The experiment to turn a horse barn into a habitable space for humans suggests that, at a macro level, one has to look at architecture from inside the capitalist system of production and consumption in order to identify ways to mitigate the increasingly devastating effects of that system on the environment. But the project also suggests that, at the micro level, one must unpack the inside of a particular project, say a barn and the way it has been assembled, to reconsider how available standardized products might be combined with technologies to bring about more accountable uses of resources. As unassuming as the barn conversion might appear, what we are dealing with here is a world architecture, for it offers viable solutions for cost- and energy-efficient building construction that is carefully integrated into the circular economies of the local environment.

The same issues are also relevant to Berlin, particularly considering the controversial discussions about the lack of affordable housing in the capital. Currently, the big question is how to build in a cost-effective way while adhering to the strict standards of reduced energy consumption as specified by the German government under the framework of the Energy Turn (Energiewende) – a broad policy agenda aiming to reduce greenhouse gas emissions by transitioning to renewable resources. Do we now have to lower the standards in order to be able to build cheaper or, conversely, do we have to comply with energy saving measures and accept that housing production will become more and more expensive? To resolve this catch-22

Video stills from *99¢ Space to Fit* by Jenny Rodenhouse, 2017

problem will require nothing less than a concerted rethinking of business-as-usual practices. The architects of the 99¢ Space, among other environmentally minded practitioners, offer proof that ingenuity and creativity in taking advantage of what is already there and available on site constitutes a viable way forward in building sustainably.

Perhaps less a genius and more a bricoleur, the architect who is really trying to cope with the big planetary challenges of today – not merely paying lip service to them – must have the skills and the design knowledge to assemble what the current system is offering in an intelligent and responsible manner. It might be helpful to conclude this introduction to the exhibition with the words of Fuller himself, who stated: "All of humanity has the option to 'make it' successfully and sustainably, by virtue of our minds, discovering principles and being able to employ these principles to do more with less."

Almost Off-Grid

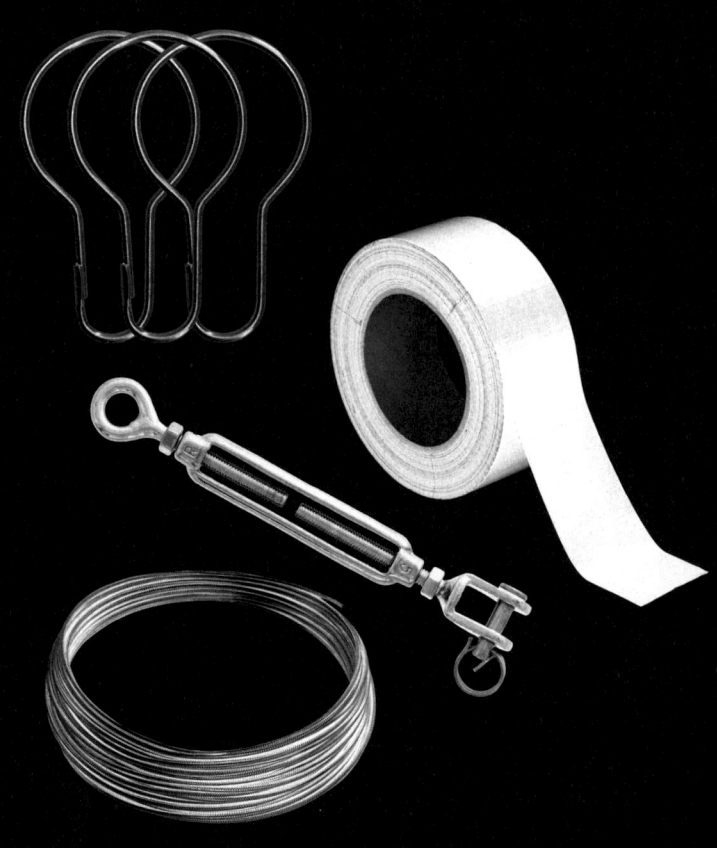

Refugio Road Ranch

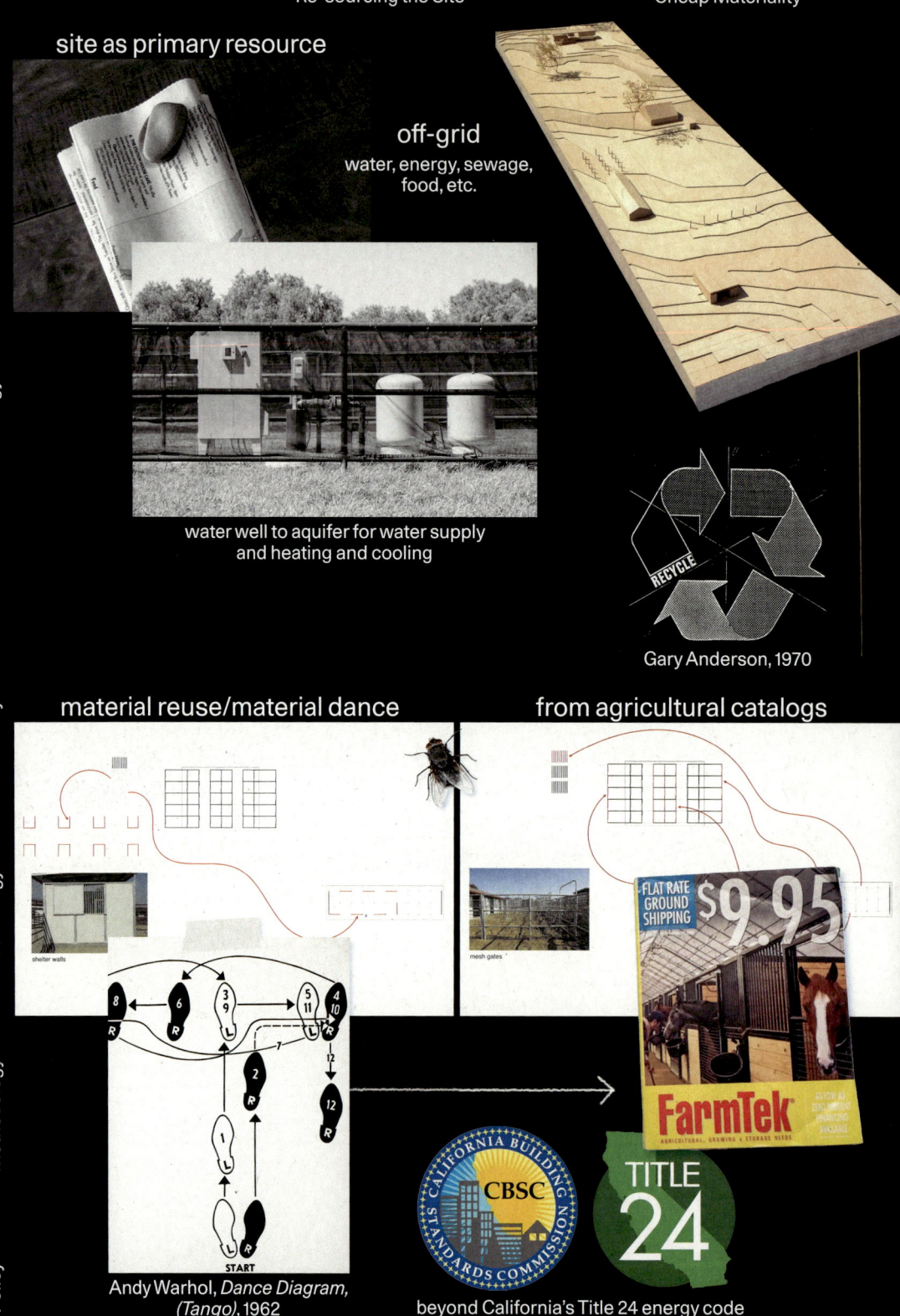

Fluxes of Common Use   An Object Lesson   The Machine in the Garden

everyday

ranch inhabitants

Leo Marx, *The Machine in the Garden*, 1964

99¢ Space

hybrid construction

300 m² PV panels
1 probe @ 150m

low-tech/farm tech
doing more with less

architect as designer, client, general contractor, developer

J. Scott Applewhite, 'silver foil' protests, Washington DC, 2018

US immigration policies

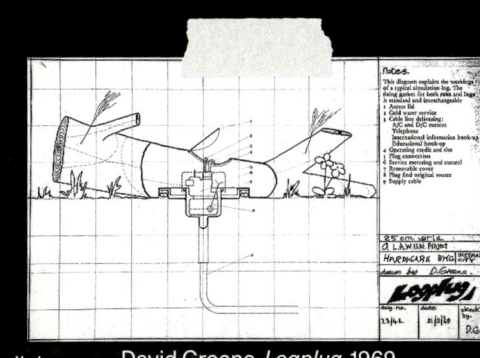

David Greene, *Logplug*, 1969

Almost Off-Grid   273

Almost Off-Grid
Refugio Road Ranch (R3), Santa Ynez, California
2015–2020

It all began with a few rounded stones casually placed on an ordinary newspaper. The stones represented what were to become the main spaces of a new ranch house overlooking the surrounding countryside of Santa Ynez (a small town just north of Santa Barbara). The newspaper, showing a map of the California coast, was cut and folded to correspond to the size of the elongated parcel of land. From this impromptu model, the first idea that came to mind was of oval-shaped structures that would allow a 360-degree view of nearby mountain ranges and valleys. Hence the stones on the folded newspaper.

    As fun as this rock-paper-scissors game may have been, it soon became clear that this was the wrong approach altogether. For one thing, ovals are notoriously expensive to build. For another, this seemed too literal an interpretation of the loose arrangement of stones on paper. Better to draw on the raw properties of the land and the qualities of the place as the basis for design than to begin with a predetermined form. More attention would be paid to the folded newspaper, meaning the agricultural plot itself. The site would be utilized as the prime resource for designing the house and the entire ranch, and the operation would begin with the ranch, its grounds, and its requisite infrastructures, whether existing or new. Hence back to the drawing board.

Refugio Road Ranch amidst elongated agricultural parcels, Santa Ynez, 2019 (Eric Staudenmaier)

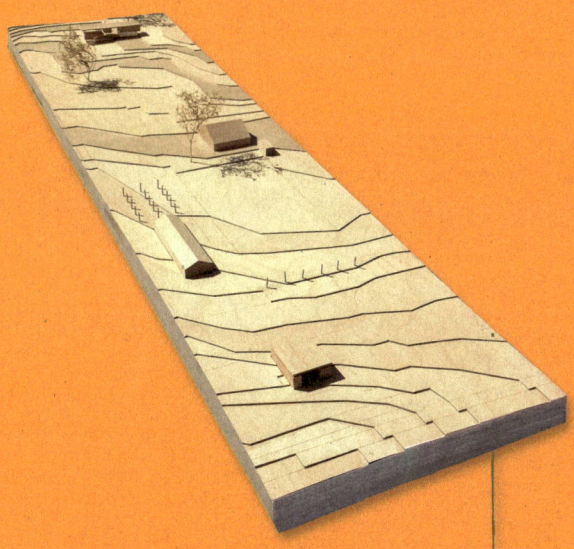

Stones on a folded newspaper representing the main units of the house on the plot of land

Site model showing the 150 m-deep well in the lower right corner

Re-sourcing the Site

How do you get a site somewhere out there in rural Santa Barbara County to work in the most ecologically minded way possible? To begin with, you become aware of what is at hand and how it is already working. Water, for starters, is no small issue, especially in a state prone to extended periods of drought; so how to best collect, store, and use it efficiently were of primary concerns when considering the general layout of the facilities. While it supposedly never rains in Southern California, or all too seldom, all rainwater was to be collected either on the ground or on roofs, used for irrigation, and then channeled through the existing topography to replenish the natural aquifer. To access this vital subterranean reservoir, a well was strategically located with a pump strong enough to draw water from some 150 m below ground – an amenity, by the way, considered important enough here to warrant its own address. Equally important given the ever-present risk of wildfires, a sufficiently sized water tank had to be placed on the highest part of the site to assist those much-revered community firefighters in case of an emergency.

After the issue of water supply had been addressed, its off-grid dispersal and the means for treating both black and gray wastewater were designed, prompting the installation of multi-chamber septic tanks and drain fields that function as on-site sewage systems. Once treated, the residual liquid percolates through the ground sediment and seeps back into the aquifer to complete the on-site water cycle. In all, water was central to the overall design of the ranch, determining not only the placement of the various structures but also fundamentally how they work together to optimize the use and reuse of an increasingly scarce resource.

Another determining factor in the overall design was the use of renewable energy to minimize the ranch's carbon footprint. Given the ample amount of sunlight in the region, a 44 kW array of photovoltaic panels was installed on the roof of an existing barn to provide all the power required for the entire property, including the well pump, the agricultural buildings, and the living units. Though the goal was to make the ranch self-sufficient with regards to energy production and consumption – off-grid, as it were – it proved to be more efficient to plug into the public utility network and, as is common practice, use this human-made energy reservoir to store any electricity produced on site for current and future needs. Any surplus generated is credited to the owner, excluding administrative costs. Not only does this system eliminate the need for costly

Site infrastructure: water tank for firefighters, rainwater cistern, septic tank, and composting facility

Pump equipment for drawing water from a 150 m-deep well

Crops are grown year-round in designated agricultural fields batteries and accordingly the toxic hazards that come with their disposal, but it also amplifies the circular economies at work in the operation of the ranch.

Concerns for water management and energy production led to discussions about what the site could yield in terms of crops for both the human and the animal inhabitants of the compound. As a matter of principle, everything planted was to be edible. Besides being a horse boarding facility outfitted with the requisite stables, pastures, and training grounds, the site would also serve as an agricultural farm, cultivated to produce fruit, vegetables, nuts, olives, eggs, and herbs for humans, as well as grass and hay as animal fodder. Any surplus food that is not consumed by the residents and friends is donated to the local nonprofit organization Veggie Rescue that provides pick-up and delivery services catering to needy communities in the area, keeping in mind that more than 20% of the region's population is threatened by food insecurity.

That said and with every effort made to get as much from a harvest as possible, a farm nevertheless produces plenty of organic waste, tons of horse manure included, all of which needs to be collected, aerated, moistened, and covered before being distributed back onto the fields and gardens as composted fertilizer. Here again, whatever is produced is reused on the property within a larger circuit in which the ranch serves the farm and vice versa.

Such measures essentially reframed landscape architecture as it is usually practiced. The site design was based on infrastructure and systems installations rather than one focusing on formal composition – no groomed lawns or manicured hedges, but rather the channeling of material and energy flows already at hand. The site itself, in other words, was 're-sourced' in view of its intrinsic operative capacities to generate, amass, and recycle in perpetual and productive loops.

This logic of landscape and resource management was established throughout the property before the house was designed or any definitive form was drawn, setting up the rules of the game for the architecture in an environmentally sound and appropriate direction.

Cheap Materiality

If the initial planning phase took into account circular economies of the site as the basis for decision-making, an economy of means would determine the construction of all habitable structures on the grounds. But prior to building the ranch house, an experiment was made to test just how cheap the process of building could really be. To this end, an existing horse barn was transformed into a live-work space for humans using available on-site materials as well as the most inexpensive industrial and agricultural supplies sourced as locally as possible, with "99¢ being the modus operandi of the overall design investigation," to quote the architects. A wordplay on the name of the American 99¢ Store franchise, this exploration of 'how low can you go' – to use another American idiom – reflected the core ambition and the overall spirit of the project.

But say 99¢ to anyone in the trade, and the first question is most likely, "99¢ per what unit?" The point here, however, was less about metrics or numbers on a spreadsheet and more about calling attention to the often-opaque pricing of building products in general. Far from mere rhetoric, the 99¢ price tag raised the broader question as to what extent one really knows how much building elements should cost in the context of today's highly competitive global market. Reflecting on this, one of the architects observed:

> We used to know how much a toilet should cost. A reliable one was US$500. Pay more and they get too complicated; pay less and they break. Now, however, we don't know anymore. With the internet, overstock supply sales, and China, we don't know how much we should pay for toilets or faucets or lights or anything else that goes into a building. And how much should we pay for shelter? Why can't we build lightly rather than with heavy, redundant layers? Building codes provide an immediate answer as to what is not allowable, but what is possible? Why can't we use the straightforward, economical systems of agriculture and industry for building shelter?

The experiment with the barn conversion was meant to address these very questions, calling for concerted deviations from business as usual. The first move, before anything new was ordered, was to take stock of all materials on the ranch that could be repurposed, either to convert the existing barn, to upgrade another barn already standing, or to construct additional animal shelters, given that what was already at hand provided a wealth of embodied energy. This stocktaking subsequently set off a veritable flow of materials across the site, be it wall elements, mesh panels, stall doors, assorted structural components, and so forth, as if tracing out coordinated lines of movement not unlike those depicted in Andy Warhol's *Dance Diagram* from the early 1960s, as referenced in the *99¢ Space* exhibition by the architects that was originally shown at the Architektur Galerie in Berlin in 2017.

Sketch of the recycling symbol by Gary Anderson, 1970

FarmTek catalog for low-cost agricultural supplies, building components, and prefab structures

The idea of circular material circuits, which was at the core of the approach to repurpose the existing barn, had been captured in a drawing from half a century ago – a drawing that in time would become the ubiquitous symbol for recycling and, as fate would have it, would be printed on so many discarded products. The drawing by Gary Anderson – a University of Southern California architecture student at the time – was the winning entry in a competition sponsored by the cardboard manufacturer Container Corporation of America in 1970. A rallying icon for 'green' awareness, the design could not be simpler. Comprised of three chasing arrows, the diagram circumscribes a closed-loop system, where one segment feeds into the next. Though usually presented as a flat, two-dimensional image, the figure recalls the seamless continuity of a Möbius strip unfolding in space. Referencing the impossible realities of M. C. Escher, the diagram implies the phenomenon of continuous return, a veritable perpetual motion machine fueling its own cyclical revolutions. The message is clear: reuse materials wherever and whenever you can.

The material shuffle at Refugio Road Ranch, involving the recirculation of bits and pieces of buildings, would yield a bare-boned framework that could be filled in and modified according to specific requirements.

In keeping with the design tenet of cheap, no-frills materiality, the next task was to identify external sources for low-cost building components beyond those available on site. The market is awash in assorted product brochures, mail-order catalogs, and e-commerce websites, each featuring the latest in construction supplies for small industrial and agricultural facilities. The search for the most affordable, most environmentally sound, and most ethically accountable product lines would generate, in due course, a substantial library that included the likes of FarmTek, MD Barnmaster, McMaster-Carr, Viagrow, 1000Bulbs, ULINE, etc., all sitting on the shelf next to standard editions on art, architecture, and literature. Having reviewed the various catalogs,

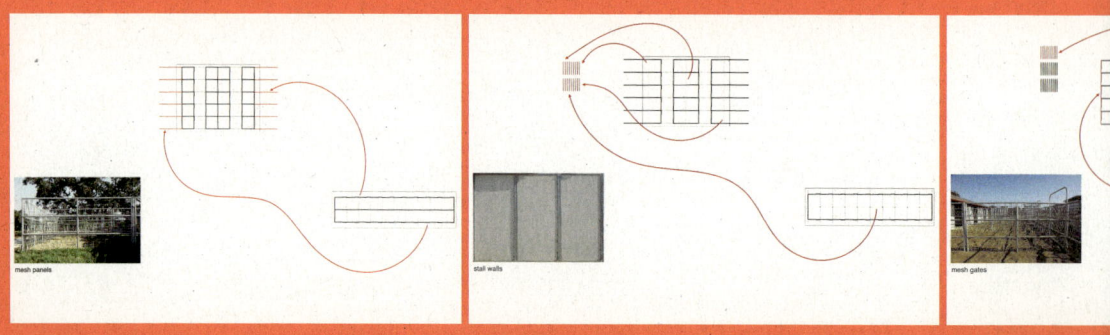
Flow diagrams showing the movement of repurposed building components

Product brochures, mail-order catalogs, and e-commerce websites advertising construction supplies

Details showing how industrial-grade products are installed from catalog to construction

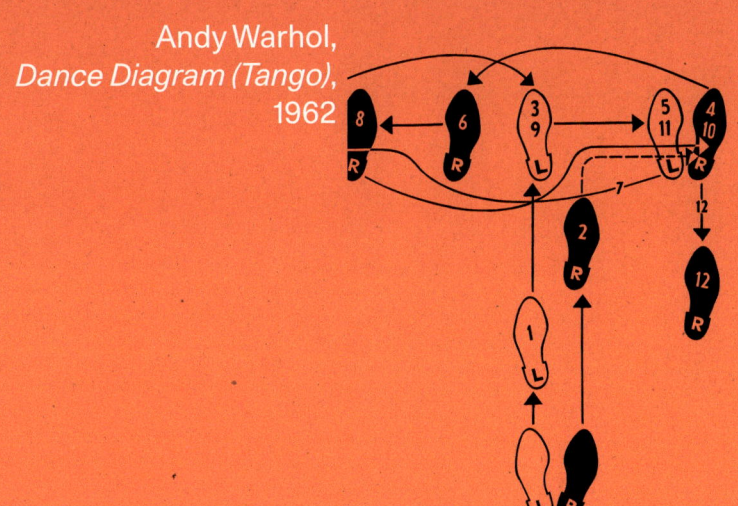

Andy Warhol, *Dance Diagram (Tango)*, 1962

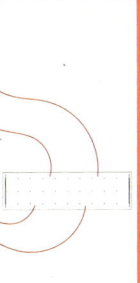
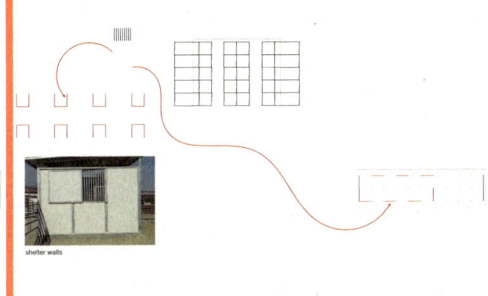

shelter walls

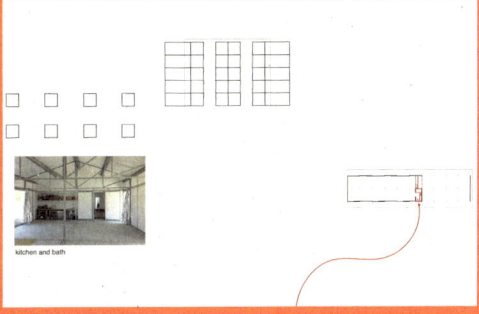

kitchen and bath

15¢ per sq. ft.

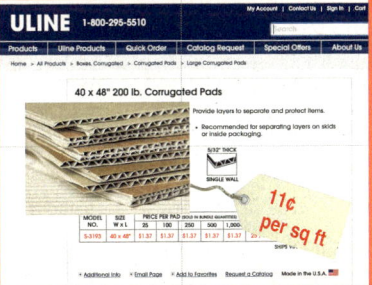

11¢ per sq ft

$1.36 per sq. ft.

Almost Off-Grid

283

Facade with various layers allowing it to be fully opened or closed

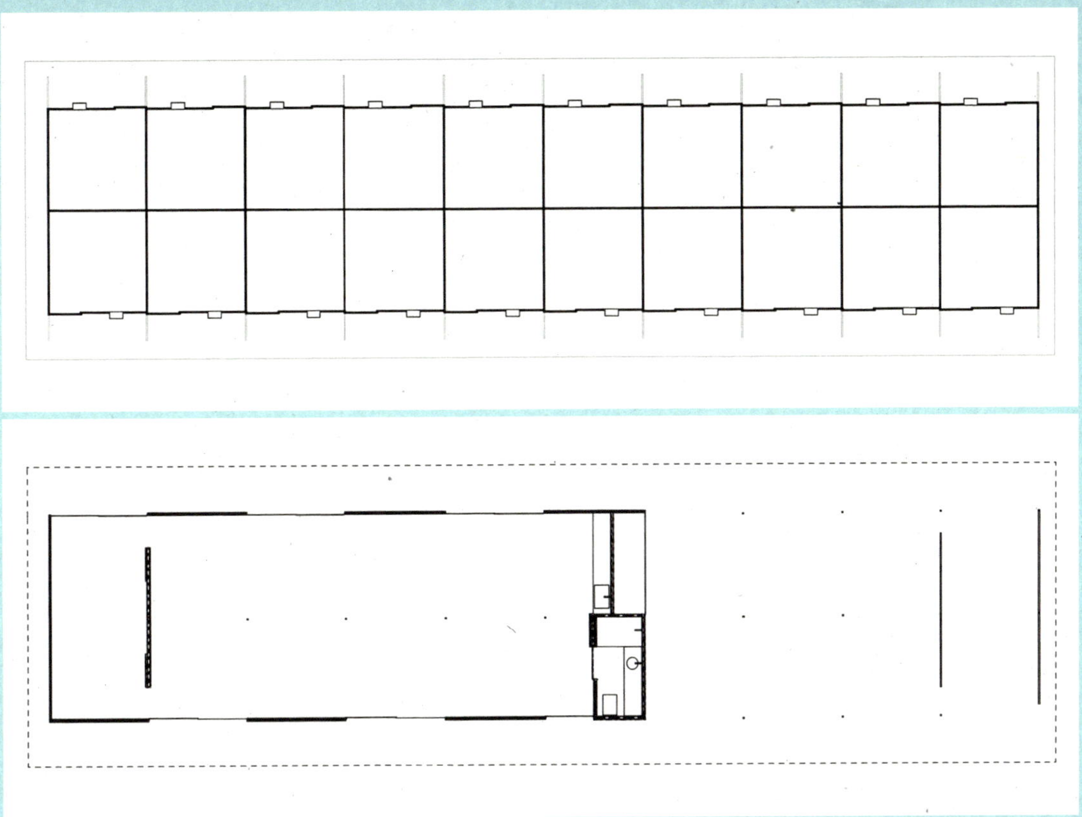

Plans showing the layout of the barn before and after its conversion

Details of the light-gauge structural framing used for the barn conversion project

Almost Off-Grid

the architects compiled an itemized list of components ranging from the very large to the most minute. Larger elements from prefabricated barn and greenhouse kits, for example, were employed as enclosure and structural framing. At the other end of the scale, items like off-the-shelf tension cables, turnbuckles, standard-gauge piping and conduits, and construction-grade plywood and corrugated cardboard were used for outfitting the interior.

The construction of the 99¢ Space, as the barn conversion was eventually named, required another approach altogether than that typically practiced by architects who labor over the resolution of precise details and finishes. On the contrary, everything assembled here was rough, raw, and ready to use. The 'lite' structural framing was pounded into place and bolted together without fuss, resulting in a pared-down pragmatism that gives the space its Spartan quality. As with the load-bearing structure, the facade is a blend of new and existing components put together in simple layers. Former stall doors were clad with recycled corrugated fiberglass sheets and then reinstalled as moveable panels on the exterior. Translucent sliding doors were mounted on the interior, allowing the space to be completely opened to the outside. A silver Mylar curtain – the only high-tech material brought in, developed by NASA but cheaply sourced through agricultural greenhouse suppliers – was hung on the inside with tension cables, duct tape, and magnets as attachment hardware. In addition to providing privacy and regulating light, the curtain insulates the space. All in all, the investigation of cheap construction was carried through to every aspect of the work, determining design decisions large and small.

Activists using silver foils in defiance of Trump's immigration policy, Washington DC, 2018 (AP Photo/J. Scott Applewhite)

By sheer coincidence, silver Mylar foil would take on a new significance far beyond the ranch, becoming in a broader political sense a symbol of resistance amidst the controversy over President Trump's immigration policies. Just after construction had begun at Refugio Road Ranch, widespread media coverage showed migrant detention camps where children separated from their parents had

Range of everyday activities and special functions in the 99¢ Space

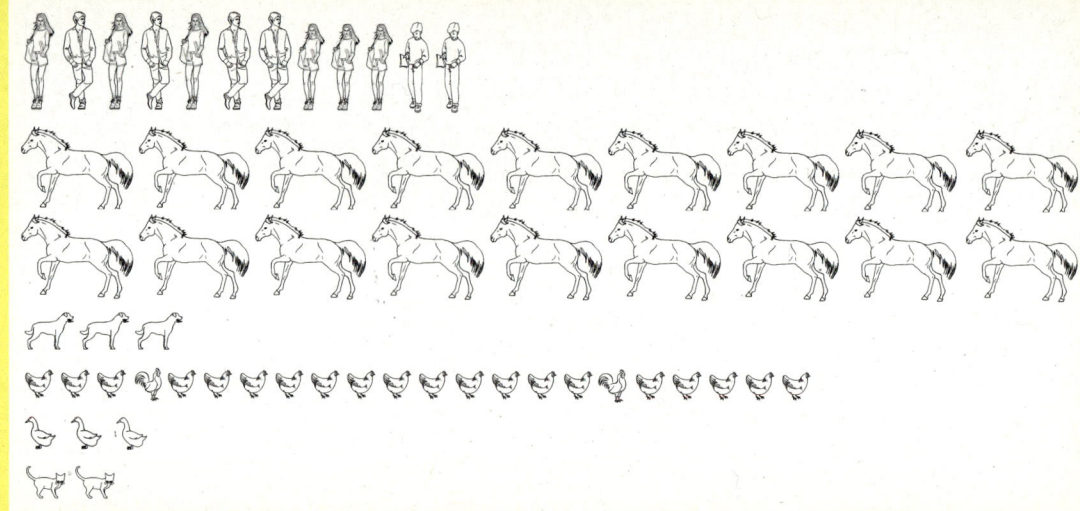

Ranch inhabitants

Elevation of the repurposed barn; habitable spaces on the left and storage facilities on the right

Toolshed for storing equipment, repairing machinery, and constructing items for ranch operations

been wrapped in Mylar blankets. It would not be long before mass protests broke out over such inhumane treatment, with demonstrators from coast to coast wearing silver foil as a sign of defiance. This is no small issue in a state like California, where a large portion of its population is made up of immigrants from south of the border, both legal and illegal. And this was no small issue on the ranch itself, since the Mexican families who live and work there expressed their immediate concern about the unfolding political events at the time, cheap materiality notwithstanding.

Fluxes of Common Use

While inexpensive in its construction and maintenance, the 99¢ Space is rich in its variability of use. The open space allows for a high degree of adaptability for all types of indoor and outdoor functions. At one end, there is always someone going in or out of the toolshed for a shovel, rake, or axe, or someone repairing something, while someone else on a tractor is busy loading or unloading bales of hay. At the other end of the building, the multifunctional room buzzes with residents going about their daily business, be it drying herbs and peppers, cleaning vegetables and fruit, making a variety of preserves, building cabinetry, simply sharing lunch, or children doing their homework. Later, the 99¢ Space was christened "the schoolhouse" by kids forced to stay home during the COVID-19 pandemic, as this was where they studied.

Within the space, all of the furniture is on wheels and can accordingly be arranged at will. The space can also accommodate periodic guests, with tables designed to be converted into beds and mobile storage units rolled out to become nightstands. There is also a small kitchen and bathroom that are closed off with sliding stall-door panels. The flux of everyday activities brings this modest building to life as the hub of a ranch that is home to 12 people, 18 horses, 22 chickens, 3 geese, 3 dogs, and 2 cats, not to mention the assorted wildlife that regularly wanders onto the premises – a mix ensuring that there is always something going on and, of course, always something to fix.

Just as the 99¢ Space is open to commonplace uses it is also appropriated by residents for special events. There are frequent barbecues, occasional horse clinics, and the annual Cinco de Mayo festivities. The space is used for the yearly Christmas party held in honor of the workers and their families. When rearranged for celebrating the First Communion of one of the children living on the ranch, the space was redressed with colorful paper lampions, garlands, and a piñata hung from the trusses. The wedding for one of the resident family's relatives was even more elaborate, with a very loud mariachi band playing just inside the main space to a sizeable audience drinking, eating, and dancing outside. And who knows what else is in store for the 99¢ Space? Not only a lively hub, it has since evolved into a kind of commons for life on the ranch and the community beyond.

An Object Lesson

The barn conversion proved to be instructive as an experiment in doing more with less, inasmuch as those earlier concerns about resourcing the site, cheap materiality, and fluxes of use informed the concept, spaces, and detailing in the design and construction of the new house. What had begun as a few stones laid on a newspaper became a collection of indoor and outdoor spaces assembled under one large roof – three porches, two living units, and one workspace. They all fit together like pieces of a jigsaw puzzle through which the occupants move in and out while going about their everyday activities. A freestanding object in the field, the ranch house has varying degrees of transparency and opacity. In places, it is fully open to frame views of the landscape beyond; in others, the house stands out sharply from the surroundings as a human-made silhouette, thereby enmeshing the artificial and the natural.

What is key to the project's circular economy is that the house is plugged into the off-grid systems of the ranch, the most important parts of which are the water well, the photovoltaic array, and the on-site septic sewage system, together forming the necessary base infrastructure for water power, and human waste management. With this hands-on interlinking of systems, the site itself functions as the key resource and main facilitator of the house's operations.

Additionally, the well at the eastern end of the property provides not only potable water but also the water needed to cool or heat the spaces of the house. Once the water is drawn from the aquifer (in

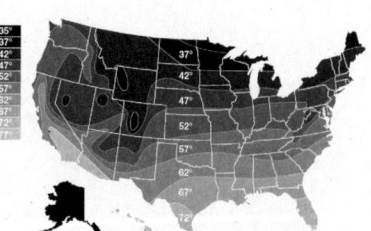

Groundwater temperature across the United States (US Geological Survey)

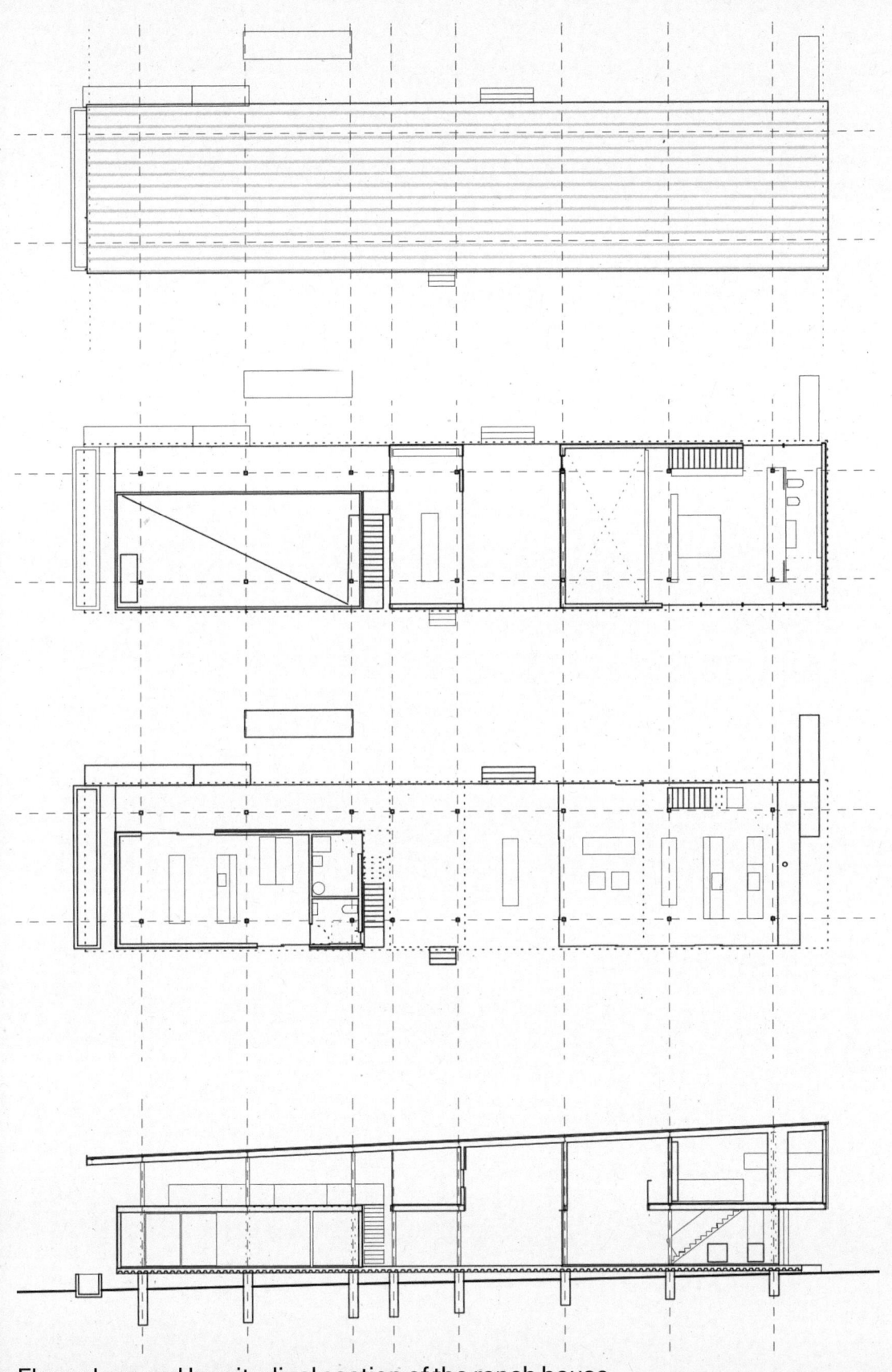

Floor plans and longitudinal section of the ranch house

Hybrid construction comprised of concrete slabs, steel skeleton, and wood framing this case considered as an energy reservoir), it is routed to a heat pump and a buffer tank, both regulating the temperature difference between the water in the ground and that used for the in-floor heating and cooling system. Considering that the temperature of the groundwater in the region is relatively moderate (62°F/17°C), little energy is needed to either cool or heat the building. In short, aquifer, water well, heat pump, buffer tank, and in-floor coils are all connected to condition the interior environment of the house. An app on a mobile device is used to control the temperature throughout, putting the occupants inside the machinery, as it were, wherever they may be.

Covered in corrugated galvanized metal, a common agricultural building product, the roof is as much an integral piece of site infrastructure as it is a functional component of the house itself. The long south-facing plane, conceived as a large umbrella lifted slightly above the roof construction, protects the indoor and outdoor spaces from direct sunlight. It is sloped to channel rainwater to a cistern at one end that is used for irrigating the fields. Given its size, the roof could also accommodate an array of solar panels should an extension to the existing installation ever be necessary.

To reduce the house's environmental footprint and considering that everything needed for new construction had to be brought to the site, material flows were kept to a minimum. No grading was made to the land itself, since the house sits on a concrete platform hovering just above the existing topography. Likewise, no earth was moved off-site for the construction of the foundations, their number and dimension reduced to what was structurally feasible. The slab and grade beams are made of carbon-reduced concrete, utilizing locally sourced aggregate and recycled fly ash that lowers the required amount of Portland cement (estimated CO_2 reduction of 20%). The concrete floor is exposed throughout, giving expression to the doing-more-with-less approach and the logic of reduced layers and materials.

In terms of the load-bearing structure, only a few slender columns support the house. The steel moment-frame was produced locally with just over 90% recycled content, its dimensions purposely minimized as well. Standard wood framing for walls and floors complements the concrete and steel, all coalescing to form a hybrid construction that draws on the interplay of distinct material qualities working in unison. Often hidden but here exposed, these combined efforts to lessen the house's environmental impact, starting from the ground up, resulted from a lively back-and-forth exchange (another dance of sorts) among the architects, engineers, and contractors.

East facade highlighting its varying degrees of transparency, 2019 (Eric Staudenmaier)

Model of the ranch house shown in silhouette as an assembly of indoor and outdoor spaces under a large roof

Ranch house terrace, 2019 (Eric Staudenmaier)

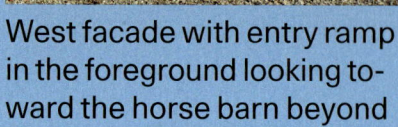

West facade with entry ramp in the foreground looking toward the horse barn beyond

Living room of the ranch house, 2019 (Eric Staudenmaier)

The house was constructed with standard farm-tech products, some sourced straight from those agricultural and industrial catalogs used for the barn conversion yet tweaked here and there to enhance the building's environmental performance. A case in point is the double layering of the facade, a principle infrequently employed in the United States, though common in Europe. The inner wall, a basic steel frame with wood infill, is complemented by an outer rainscreen made of industrial-grade perforated metal sheeting or unpainted mineral-fiber cement boards. The space between the layers serves as a thermal buffer, perhaps explaining why the construction crew nicknamed the building, although technically inaccurate, "the thermos bottle." This was their expression of appreciation for the overall approach to sustainable construction.

The Title 24 California Building Standards Code – a broad set of requirements for "energy conservation" and "green design" – does not have explicit specifications for 'thermos bottles' per se, let alone for a house heated and cooled by solar and geothermal energy. When the plans and performance-based analysis of the building envelope were submitted for the permit, the calculation standards had to be modified, insofar as no energy was being drawn from the state's power grid, and geo-cooling was not even in their evaluation system. Local authorities simply did not have a way to approve the project, for the numbers did not add up to any passing grade and the energy use was too low for the spreadsheet. Despite the state's stringent environmental policies, the ranch house stood outside the norm, even though much effort had been made to apply common sense to building with less, and more responsibly. Public officials had to help figure out how to get the necessary approvals, as if tacitly acknowledging that a revision of the code was long overdue.

The Machine in the Garden

Leo Marx, *The Machine in the Garden: Technology and the Pastoral Ideal in America*, 1964

All told, construction on the ranch house proceeded experiment by experiment. As with the trial-and-error approach to site planning, as well as the 99¢ Space conversion, the tests carried out on the new house attempted to push the limits of standard building products and practices alike. The land and the ranch facilities are managed as an ecosystem. Natural and artificial processes are integrated, each drawing on the other. Refugio Road Ranch is a mosaic of ideas and solutions aimed at connecting things that often remain unconnected. Far from confirming the bucolic cliché of country life, the project reconsiders what a contemporary ranch can be as a shared habitat for humans and nonhumans, and what it can do environmentally, economically, and socially as an inhabitable hybrid. Not just "a machine in the garden," to recall another American trope examined by Leo Marx in his 1964 book of the same name, where the technical and the natural are held apart as distinct realms, the project explores ways to put their entanglement to work in mutually reinforcing loops of give-and-take.

What might once have seemed an apt diagnosis of the disharmony between a pastoral ideal and the advance of civilization, Leo Marx's machine-in-the-garden metaphor still upheld the common view of an idyllic nature encroached upon by invasive technology. Even today, we may indeed still think unreflectively in terms of 'nature' on one side and 'technology' on the other. But contrary to this culturally engrained view, the Refugio Road Ranch experiment works to reconcile polarities between the artificial and the natural, and the technological and the pastoral, as well as the machine and the garden.

What results is something along the lines of David Green's *Logplug* from the late 1960s showing a working drawing of a tree trunk outfitted with mechanical installations and plugged into a subterranean infrastructural network. Here, the idea of "a full-service natural landscape" was part of a vision for a fully integrated technological environment. And this goes for the ranch as well. Cultivating a collaboration of nature and technology through design, the project operates as an aggregate of relations and reciprocal dependencies played out in and with the existing landscape – from water pump to in-floor coils, from cistern to irrigation network, from solar panels to electrical boilers. Technology, in this respect, is not an invader of some primordial setting, but is rather a constituent part of a larger operating system, whereby the machine is the garden and the garden the machine.